A DREAMSPEAKER CRUISING GUIDE, VOLUME 1

Gulf Islands & Vancouver Island

VICTORIA & SOOKE TO NANAIMO

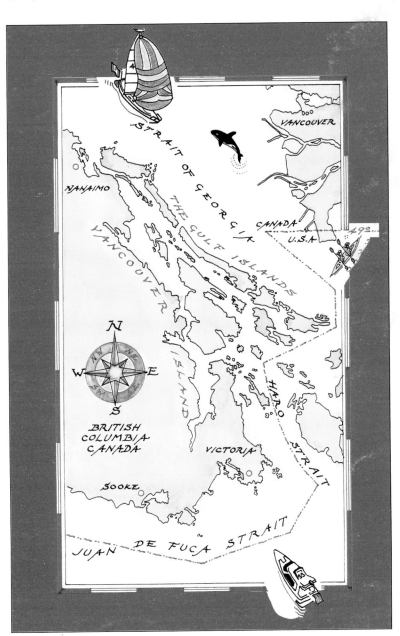

A N N E & L A U R E N C E Y E A D O N - J O N E S

RAINCOAST BOOKS

Vancouver

FOREWORD

In planning a journey, whether by land, sea or air, one is well advised, and sometimes required, to obtain and use official publications designed to assist the traveller. As helpful as these documents may be, the advice and experience of someone who has been to your proposed destination is invaluable and plays a large role in the success of your journey. In a user-friendly manner and in comprehensive terms, Anne and Laurence Yeadon-Jones accurately portray this guide's unique focus area – the waters bounding southern Vancouver Island and the adjacent Gulf Islands. The information provided here truly supplements and enhances the available maps and charts, not only by stressing the safety aspects of the journey but also by providing an attractive montage of sketches, descriptions and insights into what you will find upon arrival.

"Serendipitous" would describe the timing of this well-researched boating publication. It coincides with the decision of the Canadian Hydrographic Service (CHS) to cease publication of its *British Columbia Small Craft Guides,* and it follows publication of a Small Craft Nautical Map covering the area from Sooke to Nanaimo (the latter being the result of a joint venture between H & R Nautical Ventures and the CHS). *A Dreamspeaker Cruising Guide: Volume 1,* describes in detail, and cross-references, selected areas covered by both the Small Craft Nautical Map and the CHS *Gulf Islands Cruising Atlas* (Chart 3313), and it does so in fine style.

Serendipity aside, while the CHS maps and charts will get you there, the *Dreamspeaker Cruising Guides* will enhance your safety and enjoyment along the way.

A. D. O'Connor
Director, Pacific Region
Canadian Hydrographic Service

Copyright © 1998 by Anne and Laurence Yeadon-Jones

All rights reserved. No part of this publication may be reproduced or transmitted in any form or by any means, electronic or mechanical, including photocopying, recording or by any information storage and retrieval system, now known or to be invented, without permission in writing from the publisher.

First published in 1998 by Raincoast Books, 9050 Shaughnessy Street, Vancouver, B.C., v6p 6E5. (604) 323-7100.

2 3 4 5 6 7 8 9 10

CANADIAN CATALOGUING IN PUBLICATION DATA

Yeadon-Jones, Anne.
A Dreamspeaker cruising guide

Contents: Vol. 1, The Gulf Islands and Vancouver Island from Sooke to Nanaimo.
ISBN 1-55192-150-2

1. Dreamspeaker (Yacht). 2. Pacific Coast (B.C.) – Guidebooks. 3. Boats and boating – Pacific Coast (B.C.) – Guidebooks. I. Yeadon-Jones, Laurence. II. Title.

FC3845.P2A3 1998   797.1'09711'1   C97-910980-9
F1089.P2Y42 1998

Chart data of Canadian waters are reproduced under Licence Agreement 19970004 with the Canadian Hydrographic Service. Reproduction of information from Canadian Hydrographic Service charts is for illustrative purposes only. Such reproductions do not meet the requirements of the Canadian Charts and Nautical Publications Regulations and are not to be used for navigation. The appropriate charts, corrected up-to-date, and the relevant complementary publications required under the Charts and Nautical Publications Regulations of the Canada Shipping Act must be used for navigation.

Caution: This book is meant to provide experienced boaters with cruising information about the waters covered. The suggestions offered are not all-inclusive and, due to the possibility of differences of interpretation, oversights and factual errors, none of the information contained in this book is warranted to be accurate or appropriate for any purpose other than the pursuit of great adventuring and memorable voyages. A Dreamspeaker Cruising Guide should be viewed as a guide only and not as a substitute for official government charts, tide and current tables, coast pilots, sailing directions and local notices to boaters. Excerpts from CHS charts are for passage planning only and are not to be used for navigation. Shoreline plans are not to scale and are not to be used for navigation. The publisher and authors cannot accept any responsibility for misadventure resulting from the use of this guide and can accept no liability for damages incurred.

PRINTED IN ITALY

Raincoast Books gratefully acknowledges the support of the Government of Canada through the Book Publishing Industry Development Program, the Canada Council for the Arts and the Department of Canadian Heritage. We also acknowledge the assistance of the Province of British Columbia, through the British Columbia Arts Council.

WE WOULD LIKE TO HEAR FROM YOU!

We hope you enjoyed using Volume 1 of *A Dreamspeaker Cruising Guide.* We welcome your comments, suggestions, corrections and any ideas about what you would like to see in future editions of the guide. Please drop us a line at our address above (c/o Dreamspeaker), or send an E-mail to:

dreamspeaker@raincoast.com

TABLE OF CONTENTS

1 The Gulf Islands & Vancouver Island   5
How to Use This Book Charts and Nautical Publications

2 Victoria   9

3 Sooke   25

4 Sidney   40

5 Swartz Bay   53

6 Saanich Inlet   66

7 Plumper Sound   77

8 Active Pass   98

9 Trincomali Channel   104

10 Porlier Pass   123

11 Sansum Narrows   138

12 Stuart Channel   152

13 Gabriola Passage   167

14 Nanaimo   178

Selected Reading   190

CHS Chart Dealers   191

Index to Featured Destinations   192

To Helen, Stella, Wally and Roberto, for encouraging our dreams.

RESEARCH CRAFT:

Dreamspeaker, a She 36 sloop rigged sailboat.
Fox Victor India, a Bell Jet Ranger helicopter.

SPECIAL THANKS TO:

Joseph Blackburn, aerial photography.
Wilson Southam, pilot, Silverstar Helicopters.

GRATEFUL APPRECIATION TO OUR SPONSORS AND THEIR SUPPORT:

Nautical Data International (NDI), Electronic Navigational Charts for Canadian Waters.
Fugawi Pinpoint Systems, Moving Map Software for GPS Receivers.
Nobeltec Corporation, Visual Navigation Suite and Navtrek.

ACKNOWLEDGEMENTS:

Extra special thanks to A. D. O'Connor, Ronald D. Bell, Ardene Philp, David L. Fisher, Brian M. Watt and Terry Curran, Canadian Hydrographic Service, Pacific Region. We would also like to thank J. Richard MacDougall, Canadian Hydrographic Service, Ottawa; Robert Austad, Rick Whetter, Barb Clark and Selma Low, B.C. Provincial Parks South; James W. Mulchinock, Capital Regional District Parks; Dale Mumford, Canadian Heritage Parks Canada; Alan Rycroft, B.C. Ferry Corporation; Chris Seeley and Paul James, Canadian Coast Guard; Brian Jensen and Owen Lange, Environment Canada; Kevin Obermeyer, harbour master, Port of Nanaimo; Brian Henry and Michael Pardy, Ocean River Sports; Adam Hellicar, Ocean Explorations; Chris Thody, Island Cruising; Aurelia Jacobsen, Inform Enterprises; Pam Taylor and Matthew Schoenfeld, Galiano Bicycle; Maluca van den Bergh, word processor extraordinaire; Duart Snow, Pacific Yachting; Gamma Pro Imaging Inc., for film and professional processing; Maggie Finnigan, for graphic inspiration; Caroline Stewart, for help with the book proposal; David and Anne Benson and family, for their insight and encouragement; Mark Stanton, president and publisher, Raincoast Books, for going nautical; the rest of the publishing gang at Raincoast Books, Brian Scrivener, Rachelle Kanefsky and Ruth Linka; and, finally, our family and friends, for their patience and enthusiastic support.

Chapter 1
The Gulf Islands & Vancouver Island

So one day, when the sun shone bright and turned all the gulf waters into a shimmering sheet of liquid silver, I set forth to discover this strange kingdom.
— Lukin Johnston, "An Island Eden," *The Call of the Coast*

THE GULF ISLANDS & VANCOUVER ISLAND

Marina facilities frequently dot the coastline. Pictured here is Pedder Bay Marina 3.2

TIDES & CURRENTS

Refer to *Canadian Tide and Current Tables, Volume 5: Juan de Fuca Strait and Strait of Georgia*. Published annually by the Department of Fisheries and Oceans, Ottawa.

WEATHER

Refer to continuous marine weather broadcasts on the following VHF channels and frequencies: WX1: 162.55 MHZ; WX2: 162.40 MHZ; WX3: 162.475 MHZ; 21B: 161.65 MHZ. Alternatively, phone the following continuous marine weather recordings: Vancouver, (604) 666-3655; Victoria, (250) 656-2714 or 7515; Nanaimo, (250) 245-8899. For further information on weather products and services, contact Environment Canada at (604) 664-9033, or visit their web site at *www.weatheroffice.com*.

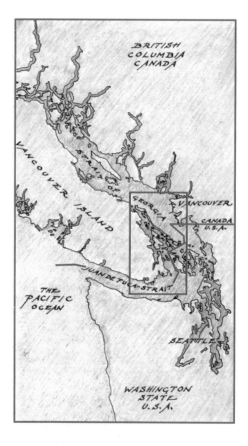

Dreaming of the ideal cruising destination or planning a voyage's itinerary gives us all a sense of thrill and adventure. However, turning the dream into reality and actually discovering wonderful anchorages or secluded bays is far more challenging and time consuming than one ever imagines.

With this in mind, we set out in our trusty 11-m (36-ft) sloop *Dreamspeaker* and compiled this efficient and friendly cruising companion that includes our selected, well-researched destinations and personal discoveries. We also provide photographs and hand-drawn shoreline plans accompanied by detailed information, which will make your journey, and especially your arrival, safer, less stressful and much more fun.

Covered in this first *Dreamspeaker Cruising Guide* is part of Canada's majestic Pacific Coast, a beautifully diverse and natural cruising ground that offers the boater an alluring and accessible pocket of paradise. Featured are the southern Gulf Islands and southeastern Vancouver Island from Sooke to Nanaimo, with the historic capital and port of Victoria providing a convenient and central urban base. The cruising boater will be charmed by each island's distinctive character and lured by clean sandy beaches, sheltered bays, hideaway anchorages, spectacular sunsets and abundant wildlife. In addition, the area's marine parks are unique to British Columbia's coast and are often only accessible by water.

From kayak to mega-yacht, all are welcome to these islands as long as due respect is paid to their sensitive ecosystems and their extensive, varied wildlife. The popular cruising months usually fall between May and October, when more favourable weather conditions prevail. Fuel, water and fresh produce are available at most major provisioning stops, and many islands provide well-developed boating facilities while managing to retain their relaxed outlook and charm.

Finally, once on your cruise, the way to really appreciate the splendour and serenity of the Gulf Islands is to ease back the throttle, slow down your pace and fall into the easy rhythm of leisurely island life. So, whatever size your craft, we wish you great adventuring, safe cruising and memorable voyages.

CUSTOMS

The main ports of entry covered by this guide for recreational boaters entering Canadian waters are located in Victoria, Sidney, Bedwell Harbour and Nanaimo (see Index to Featured Destinations for more details). Contact Canada Customs toll-free at 1-888-226-7277.

CANADIAN COAST GUARD

For a copy of their *Safe Boating Guide,* call 1-800-267-6687. For search and rescue: 1-800-567-5111 (cellular *311) or VHF channel 16.

EMERGENCY RADIO PROCEDURES

MAYDAY: For *immediate danger* to life or vessel.

PAN-PAN: For *urgency,* but *no* immediate danger to life or vessel.

For MAYDAY or PAN-PAN, transmit the following on VHF channel 16 or 2182 kHz.

1. MAYDAY, MAYDAY, MAYDAY (or PAN-PAN, PAN-PAN, PAN-PAN), this is [vessel name & radio call sign].

2. State position and nature of distress.

3. State number of people onboard and description of vessel [length, make/type, colour, power, reg. number].

HOW TO USE THIS BOOK

This sample layout identifies the various features of this cruising guide that will help you to reach your destination safely and well informed.

Chapter & featured destination reference

Chapter legend

Destination locator

Ballpark latitude & longitude

Tips on best approach & anchorages

Depths reduced to lowest normal tide (zero tide)

Cautionary note

Solid black line indicates high water mark

White area indicates shoreline that covers & uncovers with the tide

Red broken line indicates a safe approach course

Boats at anchor

Dark blue area indicates shallower water

Light blue area indicates deeper water

Depth contour (approximate position). Depths reduced to lowest normal tide (zero tide)

Green area indicates land above high water mark

Aerial approach or ambient photograph

HW: *high water*
LW: *low water*

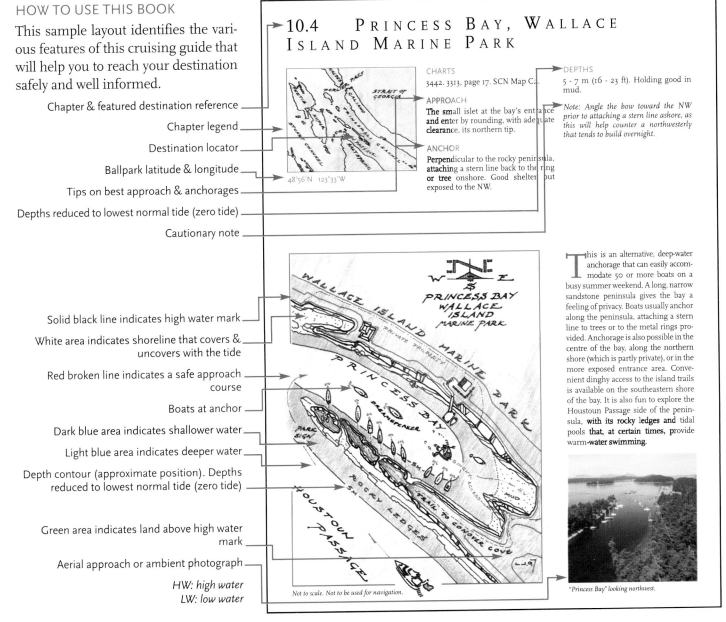

10.4   PRINCESS BAY, WALLACE ISLAND MARINE PARK

48°56'N 123°33'W

CHARTS
3442. 3313, page 17. SCN Map C2.

APPROACH
The small islet at the bay's entrance and enter by rounding, with adequate clearance, its northern tip.

ANCHOR
Perpendicular to the rocky peninsula, attaching a stern line back to the ring or tree onshore. Good shelter but exposed to the NW.

DEPTHS
5 - 7 m (16 - 23 ft). Holding good in mud.

Note: Angle the bow toward the NW prior to attaching a stern line ashore, as this will help counter a northwesterly that tends to build overnight.

This is an alternative, deep-water anchorage that can easily accommodate 50 or more boats on a busy summer weekend. A long, narrow sandstone peninsula gives the bay a feeling of privacy. Boats usually anchor along the peninsula, attaching a stern line to trees or to the metal rings provided. Anchorage is also possible in the centre of the bay, along the northern shore (which is partly private), or in the more exposed entrance area. Convenient dinghy access to the island trails is available on the southeastern shore of the bay. It is also fun to explore the Houstoun Passage side of the peninsula, with its rocky ledges and tidal pools that, at certain times, provide warm-water swimming.

Not to scale. Not to be used for navigation.

"Princess Bay" looking northwest.

CHARTS AND NAUTICAL PUBLICATIONS

We have carefully designed this cruising guide to work in conjunction with Canadian Hydro- graphic Service (CHS) charts and nautical publications. For the most part, we reference the largest scale chart, as this shows maximum detail. At the beginning of each featured destination the charts you will require are listed in the following order:

• Individual chart number.
• Chart 3313 (*Gulf Islands Cruising Atlas*) and page number.
• Small Craft Nautical (SCN) Map and sheet number.

Individual charts are the primary tools of the professional mariner. However, their size is often a problem on a small craft. CHS has specifically designed the *Gulf Islands Cruising Atlas* (Chart 3313) for the recreational boater. Chart 3313 is also a navigational resource with extensive supplementary information, extracts from *Sailing Directions* (see Nautical Publications below) and approach photographs of certain anchorages and passes. We strongly recommend Chart 3313 for its size, comprehensive coverage and excellent value. The Small Craft Nautical (SCN) Maps are primarily aimed at the open boater, sport fisherman, kayaker or canoeist who requires a small, foldable package.

ELECTRONIC CHARTS

Electronic charts are raster scans of CHS individual charts, produced under licence by Nautical Data International (NDI) (1-800-563-0634). They may be viewed independently on your computer or, with the appropriate navigational software, used as an onboard aid to navigation. The following software systems are compatible with NDI charts: Fugawi Moving Map Software for GPS Receivers (416-920-0447) and Nobeltec Inc. Visual Navigation Suite and Navtrek (1-800-495-6279).

PUBLICATIONS

We recommend the following publications to accompany your copy of *A Dreamspeaker Cruising Guide*. For futher reading, consult the Selected Reading list at the back of this book.

NAUTICAL PUBLICATIONS, CHS

Canadian Tide and Current Tables, Volume 5: Juan de Fuca Strait and Strait of Georgia.

Catalogue of Nautical Charts and Related Publications: Pacific Coast 2. (Also includes a full list of nautical publications available.)

Sailing Directions: British Columbia Coast (South Portion).

Symbols and Abbreviations Used on Canadian Charts: Chart 1.

WEATHER PUBLICATIONS, ENVIRONMENT CANADA

Marine Weather Hazards Manual – West Coast: A Guide to Local Forecasts and Conditions.

Mariner's Guide: West Coast Marine Weather Services.

BOATING SAFETY PUBLICATIONS, CANADIAN COAST GUARD

The Canadian Aids to Navigation System: Marine Navigation Services Directorate.

List of Lights, Buoys and Fog Signals: Pacific Coast.

Protecting British Columbia's Aquatic Environment: A Boater's Guide.

Radio Services: Marine Communications and Traffic Services.

Safe Boating Guide.

Chapter 2
VICTORIA

Fisgard Lighthouse emerging from the morning fog.

Chapter 2
VICTORIA

TIDES
Reference Port: Victoria

Secondary Ports: Esquimalt & Oak Bay

CURRENTS
Reference Station: Race Passage

Secondary Station: Baynes Channel

WEATHER
Area: Juan de Fuca Strait, Haro Strait

Reporting Stations: Race Rocks, Victoria Gonzales, Trial Island, Discovery Island

Empress Wharf and B.C. Parliament Buildings, Victoria Inner Harbour   2.2

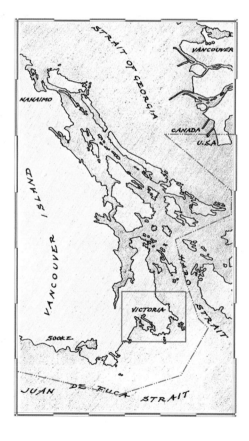

The grand city of Victoria, with its historic downtown and green suburbs, offers some of the most fascinating and diverse city moorage anywhere in North America. A city where locals display genuine island friendliness, Victoria is central to this chapter, which encompasses the sweep of coastline from Esquimalt in the west to the Chatham Islands in the east.

Victoria Harbour is an exceptionally busy international port, accommodating berths for cruise liners and container ships, floatplane and ferry traffic, tugs and barges. Right-of-way must be given to all commercial ships, which are unable to manoeuvre freely in this restricted waterway. Beyond Laurel Point the Inner Harbour opens out to James Bay and the downtown core. Ship Point is often home to visiting mega-yachts and, because the downtown wharves are all public, visitors and locals alike make yacht spotting part of a day's events.

For a little peace and quiet within close proximity to the city, try West Bay or Erie Street Wharf (Fisherman's Wharf). Fleming Bay, just west of the outer harbour, provides a pleasant setting and good anchorage. The Fisgard Lighthouse and Cole Island anchorages in Esquimalt Harbour make for a historic, fun day out. The harbour is also the Pacific headquarters of Canada's Navy. If venturing east, you will be rewarded with the modern amenities of the well-appointed Oak Bay Marina. A lovely sandy beach awaits you in Cadboro Bay. Finally, discover the allure of the tranquil Chatham Islands anchorages and the charm of Discovery Island Marine Park.

CAUTIONARY NOTES

Moderate to strong S and SW winds are common in the summer months and turn the southern steeply bluffed shoreline into a lee shore.

Fog is common and swiftly blankets the coast, often leaving you with zero visibility.

Shoal patches and strong currents, especially on the flood tide, are found in Enterprise, Mayor and Baynes Channels.

FEATURED DESTINATIONS

2.1 Victoria Harbour 12

2.2 Victoria Inner Harbour & Downtown 14

2.3 West Bay, Victoria Harbour 16

2.4 Fleming Bay, Esquimalt 17

2.5 Fisgard Lighthouse, Esquimalt Harbour 18

2.6 Cole Island, Esquimalt Harbour 19

2.7 Oak Bay & Village 20

2.8 Cadboro Bay & Village 21

2.9 Rudlin Bay & Discovery Island Marine Park 22

2.10 Puget Cove & Arbutus Cove, Chatham Islands .. 23

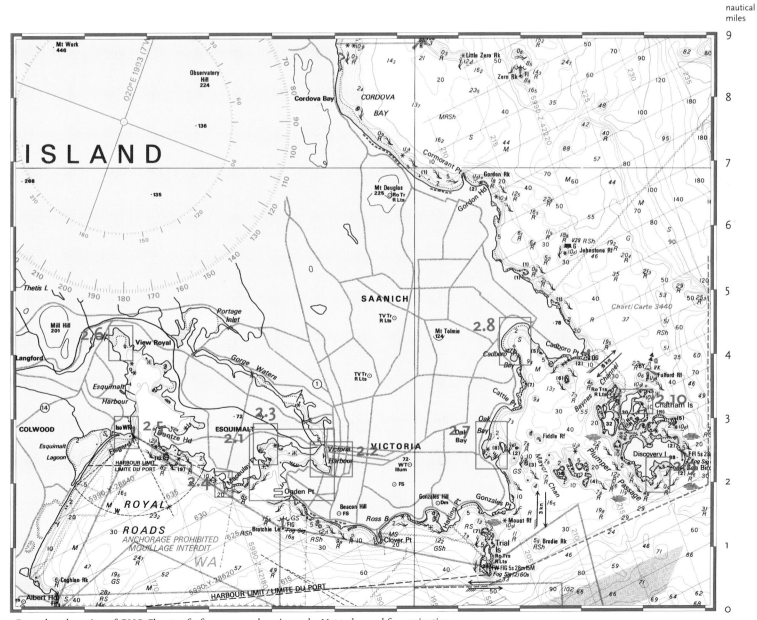

Reproduced portion of CHS Chart 3462 for passage planning only. Not to be used for navigation.

2.1   VICTORIA HARBOUR

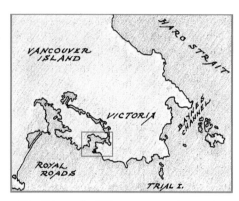

48°25'N   123°23'W

An express ferry rounds the Ogden Point breakwater.

The first welcoming sign on approaching the harbour entrance will be a classic-style light on the Ogden Point breakwater, often backed by an imposing cruise liner. Initially the outer portion of the harbour resembles a commercial seaport, with the McLoughlin fuel terminal to port and the big ship docks and warehouses to starboard. West Bay opens to the NW. Note that there are no pleasure-craft facilities between Ogden and Shoal Points.

Beyond Shoal Point the Inner Harbour extends eastward, revealing comfortable urban surroundings. Traditionally styled condominiums within a park setting perch on the rocky N shore. A floatplane operation zone extends from Shoal to Laurel Point, with planes regularly taking off and landing. The extensive public wharf at Erie Street has a fuel jetty and floats extending along the southern shore.

Once through the passage between Songhees and Laurel Points, boaters will experience a sense of elation as they enter James Bay and the majestic old harbour of Victoria.

Victoria Harbour extends N beyond the twin lifting road/rail bridges at Johnson Street, allowing access for commercial and local pleasure craft to the Upper Harbour.

Victoria is home to a large commercial fishing fleet, which, when in harbour, is tightly packed into ERIE STREET WHARF, known locally as FISHERMAN'S WHARF. In the summer months, when the fishing fleet is out, this friendly location becomes a quieter alternative to the downtown wharves. There is a park adjacent, and the frequent service of VICTORIA HARBOUR FERRY (mid-March to end of October) will transport you downtown. The LITTLE GEM grocery store carries good basic provisions and is just a 5-minute walk away, while THRIFTY FOODS and a B.C. LIQUOR STORE are a good 15-minute walk. Fresh fish is available at the floating fish store, and BARB'S FISH & CHIPS is renowned for its fare as far as Port Angeles. For an exciting experience in West Coast whale watching, join OCEAN EXPLORATIONS (1-888-442-6722) at the COAST HOTEL.

Shoal Point and the Erie Street Wharf.

CHARTS

3415. 3313, page 3. SCN Map A4.

APPROACH

Enter Victoria Harbour between the Ogden Point breakwater and Macaulay Point. The Inner Harbour extends E from Shoal Point. The Upper Harbour lies N of Johnson Street Bridge (lifting). Bridge monitors VHF channel 12. Operates 9:00 a.m. to 4:00 p.m., 6:00 p.m. to midnight.

PUBLIC WHARF

Extensive public moorage is available at ERIE STREET WHARF. Wharf manager monitors VHF channel 73. For Inner Harbour, see pages 14-15.

BOAT LAUNCH

Public at Camel Point.

FUEL

A fuel jetty and float lie W of the Erie Street Wharf.

CUSTOMS

Located in James Bay. See Victoria Inner Harbour & Downtown, page 15.

Notes: A floatplane operation zone lies between Shoal and Laurel Points. A strobe beacon on Berens Island is activated when an aircraft is intending to land or take off. VICTORIA HARBOUR FERRY operates a fleet of tour and transportation ferries (mid-March to end of October) and monitors VHF channel 67.

There is no official designated anchorage for pleasure craft within the harbour limits. The marina fronting the COAST HOTEL is private.

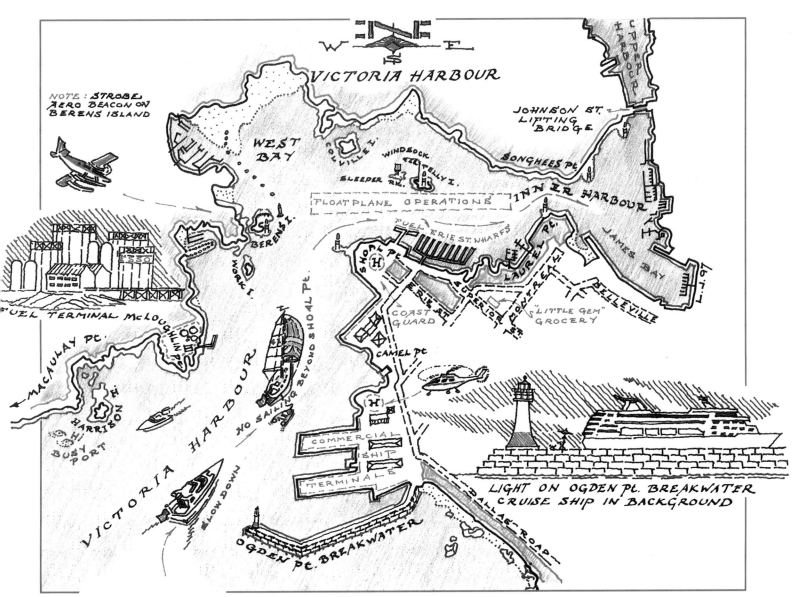

Not to scale. Not to be used for navigation.

2.2 VICTORIA INNER HARBOUR & DOWNTOWN

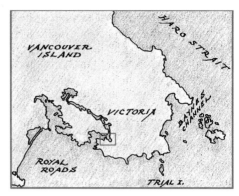

48°25'N   123°22'W

East from Shoal Point lies the Inner Harbour and downtown.

The Victoria Marine Adventure Centre, Ship Point and Empress Wharf, James Bay.

The harbour traffic from the private marina at the Coast Hotel.

Victoria, British Columbia's capital and oldest city, is a wonderful mix of English charm and West Coast style. The Inner Harbour penetrates deep into the heart of this historic city, giving the visiting boater a chance to experience downtown Victoria and savour its fascinating diversity.

The B.C. Parliament Buildings lend a gothic air to the southern end of James Bay. Here you will find the EMPRESS WHARF, backed by the famous, ivy-covered EMPRESS HOTEL. This is a popular spot in the summer months, when street performers entertain eager crowds well into the evening. VICTORIA HARBOUR FERRY also operates from here (mid-March to end of October) and is an efficient and fun way to get around the city shoreline (250-480-0971).

A little further N, extensive and less noisy moorage is available at the WHARF STREET public wharf, also home to an interesting variety of mega-yachts. Both public wharves are run by friendly and informative staff who can also be contacted for information regarding ice, showers and laundry facilities, which are located below the visitor information centre on the corner of Wharf and Government Streets. (Visitor info: 250-953-2033.)

The ALPINE FLORIST & FOOD MARKET on Fort and Blanshard Streets offers a good selection of basics, fruits and vegetables, as well as hot snacks and lunches to take out. The B.C. LIQUOR STORE is located in the EATON CENTRE next to MARKS & SPENCER, which has a food department that carries a scrumptious selection of English biscuits and specialty frozen and tinned foods. THRIFTY FOODS is a good 20-minute walk away on Simcoe and Menzies Streets. For coffee try JAVA COFFEE on Yates Street or MURCHIE'S TEA & COFFEE on Government Street. Victoria has a wonderful selection of mouthwatering bakeries: CAPTAIN COOK'S on Fort and the ITALIAN BAKERY on Quadra, to name two.

MARKET SQUARE and BASTION SQUARE are well worth a visit, offering a good mix of interesting shops and craft vendors. Charts can be found at CROWN PUBLICATIONS on Fort Street and at BOSUN'S LOCKER on Johnson Street, which also keeps a varied selection of boat chandlery. There are many interesting restaurants to choose from in Victoria, so ask the locals about their favourites or consult the visitor information centre. Your visit to Victoria might not feel complete without an afternoon tea experience. The EMPRESS TEA LOBBY serves traditional tea-time fare (250-389-2727), and POINT ELLICE HOUSE is a 15-minute ferry ride from the Inner Harbour and offers high tea and light lunches on the croquet lawn (250-380-6506).

CHARTS

3415. 3313, page 3. SCN Map A4.

APPROACH

Enter the downtown and James Bay portion of the Inner Harbour between Laurel and Songhees Points.

PUBLIC WHARF

Extensive public moorage is available at the EMPRESS WHARF and at the WHARF STREET public wharf. Very large pleasure craft may moor at Ship Point and Wharf Street public wharf. The wharf managers monitor VHF channel 73.

MARINA

The VICTORIA MARINE ADVENTURE CENTRE has moorage for transient visitors. Monitors VHF channel 67. Ask for V.Mac Docks.

CUSTOMS

A designated customs float is situated below the wharf managers' office with 21 m (70 feet) on either side. There is a direct phone line to customs on the float.

Note: If you require information or assistance, harbour patrol monitors VHF channel 73 and is available to guide you to an appropriate berth.

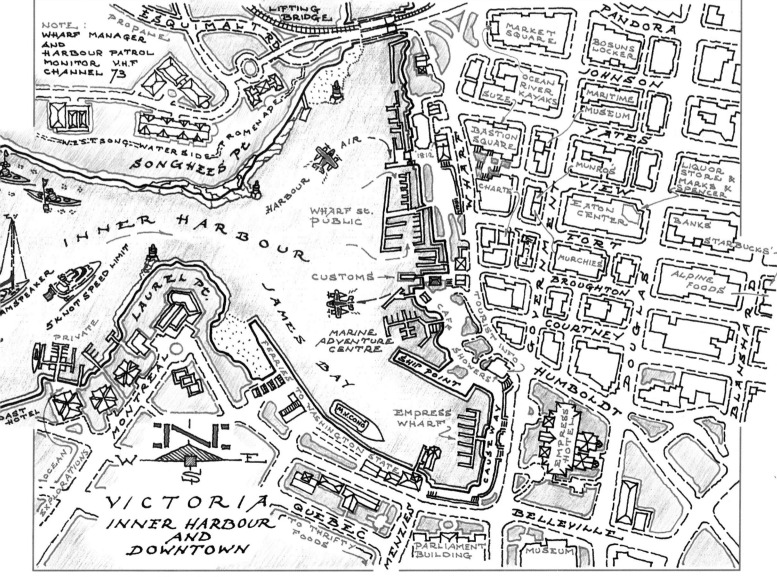

Not to scale. Not to be used for navigation.

2.3 WEST BAY, VICTORIA HARBOUR

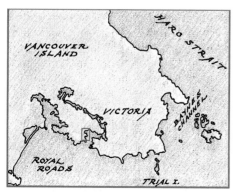

48°26'N 123°23'W

CHARTS

3415. 3313, page 3. SCN Map A4.

APPROACH

The marina via a dredged channel, which has a least depth of 1.5 m (5 ft).

MARINAS

SAILOR'S COVE MARINA (250-389-2255); HIDDEN HARBOUR MARINE CENTRE (250-388-4666); WEST BAY MARINE VILLAGE (250-385-1831). All marinas have limited transient moorage. However, West Bay Marine Village plans to upgrade its facilities with extensive moorage for the visiting boater. They also monitor VHF channel 68.

BOAT LAUNCH

At West Bay Marine Village.

Note: Although no official anchorage existed in 1997, boats have been known to anchor E of the dolphins for short periods. In future it is hoped that this area may become a designated anchorage.

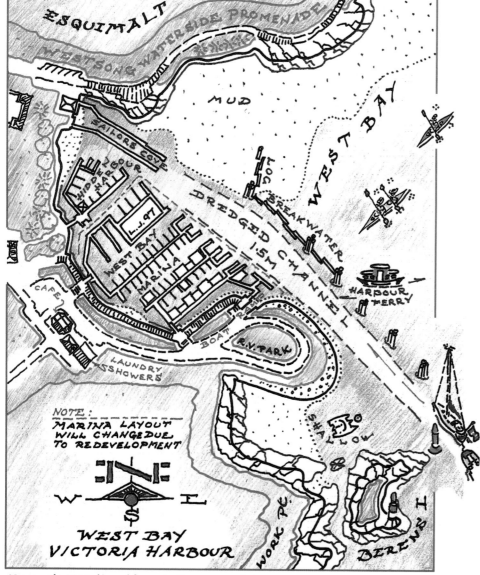

Not to scale. Not to be used for navigation.

Tucked away in the quiet western corner of Victoria Harbour is West Bay. Currently WEST BAY MARINE VILLAGE provides good shower and laundry facilities, and the local WEST BAY CAFÉ is a friendly meeting place. SUZY, a short walk up the road, carries a good stock of basic groceries. ESQUIMALT PLAZA, a 25-minute walk away, offers a supermarket and a variety of shops. A B.C. LIQUOR STORE is another 10-minute walk. West Bay is also home to the fleet of VICTORIA HARBOUR FERRY (250-480-0971). The Westsong Waterside Promenade affords a pleasant walk all the way to Johnson Street Bridge, passing through the redeveloped area of the old Songhees Village and along Victoria Harbour's rocky shoreline.

Approach to West Bay.

CHARTS

3415. 3313, page 4. SCN Map A4.

APPROACH

From the S and enter by leaving the breakwater to starboard, the tip of which is marked by a starboard-hand day beacon.

ANCHOR

Stern line to breakwater (there is limited room to swing, as boats from the boat launch need a clear channel). Good all-around shelter.

DEPTHS

3 - 4 m (10 - 13 ft). Holding and bottom condition unrecorded.

BOAT LAUNCH

Public (fee charged) with finger and dinghy float.

Note: Leave well to port the port-hand day mark on the rock E of Gillingham Islands to clear the northerly unmarked rock, which covers at high tide.

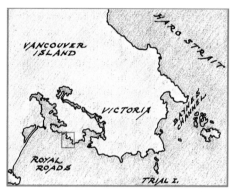

48°25'N   123°25'W

O ften overlooked, this pleasant cove provides good anchorage behind its high stone breakwater, to which a stern or bow line should be attached, as space is limited. Fleming Bay is home to the ESQUIMALT ANGLERS' ASSOCIATION, so weekends and summer months are busy with fishing boats popping in and out, or the day's catch being cleaned on a designated float in the SE corner of the bay. There is a launch ramp and dinghy dock, making it a convenient spot for kayaks and canoes. Onshore there is a grassy picnic area with wooden tables in Buxton Green. Trails lead to MACAULAY POINT PARK, with great views to the S and E.

On approach leave well to port the port-hand day mark.

Not to scale. Not to be used for navigation.

2.5   FISGARD LIGHTHOUSE, ESQUIMALT HARBOUR

48°26'N   123°27'W

CHARTS

3419. 3313, page 4. SCN Map A4.

APPROACH

Enter Esquimalt Harbour between Duntze Head and the port-hand buoy E of Fisgard Lighthouse. Approach the causeway from the NE.

ANCHOR

E of Rocky Hump. Temporary anchorage.

DEPTHS

3 - 6 m (10 - 19.5 ft). Holding good in gravel.

Note: The construction of a visitors' wharf is planned for the near future.

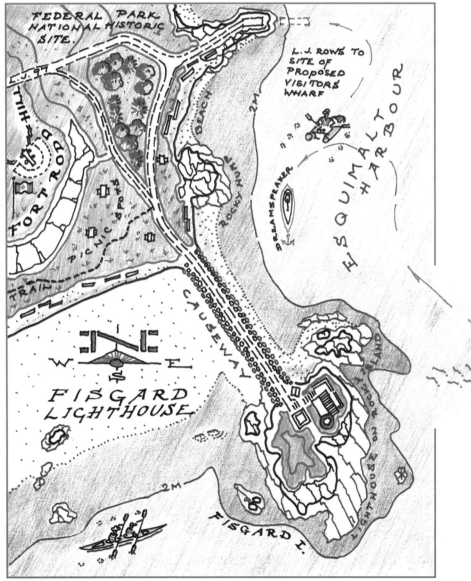

Not to scale. Not to be used for navigation.

Canada's oldest West Coast lighthouse sits commandingly on an outcrop of volcanic rock, where it has guided ships home safely for more than 135 years. This is an unexpected and delightful anchorage and makes an exciting day trip out from Victoria. The causeway that links the lighthouse to the main-land affords some protection, although this temporary anchorage is exposed to northerly winds and southerly swells. Parks Canada is planning the construction of a visitors' dock. Beach your dinghy below the restored lighthouse and explore the keeper's house, which has exhibits and photographs telling the story of Fisgard, its keepers and the terrifying shipwrecks in the graveyard of the Pacific.

A visit to Fort Rodd Hill is well worthwhile, as it is one of the best-preserved 1890s coast artillery forts in the world. (For information call 250-478-5849.)

A causeway connects the Vancouver Island shore to Fisgard Island and the lighthouse.

CHARTS

3419. 3313, page 4. SCN Map A4.

APPROACH

Within Esquimalt Harbour, approach from the SE, between Dyke Point and the mooring tripods W of McCarthy Island.

ANCHOR

Between Cole Island and Tovey Bay. Exposed to the S but protected from swells.

DEPTHS

3 - 4 m (10 - 13 ft). Holding good in mud.

Notes: At LW mud flats extend from Parsons Bridge in the N to Cole Island.

The locally acclaimed SIX MILE HOUSE PUB will welcome you with a well-earned drink and scrumptious pub fare if you decide to take a row to Parsons Bridge.

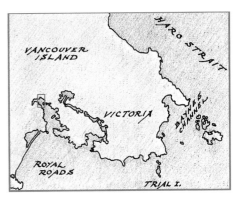

48°27'N 123°27'W

Tucked into the NW corner of Esquimalt Harbour is another unexpected anchorage steeped in history. Peaceful Cole Island, with its abandoned brick-and-stone buildings and ruined jetty, was a munitions magazine used by the Royal Canadian Navy over 130 years ago. Today you can walk along the overgrown trail to the crumbling warehouses built into the rock face. Please note that the island should be explored with extreme caution and at your own risk. No overnight camping or fires are allowed, and any use of the jetty is prohibited. Cole Island is now owned by the provincial government, so please respect and help preserve this little piece of local history. (Call B.C. Heritage at 250-356-1040 for information.) At HW take the opportunity to row or paddle across the shallows, teeming with ducks and geese, to Parsons Bridge.

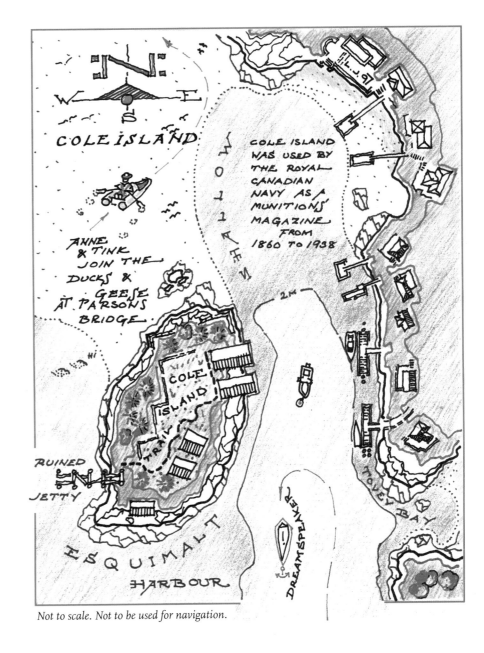

Not to scale. Not to be used for navigation.

Dreamspeaker at anchor just south of Cole Island.

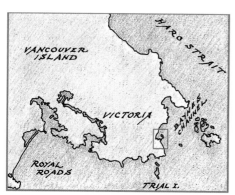

48°26'N 123°18'W

CHARTS

3424. 3313, page 3. SCN Map A4.

APPROACH

Enter anchorage and marina between breakwater at Turkey Head and breakwater projecting S from Mary Tod Island.

ANCHOR

To the NW of yellow cautionary buoys, between or N of boats on mooring buoys.

DEPTHS

4 - 6 m (13 - 19.5 ft). Holding moderate in weed and gravel.

MARINA

OAK BAY MARINA (250-598-3369 or 1-800-663-7090) offers extensive transient moorage. Check in at fuel dock. Monitors VHF channel 68.

FUEL & CUSTOMS

At marina. Yacht service by OAK BAY BOAT WORKS (250-598-2912).

Note: The yellow cautionary buoys mark a clear channel to the marina.

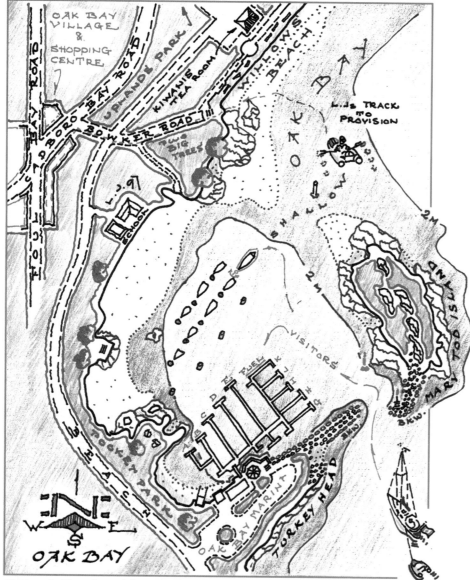

Not to scale. Not to be used for navigation.

Behind the breakwater at Turkey Head lies OAK BAY MARINA. This well-appointed establishment comes equipped with a fine restaurant, sushi bar, café and deli, and would make any homesick urbanite feel right at home. The marina is close to the OAK BAY VILLAGE & SHOPPING CENTRE, which ranks as one of the most comprehensive malls in Victoria. The B.C. LIQUOR STORE has an excellent selection of local and international wines.

Willows Beach, N of the marina, offers a lovely, sandy shoreline, and the KIWANIS TEA ROOM, just up from the beach, provides an elegant spot to relax, sip a cup of Earl Grey tea and ponder the beach's 2,500-year history as a First Nations winter village. A hike through nearby UPLANDS PARK offers 30 hectares (75 acres) of protected natural vegetation, with dramatic views across Oak Bay to Haro Strait.

Approaching the breakwater that extends out from Turkey Head.

CHARTS

3424. 3313, page 4. SCN Map A4.

APPROACH

From the SE, leaving Spurn Head and the stone breakwater to port.

ANCHOR

Best protection from southerly winds can be found in the NW part of the bay.

DEPTHS

3 - 6 m (10 - 19.5 ft). Holding good in mud.

MARINA

ROYAL VICTORIA YACHT CLUB (250-592-2441) has reciprocal moorage only. Monitors VHF channel 9. If no reply, moor at visitors' dock and check in with foreshore office or bar.

BOAT LAUNCH

Via the beach at Cadboro Bay.

Note: Although exposed to the SE, southerly swells seldom disturb the bay in the summer months.

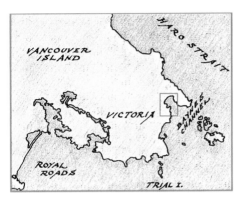

48°27'N 123°17'W

A delightful anchorage with a sandy beach, a charming shopping village and home to the ROYAL VICTORIA YACHT CLUB. The beach at the head of the bay affords a good opportunity to stretch your legs and is a favourite launch site for kayakers heading out to the Chatham Islands. Cadboro Bay's GYRO PARK is a hit with the kids, who love to climb on its oversized sea creatures. The village is a short walk up Sinclair Road and is great for provisioning or just relaxing on the patio of OLIVE OLIO'S or THE SMUGGLER'S COVE PUB. PEPPERS store has a good selection of basics, fresh fruit, meat, fish and vegetables. There is also a tempting bakery filled with "fresh from the oven" delights, an absorbing bookstore and a bank.

Spurn Head with the Royal Victoria Yacht Club and Cadboro Bay in the background.

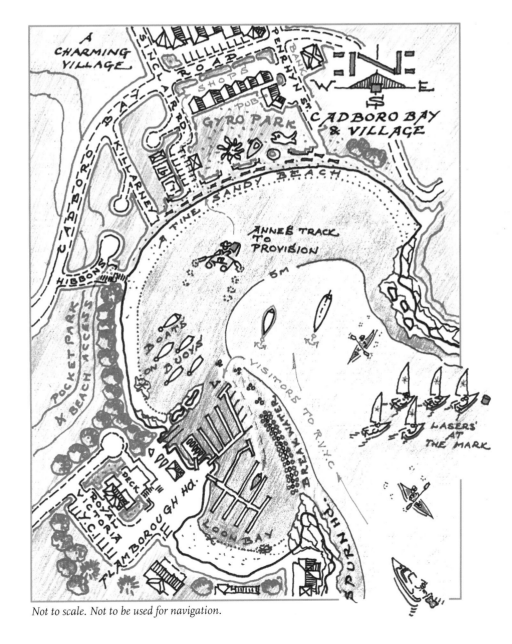

Not to scale. Not to be used for navigation.

2.9 RUDLIN BAY & DISCOVERY ISLAND MARINE PARK

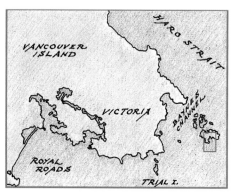

48°25'N 123°14'W

CHARTS

3424. 3313, page 4. SCN Map A4.

RUDLIN BAY

Approach from the SE. Anchor in 4 - 6 m (13 - 19.5 ft). Holding unrecorded. A daytime picnic spot only.

*Note: All anchorages in the Chatham Islands and Discovery Island group are temporary. Visit only in settled weather and approach at LW. These islands have a very rocky shoreline. **Extreme caution** must be exercised while navigating these waters.*

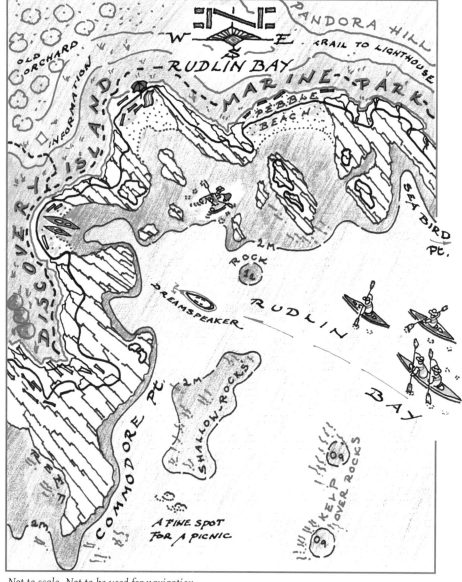

Not to scale. Not to be used for navigation.

Three lovely pebble beaches fringed by tall grass meadows make this temporary anchorage an ideal picnic stop, but keep a sharp lookout for covered rocks and shoal patches when entering Rudlin Bay. A walk to the 1886 lighthouse atop the rocky bluff at Sea Bird Point is certainly worthwhile, as along the way you may discover some of the island's wildlife. Notice the arbutus trees, formed into curious shapes by the strong southwesterly winds. Discovery Island Marine Park was once the home of Captain E. G. Beaumont, and the now neglected orchard and overgrown meadows give this end of the island a sense of calm and solitude.

Lighthouse on Discovery Island and the Chatham Islands in the background.

CHARTS

3424. 3313, page 4. SCN Map A4.

PUGET COVE

Approach from the E. Anchor in centre of bay. Holding good in gravel. Exposed to wind and swell from Haro Strait.

ARBUTUS COVE

Approach from the N. Anchor in 4 - 6 m (13 - 19.5 ft). Holding good in gravel. Most sheltered of all bays.

"Arbutus Cove" looking south.

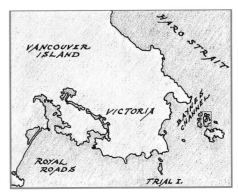

48°26'N 123°15'W

The alluring Chatham Islands, so close to Victoria, have surprisingly uncrowded anchorages. The Chathams and the N portion of Discovery Island are owned by the Songhees Band and should be respected as private. Kayakers can use Discovery Island Marine Park as their base camp when exploring around these islands.

In the northern Chatham Islands, "ARBUTUS COVE" (local name) and PUGET COVE, 2 peaceful anchorages with log-strewn beaches and rocky ledges, lie on either side of a narrow neck of land. "Arbutus Cove" is the better protected anchorage, as Puget Cove is open to southerly and easterly winds and the swell from Haro Strait. We anchored overnight in Puget Cove when a westerly was blowing and enjoyed the tranquility of this quiet hideaway.

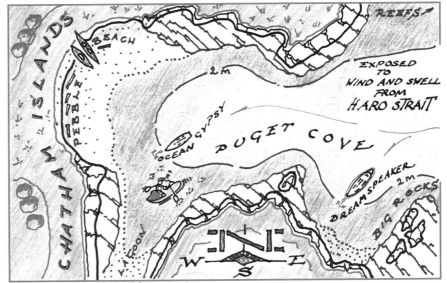

Not to scale. Not to be used for navigation.

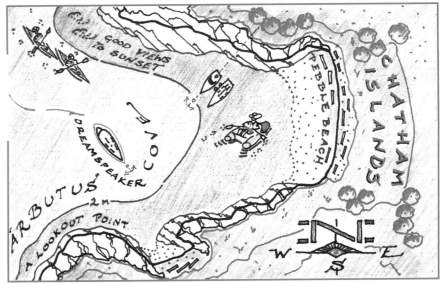

Not to scale. Not to be used for navigation.

Puget Cove looking west.

Dreamspeaker at anchor below the Fisgard Lighthouse.

Floatplane off Songhees Point, Victoria Inner Harbour, prepares for takeoff.

Powering east along the Victoria shoreline toward Enterprise Channel.

Chapter 3
SOOKE

Approaching Sooke Harbour Public Wharf 28

Chapter 3
SOOKE

The anchorage in Parry Cove   3.1

TIDES

Reference Port: Victoria
(Witty's Lagoon)

Secondary Port: William Head
(Pedder Bay)

Reference Port: Sooke

Secondary Ports: Sooke Basin &
Becher Bay

CURRENTS
Reference Station: Race Passage

WEATHER
Area: Juan de Fuca Strait

Reporting Stations: Sheringham
Point, Race Rocks, Trial Island

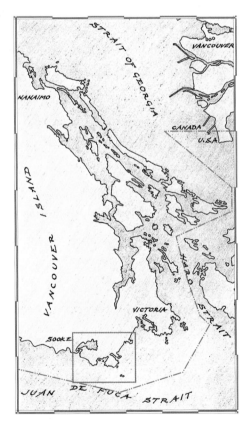

Sooke and the southeastern coastal waters of Vancouver Island have always been renowned for their excellent sportfishing opportunities. As a result, they attract a variety of craft, especially small, fast motorboats that are able to nip in or out at a moment's notice. This trend is now shifting due to the influx of boaters and kayakers who view Sooke as a new and exciting cruising destination.

The cruising waters of this chapter take in the southernmost tip of Vancouver Island, from Sooke Inlet in the west to Albert Head in the east, allowing you to savour a bite-size piece of the "real West Coast" without going too far. You can look forward to dramatic coastlines, unspoiled beaches, preserved wetlands and a diversity of marine animals, including pods of orcas. Parks are numerous and opportunities for hiking plentiful, with enough variety to satisfy all levels of experience.

Begin with a short hop from Victoria to magical Witty's Lagoon Regional Park, where a splendid sandy beach and invigorating park trails are waiting to be explored.

Farther south, Pedder Bay Marina provides a sheltered overnight stop.

Once you have safely navigated temperamental Race Passage, turn west and enter the infamous Juan de Fuca Strait. The spectacular East Sooke Regional Park is easily accessible from Campbell Cove in Becher Bay, where protected anchorage can be found.

Sooke Harbour and Sooke Basin provide good recreational anchorages and provisioning facilities. Both are convenient stopovers for boats off to cruise the West Coast of Vancouver Island or the Broken Group Islands in Barkley Sound. Marina berths for transient visitors are limited at present, but they will hopefully be expanded to accommodate more cruising boaters in the near future.

CAUTIONARY NOTES
(FOR THE SUMMER MONTHS)

Moderate to strong westerly inflow winds are common on clear sunny days, peaking in the late afternoon.

Westerly winds and waves encountering an ebbing current in Race Passage and at Beechey Head can produce chaotic, choppy seas.

Fog is frequently found rolling in from the Pacific, especially in the late summer.

Featured Destinations

3.1 Witty's Lagoon Regional Park & Parry Cove   28

3.2 Pedder Bay & Marina   30

3.3 Race Rocks & Race Passage   31

3.4 Campbell Cove & Wolf Island, Becher Bay   32

3.5 East Sooke Regional Park   33

3.6 Sooke Harbour & Sooke Basin   34

3.7 Whiffin Spit Park, Sooke Harbour   36

3.8 Sooke Harbour Public Wharf & Marina   37

3.9 Anderson Cove, Sooke Basin   38

3.10 Sunny Shores Resort & Marina   39

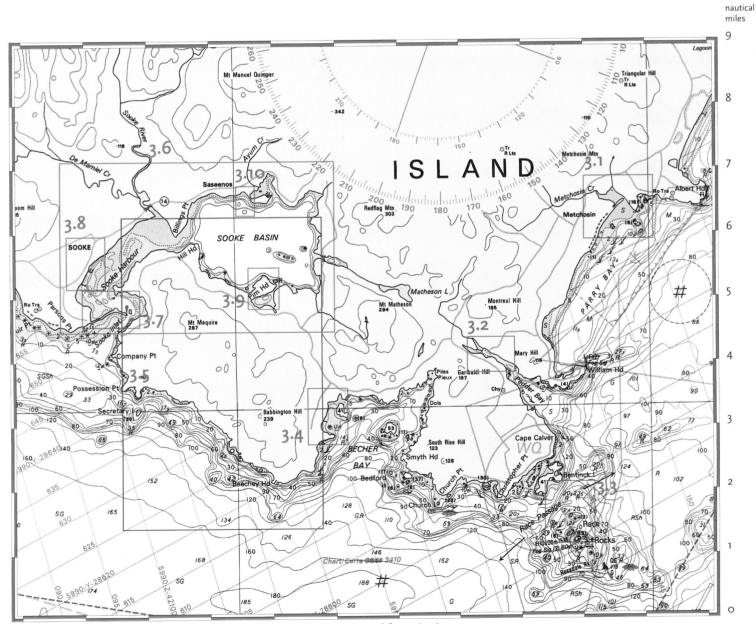

Reproduced portion of CHS Chart 3461 for passage planning only. Not to be used for navigation.

3.1 WITTY'S LAGOON REGIONAL PARK & PARRY COVE

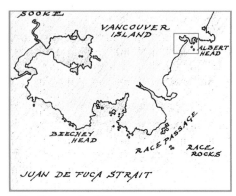

48°23'N 123°30'W

CRD Parks

Kayaker below the Sitting Lady Falls, Witty's Lagoon.

Just a short hop from bustling Victoria lies a magical picnic day stop with all the right ingredients: a fine sandy beach with warm-water swimming, a lagoon and salt marsh teeming with wildlife and a waterfall spilling over volcanic rocks. To top it all, the water here is wonderfully clear and clean. Anchorage is possible N of Haystock Islets or just off the shallows in Parry Bay. In favourable weather conditions overnight anchorage for 3 to 4 boats can be found in Parry Cove, N of Two Tree Islets (both local names). Here snoozing, snorting seals compete for drying rocks, and kingfishers flirt along the water's edge.

The park is a harmonious blend of protected natural environments, and many of the plants found in the salt marsh are a crucial source of food for wintering wildfowl. The lagoon is a birder's paradise, so pack your binoculars.

If you take your dinghy over to TOWER POINT you can explore the forest trails that lead down to pristine pocket beaches. The point is made up of pillow basalt and is one of the best examples of this intriguing geological formation in North America. This part of the park is also an equestrian area and is separated from the park's main body by private property. A narrow trail leads up to OLYMPIC VIEW DRIVE, which then connects with the park and LAGOON TRAIL. To visit the SITTING LADY FALLS continue along this trail. Alternatively, beach your dinghy at the W end of the sandy beach and follow the COAST TRAIL or, at HW, take a leisurely row to the head of the lagoon. Please note that outboards are prohibited in the lagoon. (For a detailed map and information on WITTY'S LAGOON call 250-478-3344.)

At LW it is fun to explore the sand flats that, upon drying, nearly connect with Haystock Islets. The rocks on these islets, covered with grass and scrub, resemble orderly haystacks. The surrounding waters are a favourite playground for harbour seals who, at low tide, can be found sunning themselves en masse.

Anchorage in Parry Cove. Witty's Lagoon in the background.

CHARTS

3410. 3313, page 1. SCN Map A3.

Note: Witty's Lagoon is a bird sanctuary and is not accessible to boats other than non-powered dinghies or kayaks. Even at HW, the depths within are 0.3 m (1 ft) or less.

APPROACH

Parry Cove from the E, S of Albert Head, and enter between Two Tree and Snoozing Seal Islets. (Parry Cove as well as Two Tree and Snoozing Seal Islets are all local names.)

ANCHOR

Centre of the cove; room for 3 - 4 boats. Temporary, exposed to the S and E.

DEPTHS

4 m (13 ft). Holding good in sand.

BOAT LAUNCH

Kayaks can be launched at the foot of the steps off Witty's Beach.

Note: Enter Parry Cove at LW to ascertain clearance over rocks that cover. Anchoring is possible in settled weather off the edge of the sand spit that extends out from the lagoon.

Chart 3410 is required to supplement Chart 3313.

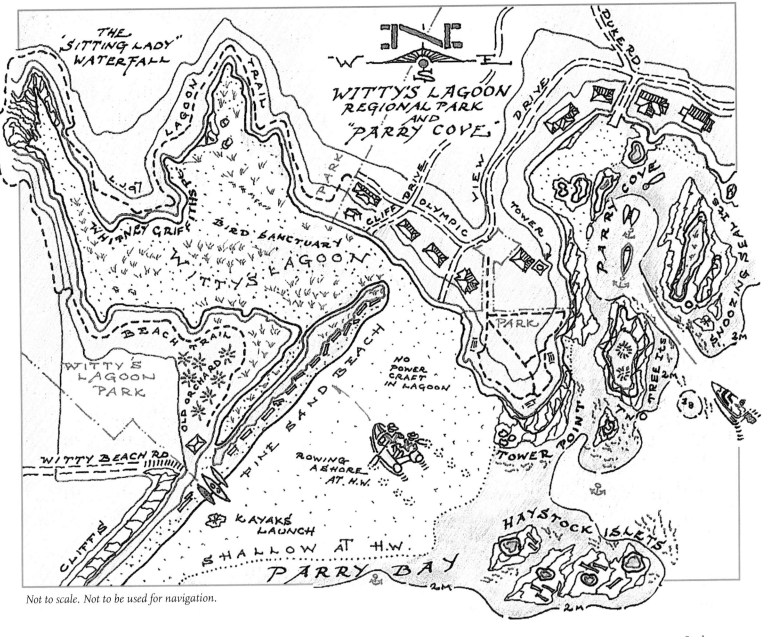

Not to scale. Not to be used for navigation.

3.2 PEDDER BAY & MARINA

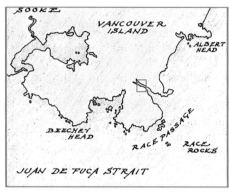

48°20'N   123°34'W

CHARTS

3410. 3313, page 1. SCN Map A3.

APPROACH

Enter the upper reaches of Pedder Bay between Weir and Watt Points. Stay in the centre of the channel, leaving the private wharf of LESTER B. PEARSON COLLEGE OF THE PACIFIC to starboard.

MARINA

PEDDER BAY MARINA (250-478-1771) lies in a dredged zone at the head of the bay. Monitors VHF channel 68.

BOAT LAUNCH

At marina.

FUEL

At marina.

If a howling westerly is blowing in the Juan de Fuca Strait or the tide is against you in Race Passage, pop into PEDDER BAY MARINA. Primarily a sportfishing marina, plans are afoot to make it more desirable to cruising boaters as a destination. At present (1997), fuel, limited transient moorage, showers and laundry facilities are available. Included in the remodelling plans are more berths for boats over 10 m (33 ft), and the shallow entrance to the marina will also be redredged.

Approach to Pedder Bay Marina. Private floats of Lester B. Pearson College in the foreground.

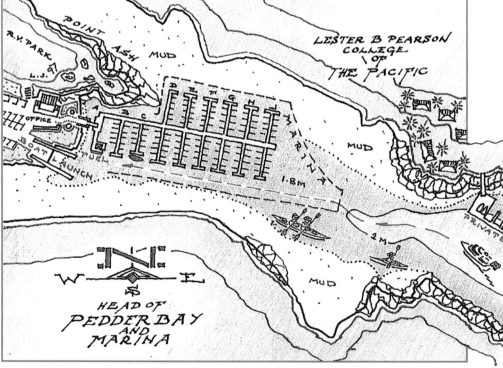

Not to scale. Not to be used for navigation.

CHARTS

3410. 3313, page 1. SCN Map A3.

RACE ROCKS

Notes: Race Rocks is a group of low, bare rocks. A lighthouse with distinctive black-and-white bands is situated atop Great Race Rock. The light is shown at an elevation of 36 m (118 ft). The fog signal consists of 3 blasts on a horn every minute. Tidal streams are tabulated for current station Juan de Fuca East. Rosedale Rock is the most southerly danger. Heavy, dangerous overfalls and races occur in bad weather.

RACE PASSAGE

Notes: Although the most direct route to Sooke, beware of tidal streams that attain 6 knots on the flood and 7 knots on the ebb. These are tabulated for current station Race Passage. The passage between Race Rocks and Bentinck Island can be used by small craft in good weather, at slack water or providing they have the power to offset the tidal stream. Favour the Bentinck Island side, keeping just outside the line of kelp. When the tide is running, dangerous tidal rips form. These can often be encountered off Christopher and Church Points.

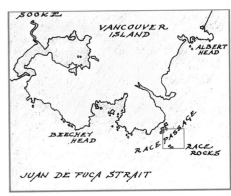

48°18'N 123°32'W

These infamous rocks mark the southernmost tip of western Canada. The surrounding area is reputed for gale-force winds, strong currents and sudden fog banks, so preparations should be made and extreme care taken when navigating these waters. The majestic black-and-white granite lighthouse, along with FISGARD LIGHT, was one of the first to be built on the British Columbia coast – and for good reason, as more than 30 boats have been lost in the surrounding waters. Race Rocks is now an ecological reserve that maintains a large variety of marine life.

Note that if red flags are being flown on Bentinck Island, indicating that the testing of explosives is in progress, vessels are advised to stay clear of the island by a 2-km (1-mi) radius. In this instance pleasure boats are advised to navigate to the S of Rosedale Rock.

The lighthouse at Great Race Rock looking south across Juan de Fuca to the Olympic Mountains.

3.4   CAMPBELL COVE & WOLF ISLAND, BECHER BAY

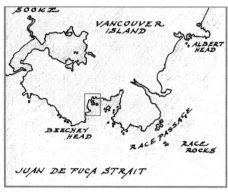

48°19'N   123°37'W

CHARTS

3410. 3313, page 1. SCN Map A3.

APPROACH

Campbell Cove and Wolf Island lie in the NW corner of Becher Bay.

ANCHOR

In Campbell Cove, N of Creyke Point. Be careful to give clearance to a rock in the centre of the bay. Or, anchor in Murder Bay, W of Wolf Island, or in the cove on the NE shore of Wolf Island. All anchorages are temporary and exposed to the E.

DEPTHS

2 - 5 m (6.5 - 16 ft). Holding good in sand and mud.

MARINA

PACIFIC LIONS MARINA (250-642-3816) currently (1997) has no facilities for boats exceeding 8 m (26 ft).

BOAT LAUNCH

At marina.

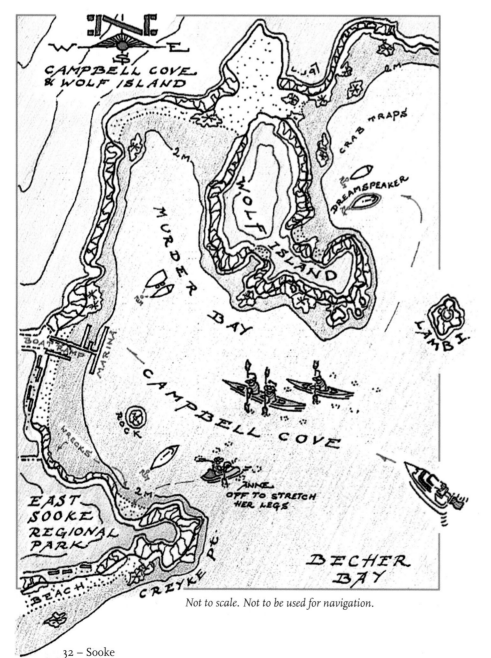

Not to scale. Not to be used for navigation.

A nchorage in Campbell Cove is protected from prevailing westerlies, but keep an eye out for the large drying rock (sometimes marked) in the middle of the bay. There are also underwater obstructions S of the bay. You can take a dinghy over to the pocket beach at Creyke Point, where access to the Aylard Farm entrance of East Sooke Regional Park is easily accessible. This is also a protected spot to beach kayaks.

Murder Bay, W of Wolf Island, affords a good anchorage, although the swell from the Juan de Fuca Strait can make it very uncomfortable. A safe and secluded 2-boat anchorage can be found in an unnamed cove behind Wolf Island. This is a truly peaceful anchorage where you can enjoy the unobtrusive company of birdlife. We have taken the liberty to name this spot "Swing Cove," as a tempting swing rope is attached to one of the trees here.

Note: Tidal streams run up to 7 knots across the mouth of Becher Bay and past Beechey Head.

CRD Parks

Views out to Juan de Fuca Strait along the park's rocky shoreline.

3410 & 3411.

Note: The map and information here are based on the Capital Regional District (CRD) Parks brochure. For full information, a copy of the brochure can be obtained from CRD PARKS in Victoria (250-478-3344).

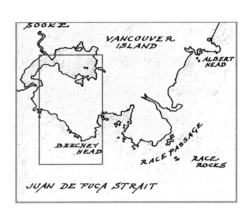

This spectacular park stretches from Aylard Farm around Beechey Head to Iron Mine Bay, then N to Anderson Cove. The brochure says it all: "Hike a windswept rocky coast, over dry hilltops, through a dark rainforest to sheltered coves." The rugged coastal trail begins or ends at the Aylard Farm entrance, but, as it is a challenging hike, careful preparation is advised. Alternatively, you can take shorter trails inland to hilltop views or just picnic on the pocket beach in the company of scampering river otters.

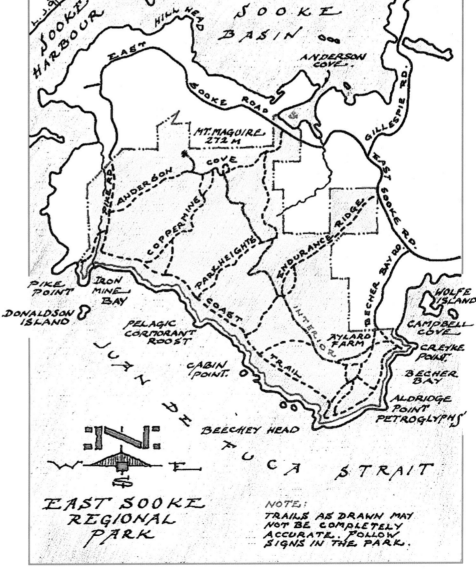

Not to scale. Not to be used for navigation.

At anchor in the lee of Wolf Island. Campbell Cove in the background.

3.6   SOOKE HARBOUR & SOOKE BASIN

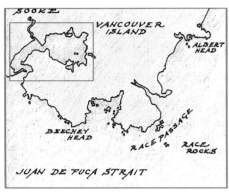

48°22'N 123°43'W

CHARTS

3411. 3313, page 1. SCN Maps A3 & A2.

SOOKE HARBOUR

APPROACH

Enter between Simpson and Parsons Points, lining up the first, outer range ("leading marks") as far out into Sooke Inlet as possible. Turn to port as soon as the second, inner range ("leading marks") aligns after rounding the tip of Whiffin Spit.

Note: Tidal streams run up to 4 knots in the entrance to the harbour. The least depth over the bar between Simpson and Parsons Points is 4.3 m (14 ft).

Sooke Harbour inner range from the tip of Whiffin Spit.

It would be foolhardy to attempt entry into SOOKE HARBOUR without adequate charts and extensive prior research and preparation. The approach, entrance to the harbour and navigation within are extremely tricky, and many boats have been known to go aground.

Make your approach from the centre of Sooke Inlet. Line up the Sooke Harbour outer range ("leading marks") before crossing the bar that extends across the entrance between Simpson and Parsons Points. When abeam of the lighthouse in the narrow part of the channel, prepare for a hard turn to port at the spit's tip to align the inner range ("leading marks"). Deep water extends in close to the tip of the spit. Take care to avoid being carried onto Grant Rocks by strong tidal streams.

Protected anchorage can be found to the N and W of the spit (see page 36). The harbour has extensive shallows, and care should be taken to stay within the marked channels.

If proceeding to SOOKE HARBOUR MARINA and the public wharf, see page 37.

SOOKE BASIN is intriguing to explore, so allow yourself enough time to relax and enjoy being in harmony with nature. Access to EAST SOOKE REGIONAL PARK can be found in Anderson Cove. This is the largest CRD Park, encompassing 1440 ha (3555 acres) of natural and protected coastal landscape that is untouched by urban development. BILLINGS SPIT is a wildlife sanctuary.

SOOKE MARINE INDUSTRIES can facilitate boat repairs for craft up to 20 m (66 ft), and the SUNNY SHORES MARINA offers fuel, limited moorage, some charts, basic provisions and ice.

Sooke Basin also offers a wonderfully safe sailing territory with few obstructions. Ideal conditions for all types of sailing, even windsurfing, occur when a westerly is blowing out in the Juan de Fuca Strait. The EDWARD MILNE COMMUNITY SCHOOL owns heritage longboat replicas and offers sailing/rowing excursions in the basin. Primarily designed for teenagers, this is a unique experience that should not be missed (250-642-6371).

Sooke Harbour outer range from Sooke Inlet.

SOOKE BASIN

APPROACH

The channel to Sooke Basin follows the E shoreline of Sooke Harbour. Between Eliza and Trollope Points the channel becomes shallow and runs between the port-hand buoy and the shore. Upon rounding the small island off Trollope Point, favour the S shore as far as Hill Head. Billings Spit extends considerably S from Billings Point.

Note: Between Eliza and Trollope Points the channel has a patch of shallow water (less than 2 m [6.5 ft] at zero tide). Entrance into Sooke Basin is best made with a flooding tide, as the currents between Trollope Point and Hill Head are fairly strong.

Off Trollope Point looking toward Sooke Basin.

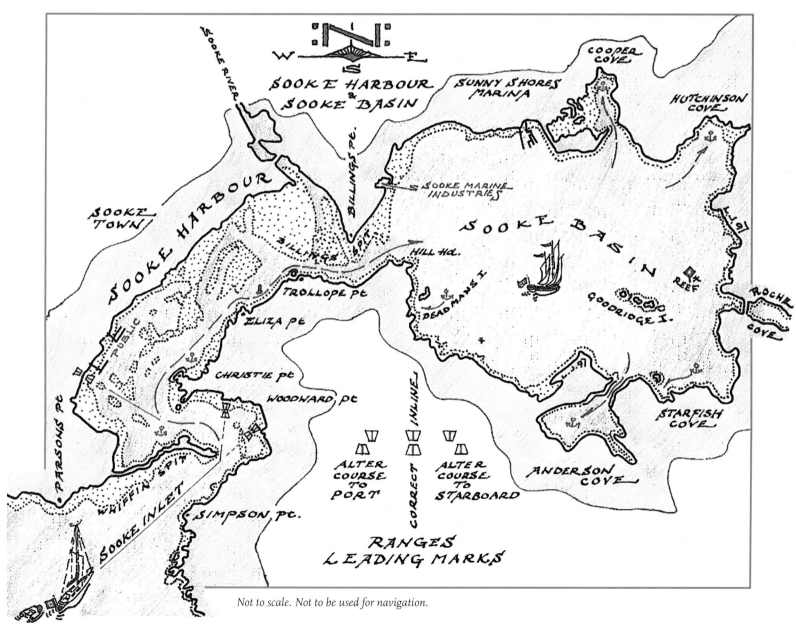

Not to scale. Not to be used for navigation.

3.7 WHIFFIN SPIT PARK, SOOKE HARBOUR

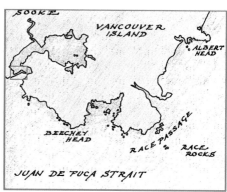

48°21'N 123°43'W

CHARTS

3411. 3313, page 1. SCN Maps A3 & A2.

APPROACH

After having negotiated the Sooke Harbour entrance at the tip of Whiffin Spit (see page 34 for directions).

ANCHOR

To the W of the channel that leads to the marina and public wharf and S of the dolphins. Good sheltered protection can be found here.

DEPTHS

4 - 6 m (13 - 19.5 ft). Holding good in mud.

BOAT LAUNCH

Kayaks can launch from the spit at the end of Whiffin Spit Road.

Note: Decades of logging operations in this area may have left debris on the bottom. An anchor trip line may be advisable.

Anchorage off Whiffin Spit from Christie Point.

This beautiful natural spit, with a lighthouse on its tip, protects Sooke Harbour from southerly and westerly winds and separates it from Sooke Inlet. Anchor NE of the spit and walk along the crushed-stone trail that runs its entire length. Respect the sensitive ecosystem of the park by keeping to the trails. The park supports an abundance of wildlife and vegetation that includes rose and willow scrub, sea asparagus, beach pea and nodding onion. Breathe in the Pacific air while surrounded by views of the OLYMPIC MOUNTAINS. In favourable weather conditions you can beach your dinghy near the head of the spit and walk through the parking lot to SOOKE HARBOUR HOUSE. Here you will experience excellent West Coast cooking, fresh from the garden and sea. Alternatively, dock at one of the marinas, where you can arrange to be picked up if Sooke Harbour House's driver is available. Crabbing is also excellent around the spit.

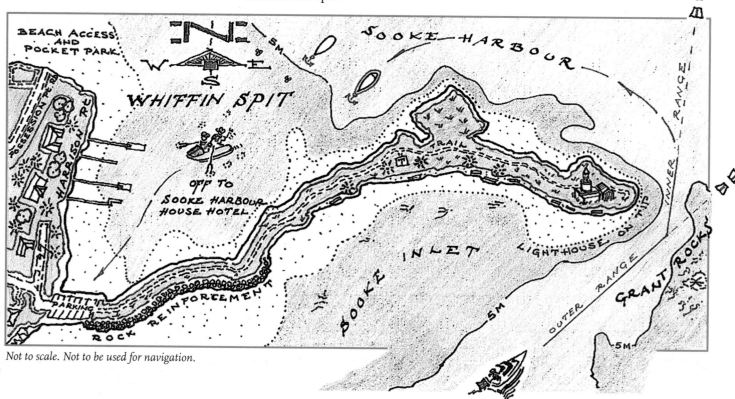

Not to scale. Not to be used for navigation.

SOOKE HARBOUR PUBLIC WHARF & MARINA 3.8

CHARTS

3411. 3313, page 1. SCN Maps A3 & A2.

APPROACH

The marina by lining up the Sooke Harbour ranges ("leading marks"), turning to starboard between the buoys that mark the channel. The outer finger of the marina lies to port. If proceeding to the public wharf, run centre channel and parallel to a line of piles to the W.

PUBLIC WHARF

Has extensive floats.

MARINA

SOOKE HARBOUR MARINA (250-642-3236) has limited transient moorage. Book well in advance.

BOAT LAUNCH

At marina.

Note: Channel between marina and public wharf shallows rapidly to the E.

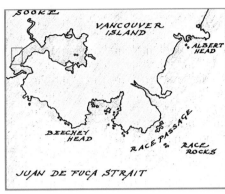

48°22'N 123°43'W

Two sets of floats make up the public wharf N of the marina. Luckily in the summer months most of the fishing boats are out and space is available. Be sure to visit PALCO'S MARINE STORE where you will find hardware and the strangest assortment of odds and ends at very competitive prices.

Provisioning in SOOKE VILLAGE town centre is very good, with banks, supermarkets, a post office, liquor store, pharmacies and hardware stores all available. The GOODLIFE RESTAURANT & BOOKSTORE provides food for the soul and books for thought and can be found on Otter Point Road. Crabbing off the end of the public wharf is also excellent.

SOOKE HARBOUR MARINA is primarily for sport fishermen and charters. They have showers and laundry facilities and a shop selling tackle and bait.

Sooke Harbour range.

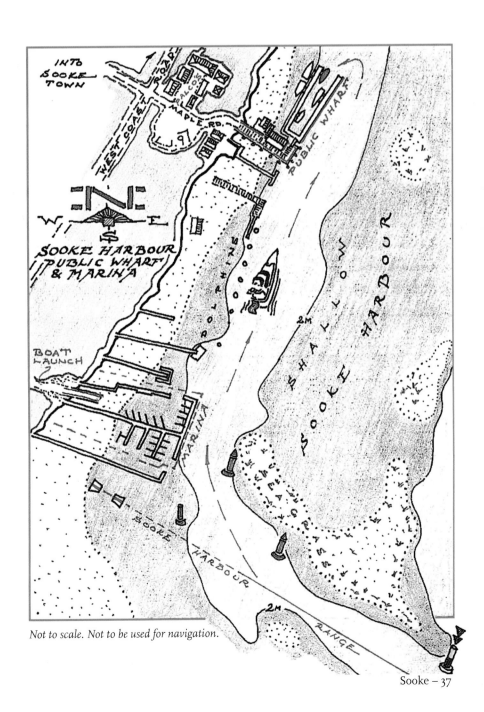

Not to scale. Not to be used for navigation.

3.9   ANDERSON COVE, SOOKE BASIN

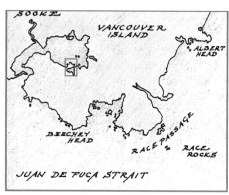

48°22'N 123°39'W

CHARTS

3411. 3313, page 1. SCN Maps A3 & A2.

APPROACH

Use great caution when navigating the rocky entrance, as the channel is very narrow. Favour the E shore and look out for rocks that protrude out from the W shore.

ANCHOR

In centre of bay.

DEPTHS

3 - 4 m (10 - 13 ft). Holding and bottom condition unrecorded.

Note: The entrance channel has patches of shallow water (less than 2 m [6.5 ft] at zero tide).

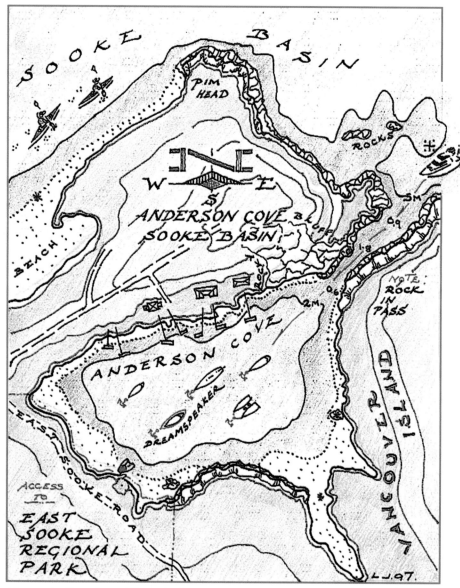

Not to scale. Not to be used for navigation.

When navigating this narrow, rocky entrance stay close to the E shore and look out for a rock in the passage. Once in, you will find a cosy and completely enclosed anchorage that is well protected. Watch out for deadheads when anchoring. Access to EAST SOOKE REGIONAL PARK can be reached from the W side of the cove and is the starting point for hikers heading to BABBINGTON HILL and MOUNT MAGUIRE, where sweeping views of the Olympic Peninsula embrace you. It is worth taking an extra day here to explore the coastal trail, which is considered one of the foremost day hikes in Canada. It is a challenging 6-hour trek that takes you across a windswept bluff with the ocean crashing at your feet, through a rainforest and then ends in a heritage apple orchard (see 3.5, page 33).

Entrance to Anderson Cove.

SUNNY SHORES RESORT & MARINA
3.10

CHARTS
3411. 3313, page 1. SCN Maps A3 & A2.

APPROACH
From the SE.

MARINA
SUNNY SHORES MARINA (250-642-5731) has limited transient moorage. Fuel is available.

BOAT LAUNCH
At marina.

FUEL
At marina.

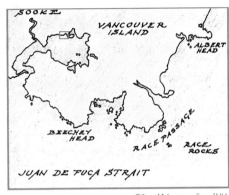

48°23'N 123°39'W

This is the only marina within the harbour and basin that provides fuelling facilities. Limited transient moorage is available, with shower and laundry facilities. The marina store provides good basic provisioning, including the biggest blocks of ice this side of Victoria. The marina also runs a resort with camping and trailer facilities, a playground, swimming pool, boat charters and a launch ramp. Nearby Cooper Cove offers protected anchorage, but its proximity to the road makes it a little noisy. Hutchinson Cove is protected and much quieter. It is possible to walk from this cove to historic 17 MILE HOUSE for a welcome beer and some hearty pub fare.

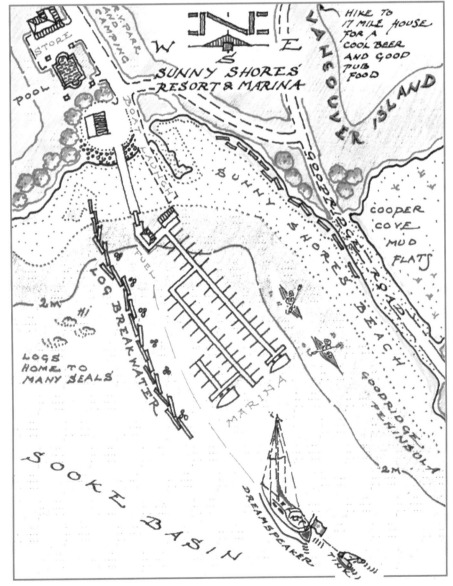

Not to scale. Not to be used for navigation.

Channel to marina fuel float.

Chapter 4
SIDNEY

TIDES

Reference Port: Fulford Harbour

Secondary Ports: Saanichton Bay & Sidney

CURRENTS

Reference Station: Race Passage

Secondary Stations: Haro Strait (Hamley Point) & Sidney Channel

WEATHER

Area: Haro Strait

Reporting Stations: Discovery Island, Kelp Reef, Saturna

Taking an evening sail in Tsehum Harbour 4.5

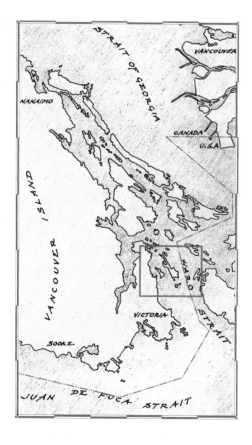

The conveniently situated port and town of Sidney, with its central position and upbeat attitude, allows visitors easy access to the many ports of call on Vancouver Island and to the Gulf Islands. On a busy summer's day, colourful fleets of pleasure boats can be seen steaming into Port Sidney Marina, which is also an official port of entry for Canada Customs. The Swartz Bay ferry terminal is nearby and the western terminus of the Washington State ferry is located south of the town. Victoria International Airport is close at hand, making Sidney an accessible destination for charter groups and boat owners who live outside the region, or even outside the country.

The waters explored in this chapter are ideal for a mini-cruise. They also allow the first-time visitor a gentle introduction to the delights of the southernmost Gulf Islands and B.C.'s unique marine parks.

Port Sidney lies near the northern end of picturesque Saanich Peninsula. Provisioning facilities here are plentiful, and this enterprising town goes out of its way to accommodate the visiting boater. A short trip east will take you over to the popular Sidney Spit Provincial Marine Park, with its long stretch of sandy beaches and tidal lagoon, a favoured refuge for migratory seabirds.

The route south via Sidney Channel provides access to the undeveloped and charming D'Arcy Island Provincial Marine Park, a favourite with kayakers and boaters alike.

Isle-de-Lis Provincial Marine Park can be reached by taking the northerly Haro Strait route to Rum Island. Although open to most winds, in favourable weather conditions this secluded anchorage is the perfect spot for lazing in your cockpit with a cool drink in hand. You can end your cruise in busy Tsehum Harbour, where good anchorage is available, marinas are in abundance and local pubs are bustling and friendly.

CAUTIONARY NOTES

Although the weather in this area tends, in the summer months, to be mainly calm, be sure to keep a sharp eye open for any changes. Don't let the generally placid weather conditions divert you from vigilant navigation, as there are numerous rocks to bump into.

FEATURED DESTINATIONS

4.1 Sidney & Port Sidney Marina   42

4.2 Sidney Spit Marine Park   44

4.3 D' Arcy Island Marine Park   46

4.4 Isle-de-Lis Marine Park   48

4.5 Tsehum Harbour   50

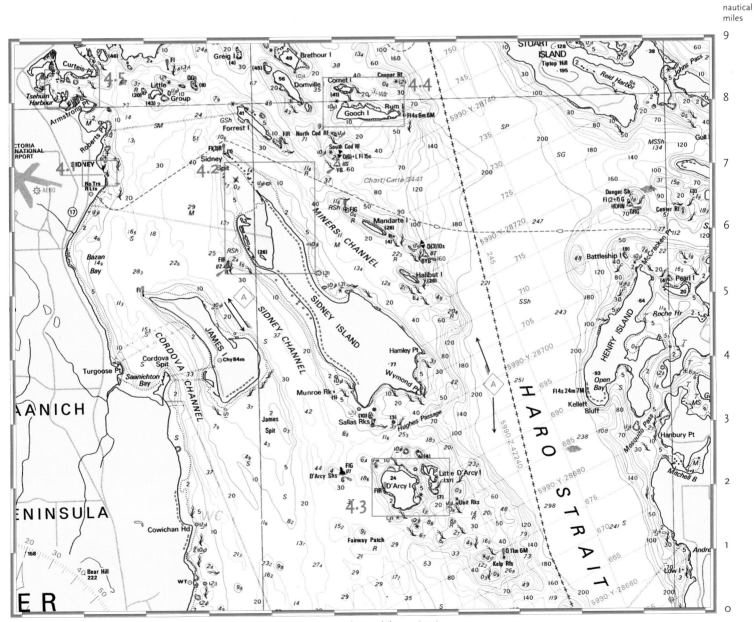

Reproduced portion of CHS Chart 3462 for passage planning only. Not to be used for navigation.

NESSUNO(A) 4.1 SIDNEY & PORT SIDNEY MARINA

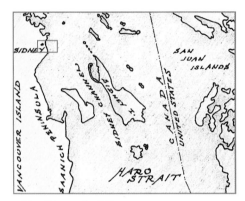

48°39'N 123°23'W

Port Sidney Marina entrance lies to the north of the public wharfhead.

Hanging baskets bursting with summer flowers and bustling dock attendants are waiting to welcome you at the refurbished PORT SIDNEY MARINA (250-655-3711). Expect a steady stream of traffic and lineups in the high summer months. Customs and check-in facilities are located at dock F under a large tent. If you have not arranged a slip beforehand, tie up here to get instructions. Showers, laundry facilities and all necessary amenities are available at the marina office building. A pet area is also provided for your sea-weary pooch at the top of the gangway. Sidney town and marina provide a wonderfully central area to freshen up, provision and visit the local attractions. To the south of Sidney lies the Washington State ferry terminal, to the west, Victoria International Airport and close by, at the tip of the Saanich Peninsula, lies the B.C. Ferries terminal at Swartz Bay. The marina offers a complimentary bus service to downtown Victoria and the Butchart Gardens from June 15 until September 5, or hop on local transit bus #70 (Pat Bay Hwy) to downtown Victoria. Bus #75 goes to the Butchart Gardens. Both leave from the corner of Beacon Avenue and Fifth Street.

The original public wharf, S of the stone breakwater, is now a private dock. The SIDNEY ISLAND FERRY (250-727-7700), servicing Sidney Spit Provincial Marine Park (hourly in the summer months) and Portland Island (Princess Margaret Marine Park), also operates from this dock. SATELLITE FISH COMPANY, a fresh fish market specializing in live and cooked crab and a variety of local, seasonal fish, is worth a visit.

The busy main street, Beacon Avenue, has a good selection of shops, lively cappuccino bars, supermarkets and diverse bookstores, as well as a bakery, liquor store and post office. For a taste of local history, visit the SIDNEY MUSEUM on Beacon Avenue. On Sunday afternoons in the summer months, live bands perform at the bandstand located next to the museum. SANCHA HALL (at Beacon Avenue and Pat Bay Hwy) showcases a selection of fine crafts and artwork in a gallery setting during the month of August. The annual SAANICH AGRICULTURAL FAIR, in existence more than 130 years, takes place on the Labour Day weekend, providing fun for all the family.

Hanging baskets burst with summer flowers at Port Sidney Marina.

CHARTS

3476. 3313, page 7. SCN Map B1.

APPROACH

The Port Sidney breakwater from the SE. The marina entrance lies to the N of the public wharfhead. Buoys mark the centre of the entrance channel. Leave to port.

ANCHOR

There is no sheltered anchorage, but on a flat, calm day a temporary spot can be found just N of the public wharf.

DEPTHS

Holding and bottom condition unrecorded.

PUBLIC WHARF

There are currently no facilities for transient overnight moorage.

MARINA

Enter PORT SIDNEY MARINA via the channel between the 2 stone breakwaters. Keep the white markers in the centre channel to port on entry and exit. The staff monitor VHF channel 68 and will guide you to custom dock F for clearance as well as into an appropriate berth.

Note: Day moorage is possible between 9:00 a.m. and 4:00 p.m.

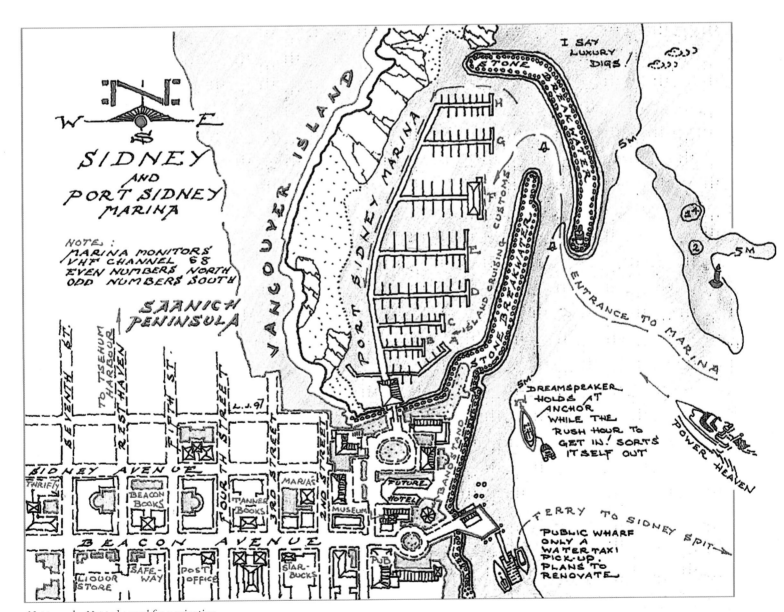

Not to scale. Not to be used for navigation.

4.2   SIDNEY SPIT MARINE PARK

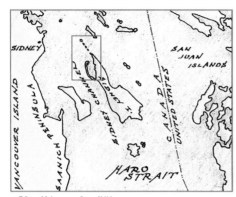

48°39'N   123°20'W

Looking south over the tip of the spit to Sidney Island and the anchorage.

Accessible by boat only, this delightful marine park is one of the most popular on the coast. Foot passengers and campers can now take the SIDNEY ISLAND FERRY (operates hourly in the summer months) from the Sidney Dock at the foot of Beacon Avenue (250-727-7700). The island was originally used as a summer camp by the Coast Salish many years ago. Today visitors still enjoy the spirit of summertime sport that remains. The park has great warm-water swimming off its long stretch of sandy beaches. Exposed at low tide, the sand heats up the incoming water to a very comfortable temperature. Winter storms also provide interesting beachcombing. The spit is a wonderful place to stretch your legs, and a hike to the light at the end of the spit and back is truly invigorating. The clay and sand banks erode easily, so make a point of staying on the trails to reduce further damage to this constantly shifting shoreline.

Arrive early if you want to pick up one of the 35 mooring buoys, or tie up at the public dock. Rafting up is discouraged, as the buoys have been known to drag in strong winds. If a summer westerly does spring up, don't panic; take the usual precautions, and be prepared for a rocky night's sleep.

The anchorage area is becoming shallower each year, so pay close attention to your depth sounder. The lagoon at the S end of the park is intriguing to explore by kayak, canoe or dinghy at HW, especially in the migration months of April and May, as well as from July to September, when shorebirds make a brief stop at the saltwater marsh.

The park is a perfect spot for kayakers and there are 24 campsites in the large field near the private wharf, with picnic tables, toilets and a hand pump for water. The only facility that can be reserved in the park is the covered picnic shelter designed for group camping (call 250-475-1341).

Looking east from Sidney Channel. Paradise Beach in the foreground.

CHARTS

3441. 3313, page 6. SCN Map B1.

APPROACH

From the W, the most conspicuous landmark being the boats either anchored or on mooring buoys.

ANCHOR

Among boats on mooring buoys or, alternatively, off the sandy hook close to the lagoon. Although exposed to the N and W, the spit offers good protection from the prevailing southerly summer winds.

DEPTHS

2 - 4 m (6.5 - 13 ft). Holding good in sand.

PUBLIC WHARF

The park has extensive moorage for pleasure craft.

Note: There are shallow areas (depths at zero tide of less than 2 m [6.5 ft]).

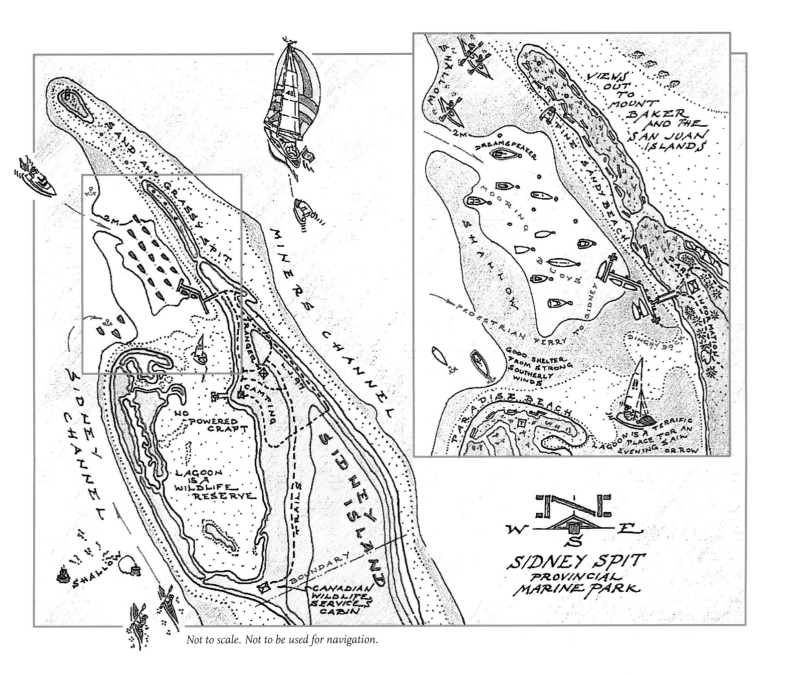

Not to scale. Not to be used for navigation.

4.3 D'ARCY ISLAND MARINE PARK

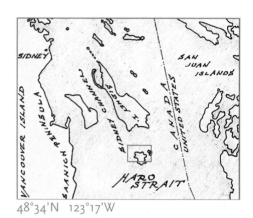

48°34'N 123°17'W

Looking north over Unit Rocks and the passage between D'Arcy and Little D'Arcy Islands.

There are many isolated rocks scattered within the passage between Little D'Arcy Island and D'Arcy Island Provincial Marine Park. Entry at LW is therefore advisable. Sunbathing seals serve as comical but useful day marks on many of the semi-submerged rocks. Beaches along the N and NE shores make this park attractive to kayakers and canoeists, who can use the public wharf in Saanichton Bay as an alternate starting point. Although the island is undeveloped, it provides 4 tempting anchorages as well as 12 basic campsites and a pit toilet. Exploring the shoreline is best done at LW, when the cleared part of the beach is exposed.

In favourable weather conditions spots 1 and 2 afford good sunsets, while spot 3 has a sweeping sandy beach and is adjacent to the campsite. In spot 4 you can anchor off a perfect crescent-shaped pocket beach.

It is probably best to put aside the island's past as a leper colony and focus instead on its present as a marine park to be both explored and enjoyed.

Little D'Arcy Island is private and, although the drying cove looks charming from a distance, on closer inspection you will find a large boathouse straddling the inner cove and a private home looking down on you.

Note: Extreme caution must be exercised while navigating the waters surrounding the D'Arcy Islands.

Sailing north to the D'Arcy Islands.

CHARTS
3441. 3313, page 5. SCN Map A5.

APPROACH
At LW is strongly advised in order to ensure visibility of the many isolated rocks.

ANCHOR
Although no real sheltered anchorage is provided by the island, in settled weather temporary anchorage with adequate protection from southerlies can be found.

DEPTHS
Depths as well as holding and bottom condition vary depending on location.

A sunbathing seal serves as a useful day mark.

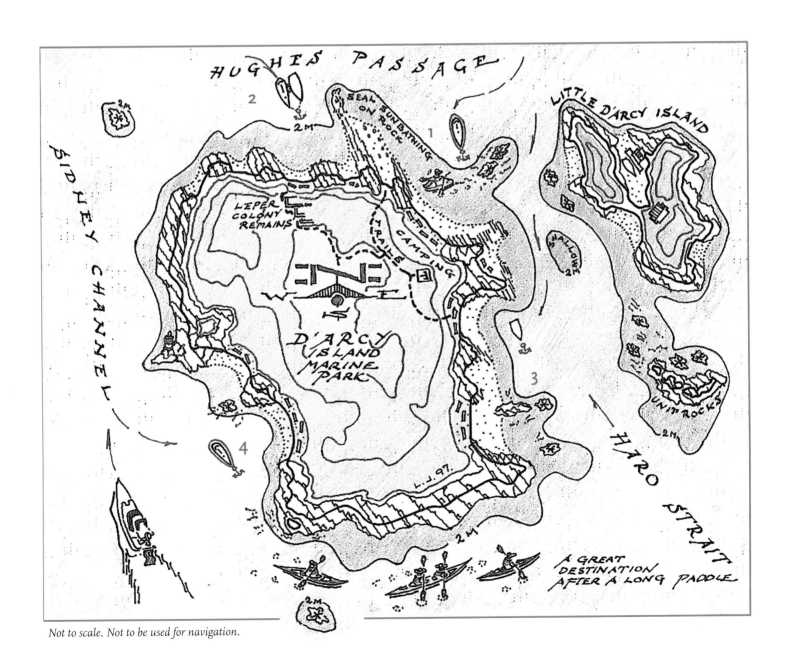

Not to scale. Not to be used for navigation.

4.4   ISLE-DE-LIS MARINE PARK

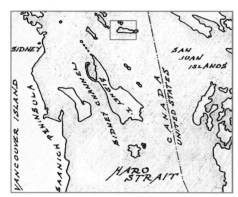

48°40'N 123°17'W

Rum Island looking east over Tom Point.

Anne rows to shore.

Isle-de-Lis Marine Park is a little-known gem on Rum Island that provides limited anchorage in either cove and is open to most winds and swells caused by passing boats or larger vessels in the nearby shipping lanes. If you plan to spend the night here at anchor, you will have to wait for a favourable weather report, but it is well worth the wait. Alternatively, you can arrive by kayak or canoe, pull up onto the gravel isthmus that joins Rum and Gooch Islands and camp beside the long grass and driftwood. A grassy campsite-with-a-view is nestled above the derelict jetty. Toilets can be found behind the park sign after following the trail E.

We have often enjoyed the restful solitude of this island, taking leisurely walks along the overgrown trails to Tom Point to watch the antics of otters at play. This is a wonderful anchorage on a still, blue-sky day, when there's time to explore the little lagoon at LW, go scuba diving along the artificial reef off Comet Island or just sit in the cockpit with a cool drink.

Anchorage between Gooch and Rum Islands.

APPROACH

From the S, giving clearance to Tom Point. From the N, taking note of the position of the wreck off Comet Island, marked by 4 white buoys. Cooper Reef to the NE is unmarked.

ANCHOR

Anchorage is possible to the N or S of the gravel isthmus that connects with Gooch Island. The northern location gives adequate shelter from the prevailing summer southerlies.

DEPTHS

4 - 6 m (13 - 19.5 ft). Holding moderate in gravel and kelp.

Note: If considering an overnight stay, wash from commercial shipping in Haro Strait can make the anchorage a little rolly.

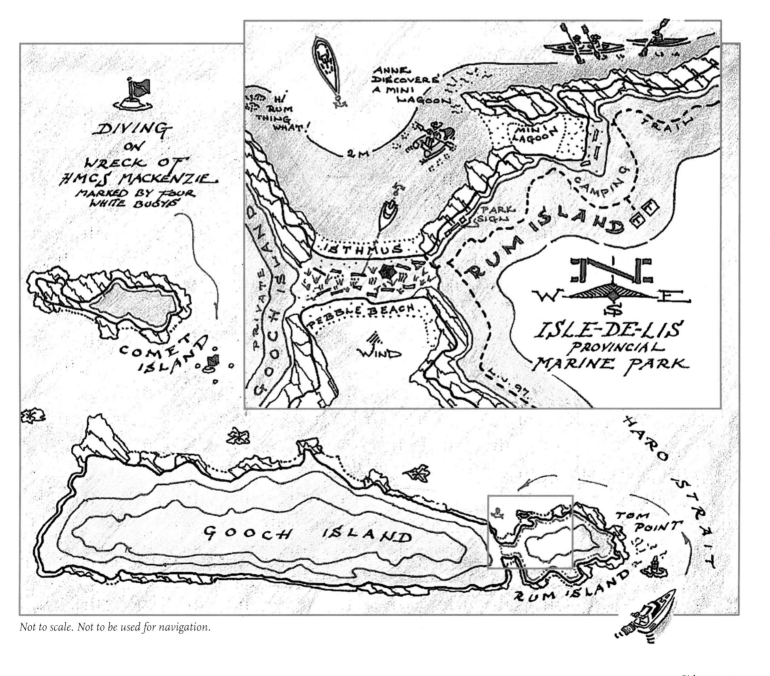

Not to scale. Not to be used for navigation.

4.5   TSEHUM HARBOUR

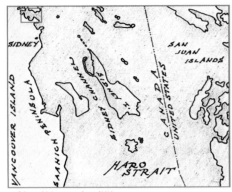

48°40'N 123°24'W

Customs and fuel float, Van Isle Marina.

This is an exceptionally busy harbour in the summer months, with adequate moorage for visiting boaters. If you need to repair, buy, build or charter a boat, you will find excellent facilities within the Tsehum Harbour industrial zone.

Good anchorage can be found to the west of VAN ISLE MARINA in the centre of the harbour, staying clear of all channels to the marinas. Gentle breezes filter through on hot days, and it is a perfect playground for kids in sailing dinghies. The public wharf is mainly commercial, although the W side of C and D docks is for transient moorage. The VAN ISLE MARINA provides visitor moorage, shower and laundry facilities, and ice is available. Their "Dock 503 Waterfront Café" serves unique and tasty lunch and supper dishes and is open seven days a week – booking ahead is essential, call 250-656-0828. SIDNEY HARBOUR CRUISE LTD. offers a shuttle service to Sidney Harbour, Canoe Bay or Swartz Bay in the summer months from 10:30 a.m. until 4:30 p.m. (250-655-5211 or pager 250-480-6930). They also monitor VHF channel 72.

Here are a few tried, tested and recommended haunts of locals and boaters alike. THE LATCH COUNTRY INN offers fine dining and/or fine sleeping if you want to celebrate a special occasion or just take a break from the boat. BLUE PETER PUB & RESTAURANT is bustling and friendly and is situated at the end of SHOAL BAY MARINA, with a convenient dinghy dock next to the ramp. The DELL on Harbour Road serves fresh baked goods and fine coffee. ALL BAY MARINE LTD. is a well-stocked and friendly marine supply centre that serves all the local boatyards. ROBERTS BAY BIRD SANCTUARY gives visitors a tranquil respite from the bustle of the harbour.

Approaching the entrance to Tsehum Harbour.

CHARTS

3476. 3313, page 7. SCN Map B1.

APPROACH

Between Armstrong Point and Curteis Point. Enter the well-marked channel into the harbour between the breakwater on Thumb Point and the lighted starboard-hand mark.

ANCHOR

In the W and centre of the harbour, away from the marked channels to the marinas.

DEPTHS

2 - 4 m (6.5 - 13 ft). Holding good over mud and gravel.

PUBLIC WHARF

An extensive public wharf is located in All Bay. Some transient moorage on C and D docks.

MARINAS

The harbour and the outer bays are home to numerous marinas. VAN ISLE MARINA (250-656-1138) has transient moorage and a customs entry float.

NORTH SAANICH MARINA (250-656-5558) and WESTPORT MARINA (250-656-2832) may have available moorage, so call ahead.

FUEL

At Van Isle and North Saanich Marinas.

Note: There is a posted and enforced 4-knot speed limit within the harbour. This applies to dinghies with outboards, too! Be sure to stay within the marked channels, as there are pockets of shallow water and reefs extend out from the shore.

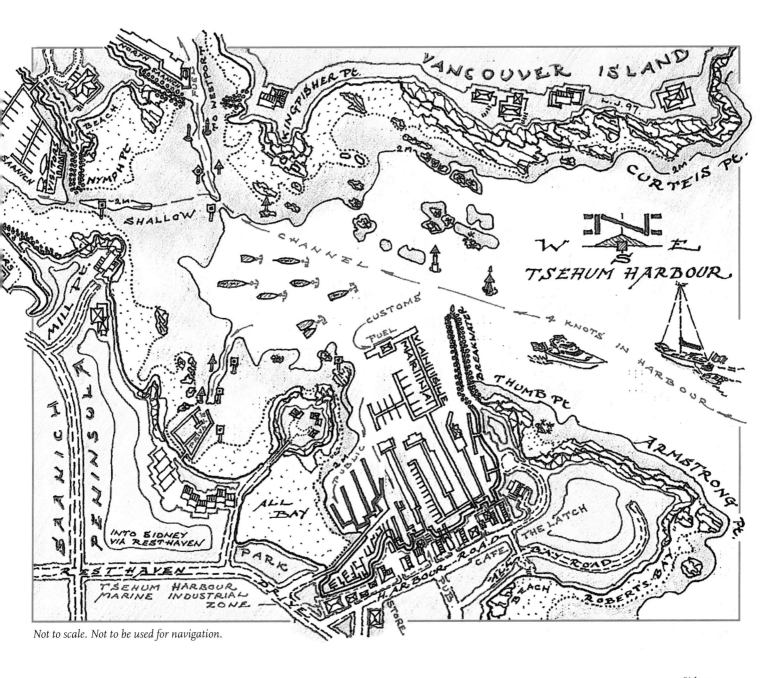

Not to scale. Not to be used for navigation.

Sailing north to Sidney.

Colourful dinghies at the North Saanich Yacht Club.

Kayakers in Canoe Cove.

Chapter 5
SWARTZ BAY

Swartz Bay ferry terminal.

Chapter 5
SWARTZ BAY

TIDES
Reference Port: Fulford Harbour
Secondary Port: Swartz Bay

CURRENTS
Reference Station: Race Passage
Secondary Station: Swanson Channel

WEATHER
Area: Haro Strait
Reporting Stations: Kelp Reef & Saturna

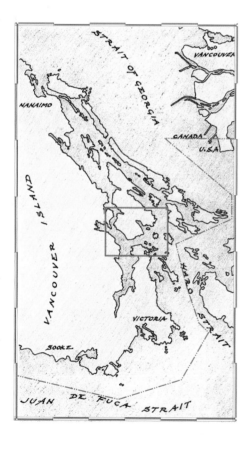

At anchor in Canoe Bay   5.1

Although Swartz Bay itself is not a featured cruising destination in this chapter, it has a tremendous influence on the areas surrounding it. As a major B.C. Ferries terminal, Swartz Bay serves six destinations by several different routes with both inter-island and mainland Superferries. It is the nearest B.C. Ferries terminal to the City of Victoria, and connection with the Washington State ferry can be made in nearby Sidney. All passages and channels in this chapter are heavily traversed by ferry traffic, but other than the occasional ferry wash, this has surprisingly little effect on the seclusion of most island coves and bays.

From the tip of Saanich Peninsula and Portland Island in the north to the southern shores of Saltspring Island, the cruising boater is offered many wonderful opportunities for invigorating hikes, quiet strolls along sandy beaches, scenic picnics or unsurpassed sunsets.

Starting from Canoe Bay, which provides a convenient pick-up point for family and friends arriving at Swartz Bay, head north to Portland Island. All of this island is an expansive and charming marine park, donated to the Province of British Columbia by Princess Margaret in 1961. You can easily spend a few restful days here.

En route to Fulford Harbour, stop for a picnic in the tiny anchorage off Isabella Island, or observe nesting oystercatchers in the unlikely anchorage near Jackson Rock. The sleepy harbour and village of Fulford provide the perfect opportunity to combine provisioning with outdoor exploration. Alternatively, while away the morning in its diverse mix of shops and cafés.

Finally, don't miss a day at the historic Ruckle Provincial Park, where you can hike, swim or picnic and enjoy the spectacular view from the bluffs overlooking Swanson Channel.

CAUTIONARY NOTES

Careful navigation is required when transiting John, Iroquois and Page Passages between Coal Island and Canoe Bay. Slow down to the posted speed limit of 7 knots, as wake in these narrow channels poses a real danger to small craft, especially kayaks. Currents in these passages can reach 3 - 4 knots on a large tide.

FEATURED DESTINATIONS

5.1 Canoe Bay (Canoe Cove)   56

5.2 Princess Margaret Marine Park, Portland Island   58

5.3 Isabella Island, Saltspring Island   60

5.4 Jackson Rock, Saltspring Island   61

5.5 Fulford Harbour & Village, Saltspring Island   62

5.6 Ruckle Provincial Park, Saltspring Island   64

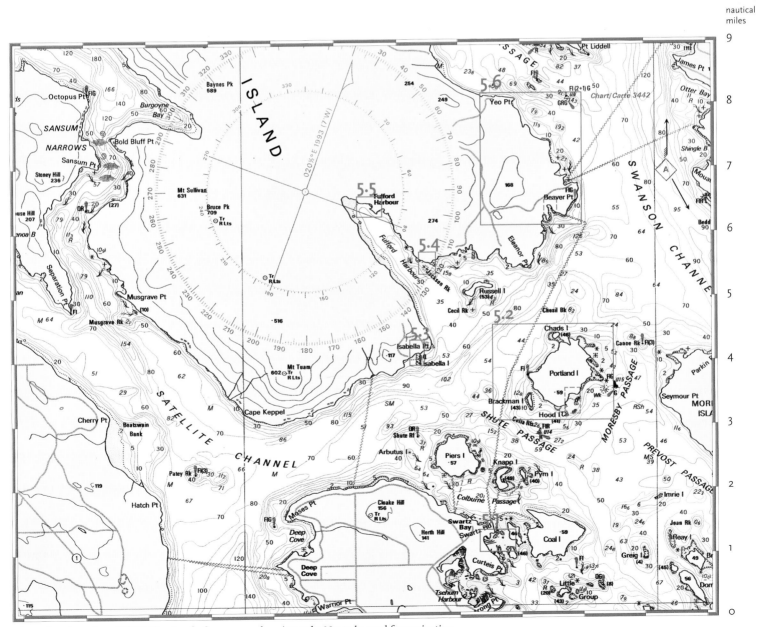

Reproduced portion of CHS Chart 3462 for passage planning only. Not to be used for navigation.

5.1   CANOE BAY (CANOE COVE)

48°41'N 123°24'W

Entrance to Iroquois Passage looking north.

Once you have navigated your way into Canoe Bay (known locally as Canoe Cove), temporary anchorage can be found between the marina and Kolb Island. Here you can swing in the back eddies of the flood and ebb currents, but note that it can be a little tight, with boats on private buoys and permanently anchored resident craft.

Alternatively, call CANOE COVE MARINA and book a transient slip. If you need to check in with customs first, tie up at the end of C dock and walk to the phone booth at the wharfhead.

The marina is extensive, providing complete boat overhaul and repair facilities. The fuel dock can be reached via a canyon of boat sheds between C and D docks. Canoe Cove is an interesting spot to explore, with a variety of boat services to choose from and artisans to visit. It is not a provisioning stop. It is also within walking distance of the Swartz Bay ferry terminal.

Here are a few selected and recommended local enterprises: The CANOE COVE COFFEE SHOP is open from 6:00 a.m. to 4:30 p.m. for breakfast and light lunches. Try the special "53 Burger" – highly recommended. The STONEHOUSE COUNTRY PUB & RESTAURANT overlooks the cove and serves up good pub grub. They also offer fine dining. If you haven't had a chance to try your hand at kayaking, OCEAN RIVER SPORTS could be the place to start. STAINED GLASS STUDIOS produces traditional stained-glass designs for that unique porthole or lamp. At MORGAN WARREN STUDIOS a busy local artist produces fine-quality bird and wildlife studies. The marina boatyard provides excellent mechanical, electrical and woodworking services. (Repairs due to rock damage average three a week.) The boatyard's marine and hardware department stocks the "business end" of boating hardware. CAMPBELL BLACK MARINE specializes in hull and fibreglass work.

Canoe Bay from Iroquois Passage.

CHARTS

3476. 3313, page 7. SCN Map B1.

APPROACH

From Iroquois Passage between Musclow Islet and Kolb Island.

ANCHOR

Between the marina and Kolb Island, where good shelter from summer winds can be found.

DEPTHS

4 - 6 m (13 - 19.5 ft). Holding moderate in dead kelp over sand.

MARINA

CANOE COVE MARINA (250-656-5566) will accommodate transient visitors if slips are available. Fuel dock, propane, customs float and full marine repair facilities.

Note: There are rocks to the N of the marina, at the end of C and D docks, that are marked with yellow poles.

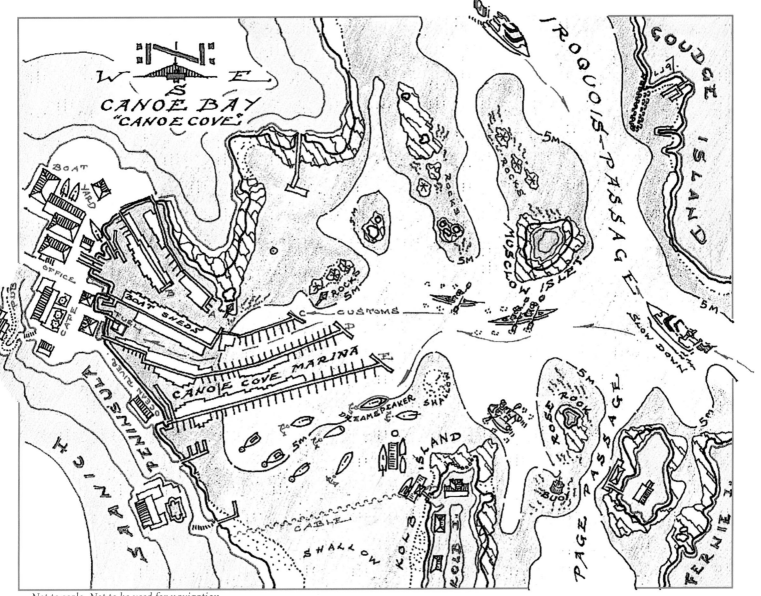

Not to scale. Not to be used for navigation.

5.2   PRINCESS MARGARET MARINE PARK, PORTLAND ISLAND

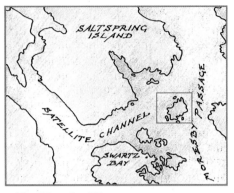

48°43'N 123°22'W

CHARTS

3476. 3441. 3313, page 9. SCN Map B6.

APPROACH

Due to off-lying hazards, approach Portland Island with extreme caution. It is strongly advised to enter the 4 featured anchorages at LW, when the rock hazards are most visible.

PRINCESS BAY (TORTOISE BAY)

ANCHOR

After entering N of and close to Tortoise Islets, swing in the centre or tie a stern line to a ring on the W shore. Temporary, exposed to the S.

DEPTHS

2 m (6.5 ft). Moderate holding in eelgrass over soft mud and shell.

Approach to Princess Bay.

Charming and popular Portland Island is perfect for leisurely circumnavigation by boat or on foot. The 2 primary anchorages are Princess Bay in the S and Royal Cove in the N. There are good, well-marked hiking trails that take you around the densely wooded island and through the meadow and orchards. Kayakers and canoeists usually come ashore in Princess Bay where beaching is easy, but Arbutus Point (local name) in the N, with its fine white-shell beach and flat areas for camping, is also very inviting. There are 20 campsites on the island, with pit toilets and a freshwater pump. There is also a fun dive site at the artificial reef, S of Pellow Islets. Note that the surrounding islands are all private. Brackman Island is an ecological reserve and is not for recreational use. The small SIDNEY ISLAND FERRY (250-727-7700) provides a daily service to the park.

After carefully navigating the narrow channel N of Tortoise Islets, you will find the attractive anchorage of Princess Bay, which is protected in most moderate summer conditions. A small private island protects the bay from easterly winds and ferry wash. There is plenty of room to swing, but on crowded weekends you can make use of the metal rings provided on the shoreline rocks. A gently sloping beach leads to the information shelter and barbecue area, which is backed by a picnic meadow and old orchard. A dinghy dock provides access to the W shoreline and is also a pick-up/drop off point for the daily ferry.

If you're unprepared, the ferry wash in Royal Cove can be somewhat alarming. Our solution was to aim the bow N into the wash, attach a stern line to a ring on the shore and take up the slack on the anchor. The upside is the cove's tranquil sunset views. Ideally this is a 6 to 8 boat anchorage; more is definitely a crowd. There are wonderful sloping rocks overlooking the anchorage, ideal for diving or picnicking. A dinghy dock near the head of the cove leads to the information shelter and hiking trails. A hand pump for fresh water can be found a short way along the middle trail.

Two delightful picnic stops can also be found to the E of Brackman Island and to the N of Pellow Islets.

Looking east to Princess Bay.

ROYAL COVE

ANCHOR

Enter the cove from the NE. It is strongly advised to tie a stern line to a ring on the shore, as this helps minimize rolling from ferry wash. Temporary, exposed to the NE.

DEPTHS

4 - 6 m (13 - 19.5 ft). Holding good in mud.

BRACKMAN ISLAND

ANCHOR

Between Portland and Brackman Islands. Entry is possible from both N and S. Day-picnic anchorage.

DEPTHS

2 m (6.5 ft). Holding good over shell and sand.

PELLOW ISLETS

ANCHOR

At the head of the tiny inlet N of Pellow Islets lies a 1- or 2-boat spot. Tuck in with line ashore. Temporary, exposed to the SE.

DEPTHS

Bottom condition unrecorded. See Chart 3476 for depths.

Note: A dive site, marked by 3 white buoys, on the sunken MV G. B. Church lies SW of Pellow Islets.

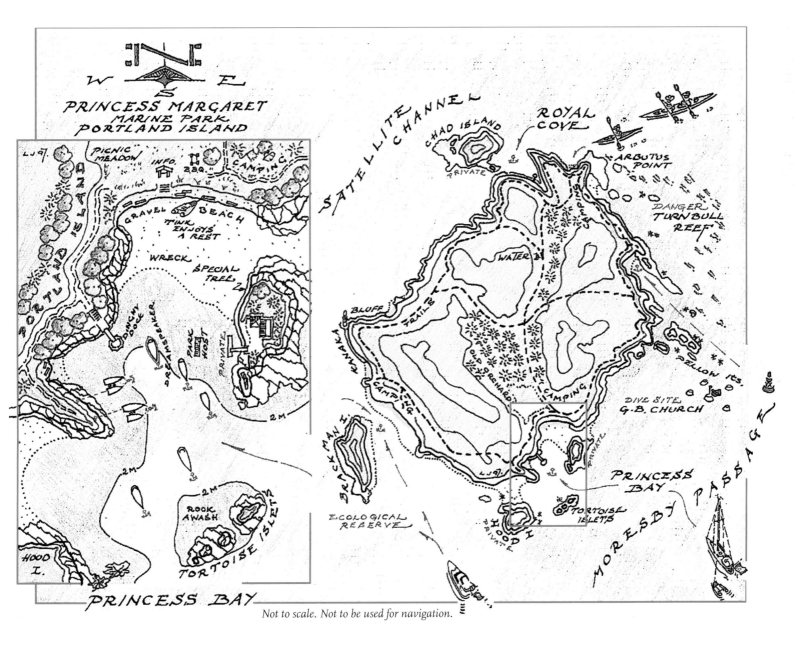

Not to scale. Not to be used for navigation.

5.3 ISABELLA ISLAND, SALTSPRING ISLAND

48°44'N 123°26'W

CHARTS

3478. 3313, page 8. SCN Map B4.

APPROACH

From the SW. The island has a light on its outer rocky point.

ANCHOR

There is temporary anchorage between Isabella Island and the Saltspring Island shore. A stern line to Isabella Island tends to minimize the effects of ferry wash.

DEPTHS

2 - 4 m (6.5 - 13 ft). Holding good in sand and mud.

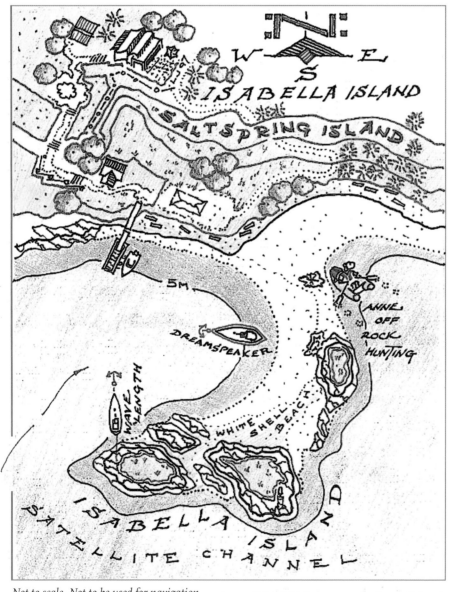

Not to scale. Not to be used for navigation.

You will find a simply perfect picnic stop where Isabella Island and 2 islets form a tiny anchorage. The foreshore is private and dominated by a beautifully designed family home, with paddocks, lawns and a private dock. Wedding preparations were in full swing the day we arrived, giving a festive air. A fun place to explore by dinghy at low tide or to take a quiet snooze in the cockpit. If the weather is favourable and you plan to stay the night, the boat "Wave Length" on the shoreline plan opposite indicates an appropriate position for reasonable protection from ferry wash.

Approach to Isabella Island.

JACKSON ROCK, SALTSPRING ISLAND
5.4

CHARTS
3478. 3313, page 8. SCN Map B4.

APPROACH
At LW, as the rocks virtually disappear at HW.

ANCHOR
Between the rock and the Saltspring Island shore. A day stop in settled weather.

DEPTHS
6 m (19.5 ft). Holding good in sand and mud.

Note: Do not take pets ashore, as the rock hosts an oystercatcher nesting area.

48°45'N 123°26'W

This temporary anchorage seems an unlikely spot to explore if passing by at HW, as 80 percent of the rock disappears. However, at low tide and in sunny weather, Jackson Rock takes on an entirely different aspect. The NW boulder is an oyster-catcher nesting area, so please keep pets off. On the Salt-spring Island shore the land is a First Nations reserve. However, a trail runs from the shoreline through the woods, and visitors are welcome as long as regard for privacy is observed.

Not to scale. Not to be used for navigation.

Jackson Rock from the Saltspring Island shore.

5.5 FULFORD HARBOUR & VILLAGE, SALTSPRING ISLAND

48°46'N 123°27'W

Approach to public wharf between marina and ferry terminal.

Saint Paul's Church.

Despite having the busiest ferry terminal on Saltspring Island, Fulford Harbour and Village give the impression of being quite laid-back. This is the perfect stop to combine provisioning with outdoor exploration. Arrive early and tie up at the FULFORD HARBOUR MARINA. They provide day and transient moorage and have extensive, well-ordered facilities, including a lookout gazebo and an onshore barbecue. At the time of writing, the FULFORD HARBOUR MARINA STORE & DELI DINER was not in operation (1997). Alternatively, anchor to the NW of the marina. Access to Fulford Village is via the public dock, which is usually filled to overflowing with local boats. Relax with a coffee at any of the local cafés before renting a bike to explore southern Saltspring Island. Friendly staff will be happy to pass on local knowledge. Don't forget a quick visit to the tiny white SAINT PAUL'S CHURCH and graveyard, where many of the old headstones carry Hawaiian family names. In DRUMMOND PARK, just past the historic FULFORD INN & PUB, a beautiful petroglyph, described as a seal, can be found in a clump of cedar trees.

Here are tried, tested and recommended stores and cafés in Fulford Village: RODRIGO'S and THE CAPPUCCINO COURTYARD are renowned for good coffee, homemade pies and a bacon, lettuce and tomato sandwich that you'll return for. MORNINGSIDE STUDIO offers both unique sculpture and accommodation. Visit SALTSPRING ROASTING CO. for freshly roasted coffee beans. JAMBALAYA sells an excellent selection of hats and unique beads. PATTERSON MARKET stocks a good all-around selection of fresh fruit, vegetables and basics. At BLACKBIRD you can treat your home or garden to a whimsical impulse. STUFF & NONSENSE is for kids big and small, and TOM GRAHAM POTTERY produces functional, quality tableware.

When entering, leaving or just getting around Fulford Harbour, take special care to stay clear of all ferry traffic.

CHARTS

3478. 3313, page 8. SCN Map B4.

APPROACH

The Fulford Harbour ferry terminal, at the head of the inlet on the E shore, provides a conspicuous landmark.

ANCHOR

To the W of the ferry terminal and marina. Although moderately exposed to the SE, the harbour provides fair protection.

DEPTHS

4 - 10 m (13 - 33 ft). Holding moderate over a sand-and-mud bottom.

PUBLIC WHARF

There are 2 public wharves, S and N of the ferry terminal. The small wharf S of the terminal is strictly for short-stay loading.

MARINA

FULFORD HARBOUR MARINA (250-653-4467). In the summer months the outer float is reserved for transient moorage.

FUEL

At marina.

Note: The interisland ferry operates regularly and resides overnight at the Fulford terminal.

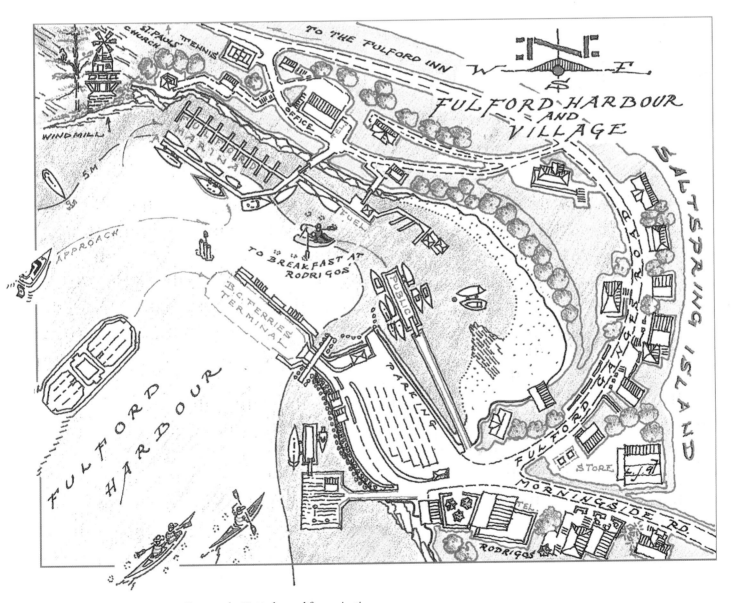

Not to scale. Not to be used for navigation.

5.6   RUCKLE PROVINCIAL PARK, SALTSPRING ISLAND

48°46'N   123°23'W

B.C. Parks

The fence to the old Ruckle farmstead.

Named by us, small "Three Beaches Cove" is on the S boundary of Ruckle Provincial Park. As an anchorage, it is exposed to the S but is more protected from ferry wash than the 2 small coves further N. The rock at the head of the bay is easy to spot, especially when it's occupied by a sunbathing seal. Campers from the park use the shaded shell-and-pebble beaches for swimming and picnicking. A trail can be found at the head of the bay, which takes you through a wooded area and along the farm fence to what remains of the original farmstead. You can take a self-guided tour around this historic farm, which has been in operation since the 1890s and is one of the oldest, continuously run family farms in British Columbia. In the summer months, slide shows are often shown in the old barn. Members of the Ruckle family still reside in the park today and oversee farming operations, so please respect private roads and fields.

Campers can set up tents on the bluffs overlooking Swanson Channel and enjoy the spectacular view, with close proximity to log-strewn pocket beaches and smooth sloping rocks. Facilities include walk-in camping, toilets, water and picnic sites.

The numerous trails are clearly indicated with red metal markers nailed to trees. If you start at the park headquarters you can pick up a map, which will give you distances and time required. Look out for bald eagles, harlequin ducks, black oystercatchers and the occasional black-tailed deer. BEAVER POINT WHARF once housed a post office and PATTERSON MARKET, which you can now find in Fulford Village.

Approach to "Three Beaches Cove." Ruckle Park in the background.

CHARTS

3441. 3313, page 8. SCN Map B4.

APPROACH

The small cove from the S.

ANCHOR

Exposed to the S. A temporary anchorage for 1 or 2 boats in settled weather.

DEPTHS

2 - 4 m (6.5 - 13 ft). Holding good in mud.

Note: Alternative anchorage can be found to the N of Beaver Point. Good access to the park is possible from "Three Beaches Cove."

Sailing toward light at Beaver Point in Ruckle Park.

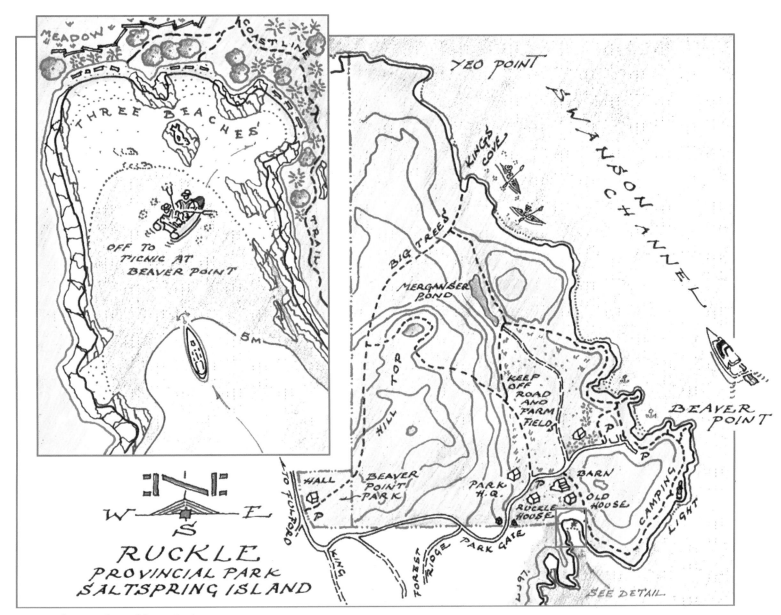

Not to scale. Not to be used for navigation.

Anchored in Tod Inlet   6.3

Chapter 6
SAANICH INLET

TIDES

Reference Port: Fulford Harbour

Secondary Ports: Patricia Bay, Brentwood Bay & Finlayson Arm

CURRENTS

Tidal streams in Saanich Inlet are weak and not specifically referenced in *Canadian Tide and Current Tables, Volume 5.*

WEATHER

The inlet is fairly well protected from the prevailing weather pattern with generally light winds in summer. It isn't adequately covered by the marine forecast.

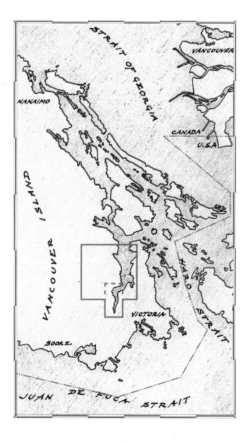

The calm waters and spectacular vistas of British Columbia's southernmost inlet are well known to locals but seldom explored by visiting boaters. Saanich Inlet's fjordlike arm reaches as far down as the popular Goldstream Provincial Park, located at the mouth of the Goldstream River. Towered over by the Malahat Ridge in the west and Mount Work in the east, it holds some remarkably unique surprises, especially in the lower reaches beyond Brentwood Bay, where steep bluffs and deep waters give the inlet a majestic but peaceful air.

In this diverse region you can choose from lively wine tasting in the warm Cowichan Valley to colourful walks through the renowned Butchart Gardens or challenging trails along the protected Gowlland Range, which is covered by an abundant show of wild flowers in spring and early summer. Beginning with Mill Bay in the north, take a leisurely trip to the southern reaches of Finlayson Arm via the inviting bays, coves and bights en route.

Mill Bay is a convenient provisioning stop and allows easy access to the fine vineyards of Vancouver Island. A short way down from Mill Bay, the anchorage at Bamberton Provincial Park has a tempting sandy beach with warm-water swimming, making it a delightful picnic stop.

The peaceful backwater of Brentwood Bay attracts visitors with its shoreline ambience, created by an extraordinary mix of pubs, restaurants and cafés that overlook the water. When visiting Butchart Gardens, access from Brentwood Bay, Butchart Cove and Tod Inlet are three options. The otherwise tranquil Tod Inlet is transformed on summer Saturday evenings, accommodating the numerous boats anchored out to watch the spectacular garden fireworks.

In sharp contrast, McKenzie Bight and Finlayson Arm provide a chance to experience the great outdoors, with trails, lakes, falls or invigorating hikes to the top of Mount Work, where the stunning panoramas are your just reward.

CAUTIONARY NOTES

Although there is a preponderance of calms in summer, the name Squally Reach indicates that occasionally strong southerlies can rocket up the inlet.

FEATURED DESTINATIONS

6.1 Mill Bay 68

6.2 Bamberton Provincial Park 70

6.3 Buchart Cove & Tod Inlet 71

6.4 Brentwood Bay 72

6.5 McKenzie Bight 74

6.6 Finlayson Arm 75

6.7 Gowlland Tod Provincial Park &
    Mount Work Regional Park 76

*Reproduced portion of CHS Chart 3462 for passage planning only.
Not to be used for navigation.*

6.1 MILL BAY

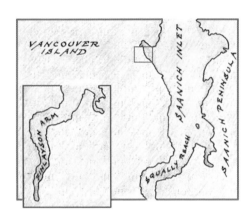

48°39'N 123°33'W

Approach to Mill Bay Marina from the southeast.

The Mill Bay ferry.

M ill Bay is completely open to the SE but provides one of the safest fair-weather anchorages in northern Saanich Inlet. Civilization is also conveniently accessible via Handy Road to the MILL BAY SHOPPING CENTRE. Here you will find a comprehensive selection of shops and services, including a well-stocked supermarket, bakery, liquor store, hardware store, bank, library and information centre. There are also numerous cafés and coffee shops to relax in after shopping, as THRIFTY FOODS will deliver your groceries by arrangement. MILL BAY MARINA, with its charming, tumbledown character, has visitor moorage and friendly service readily available.

Cowichan Valley is fast becoming known for its quality vineyards and cidery. Take the opportunity to visit at least one of them during your stay. CHERRY POINT VINEYARDS produces lively varietal wines, which you can taste and buy in their wine shop. They also sell picnic lunches to spread out on the grass or on wooden tables, and they even have an art gallery that houses the work of local artists. They claim to offer the only winery bed-and-breakfast in British Columbia. Advance arrangement to be picked up from Mill Bay can be made if convenient (call well in advance, 250-743-1272).

VIGNETI ZANATTA VINEYARDS makes their wines using the traditional Italian method. They offer seasonal tastings between 1:00 p.m. and 4:00 p.m. and have a small restaurant that serves lunch and dinner. Advance arrangement to be picked up from Mill Bay can be made if convenient (call well in advance, 250-748-2338).

MERRIDALE CIDER WORKS – British Columbia's first estate cidery – owns Canada's only orchard dedicated solely to cider production, using quality cider apples introduced from Europe many years ago. Call the owner, Al Piggott, ahead of time to be picked up from Mill Bay for a tour and tasting (250-743-4293).

Alternatively, you can take a self-conducted tour (brochure available at information centre). Tours usually operate during the harvesting months of September and October. They include the above vineyards and cidery, with a delicious lunch or lamb barbecue supper at Cherry Point Vineyards.

CHARTS

3441. 3313, page 13. SCN Map B2.

APPROACH

From the E and S of Whisky Point.

ANCHOR

Either to the N of the marina or S between the marina and public wharf. Exposed to the SE.

DEPTHS

6 - 10 m (19.5 - 33 ft). Holding good over sand and mud.

PUBLIC WHARF

With 15 m (49 ft) on either side. Mainly used by locals for temporary stops.

MARINA

MILL BAY MARINA (250-743-4112) monitors VHF channel 68. Transient moorage available. Check in at fuel dock.

BOAT LAUNCH

At the foot of Handy Road.

FUEL

At marina.

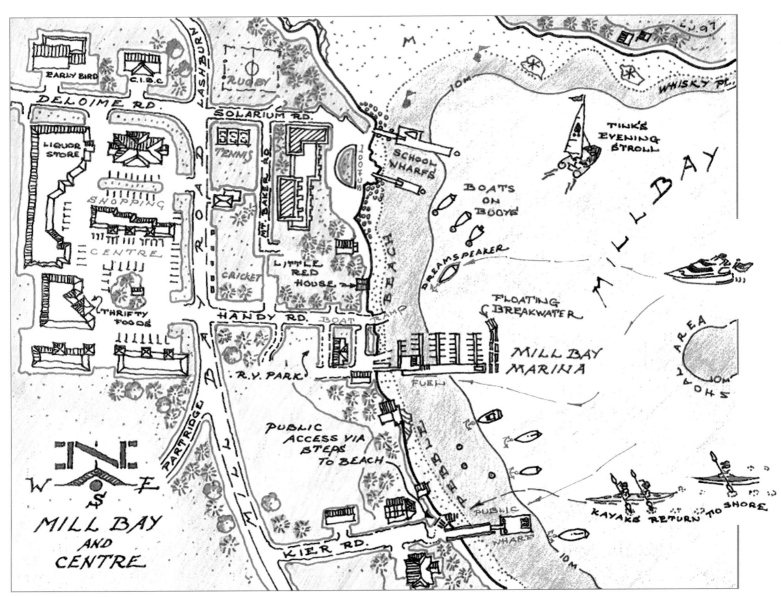

Not to scale. Not to be used for navigation.

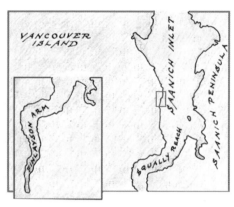

48°36'N   123°31'W

CHARTS

3441. 3313, page 13. SCN Map B2.

APPROACH

From the E and S of the B.C. Ferries terminal on the Mill Bay side. Use the park pavilion as a landmark.

ANCHOR

On a rising tide, off the sand shelf that extends a considerable way out from the park. Only a temporary day stop.

DEPTHS

2 - 4 m (6.5 - 13 ft). Holding moderate over eelgrass and sand.

Note: The drop-off away from the sand ledge is very steep.

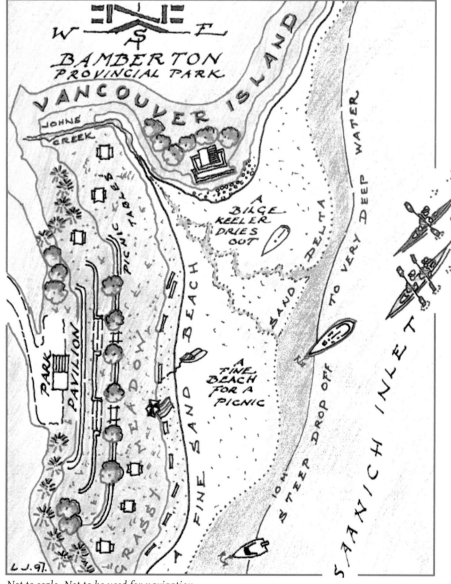

Not to scale. Not to be used for navigation.

On the W side of Saanich Inlet, just down from Mill Bay, lies a lovely sandy beach. This perfect picnic spot has the added advantage of warm-water swimming, and you can anchor quite close in, as there is a steep drop-off beyond the shallow ledge. To be safe, anchoring on a rising tide is advisable. The view E stretches across the Saanich Peninsula to the Gulf Islands, with Mount Baker beyond. Rising sharply to the W are the mountains of south Vancouver Island. Picnic tables are dotted in the grassy meadow backing the beach, and the campground N of the beach has 47 sites, with toilets, water and wood available. There is also a change house with toilets on the beach. The park has some fine examples of large arbutus trees. In the interest of protecting the park's ecology, rock collecting is not permitted.

The beach at low water.

CHARTS

3441. 3313, page 13. SCN Map B2.

APPROACH

Tod Inlet from the W via Brentwood Bay's southern shores and N of Willis Point. Butchart Cove lies E of the narrow entrance.

ANCHOR

In the lower reaches of Tod Inlet. Good all-around weather protection can be found. Alternatively, pick up 1 of the 4 mooring buoys in Butchart Cove if you intend to visit BUTCHART GARDENS. A stern line is advisable.

DEPTHS

Tod Inlet: 4 - 6 m (13 - 19.5 ft). Holding good over a mud bottom.

Note: Trails are currently being upgraded from Tod Inlet to Durrance Lake (1997). See page 76 for trails in the newly formed Gowlland Tod Provincial Park.

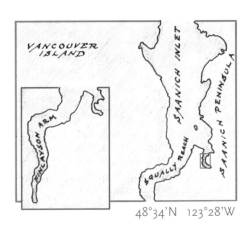

48°34'N 123°28'W

Butchart Cove provides a small boat entrance to the W side of BUTCHART GARDENS. In the cove you will find 4 mooring buoys and a dinghy dock, which is also used by sea-planes on its N side. The spectacular Butchart Gardens, open year-round, contain over 5,000 varieties of flowers, shrubs and trees, with an extensive seed catalogue available at the BENVENUTO SEED & GIFT STORE. Restaurants, cappuccino bars and cafés abound (250-652-4422).

Tranquil Tod Inlet, with its steep-sided cliffs, is captivating. Although this is a well-protected anchorage, the wind can whistle down the inlet at times. To enjoy the extended evening light, anchor near the head of the inlet. Gowlland Tod Provincial Park is accessible from the N shore.

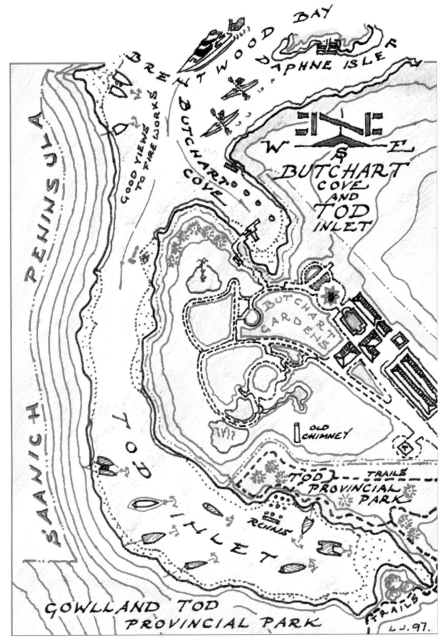

Tod Inlet anchorage.

Not to scale. Not to be used for navigation.

6.4 BRENTWOOD BAY

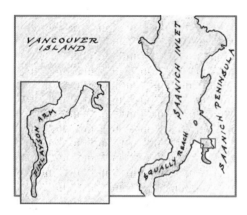

48°35'N 123°28'W

Approach to public wharf and Anglers Anchorage Marina.

Brentwood Bay is situated in a peaceful backwater and provides all essential comforts, including glorious sunsets over the Malahat Ridge. To do any serious provisioning, you will have to go into BRENTWOOD TOWN CENTRE, a good 20-minute walk from the public wharf. Here you will find a good selection of shops, including a supermarket, bakery and liquor store. BRENTWOOD GENERAL STORE, near the Mill Bay ferry terminal, has basic groceries, pop, ice cream and local First Nations art.

Whether your choice is the public wharf, one of the marinas or anchoring out, you will still be able to enjoy the shoreline ambience provided by an extraordinary mix of pubs, restaurants and cafés. CLINKER'S GALLEY at the RUSTY DUCK MARINA is adjacent to the ferry ramp and serves up good home cooking. Their hearty breakfasts are a must on weekends, and they also display the work of local artists. Look out for Aurelia Jacobsen's local "lifecatching" art (250-544-1299). Boats and kayaks are available for rental at SEASCAPES, and there is beach access for kayak launching nearby. The BRENTWOOD INN RESORT (250-652-2413) houses the well-known OAK 'N' BARREL RESTAURANT, a pub and JACKY'S BEACH HOUSE, a Caribbean-style restaurant. Behind the ANGLERS ANCHORAGE MARINA, trails and a path lead to pocket beaches and along the water's edge, eventually joining the boardwalk that fronts the PORT ROYAL complex.

Note: Drying rocks lie between the starboard-hand buoy and the shore just S of Brentwood Inn Marina. The speed limit within Brentwood Bay is 4.3 knots.

The Rusty Duck Marina, ferry ramp and Brentwood Inn Marina.

CHARTS

3441. 3313, page 13. SCN Map B2.

APPROACH

Brentwood Bay centre from the NW between Sluggett and Willis Points. The ferry terminus and BRENTWOOD INN RESORT are conspicuous landmarks to the N, as well as the PORT ROYAL complex in the S.

ANCHOR

Within the vicinity of the public wharf.

Temporary anchorage. Exposed to the W and N.

DEPTHS

6 - 8 m (19.5 - 26 ft). Holding good in mud.

PUBLIC WHARF

25 m (82 ft) on either side. Depths alongside of 4.2 m (13.5 ft).

MARINAS

PORTSIDE MARINA (250-652-2211) has

moorage only if slips are available. RUSTY DUCK MARINA (250-544-1441) has 1 berth for boats visiting CLINKER'S GALLEY. The BRENTWOOD INN MARINA (250-652-2413) has dedicated moorage for visitors on D and E docks. The ANGLERS ANCHORAGE MARINA (250-652-3531) has some guest moorage and a customs clearance phone.

BOAT LAUNCH

Kayakers can launch from small beach adjacent to ferry ramp.

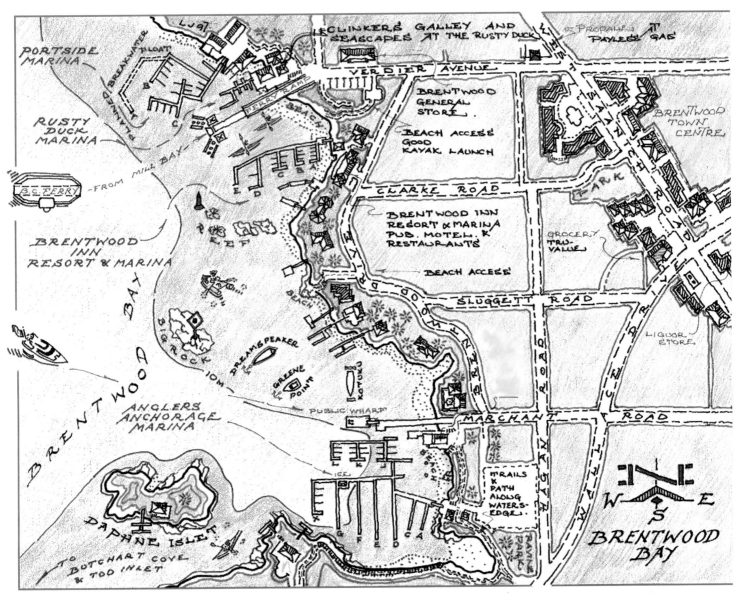

Not to scale. Not to be used for navigation.

6.5   MCKENZIE BIGHT

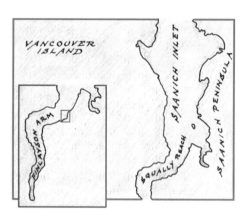

48°33'N   123°30'W

CHARTS

3441. 3313, page 13. SCN Map B2.

APPROACH

From the W. The bight is difficult to spot from a distance. However, deep water extends close to shore.

ANCHOR

On a rising tide, at the edge of the sand shelf that extends out from the creek. Temporary picnic spot.

DEPTHS

2 - 4 m (6.5 - 13 ft). Holding good in sand.

Note: The drop-off to deep water at the edge of the shelf is very steep.

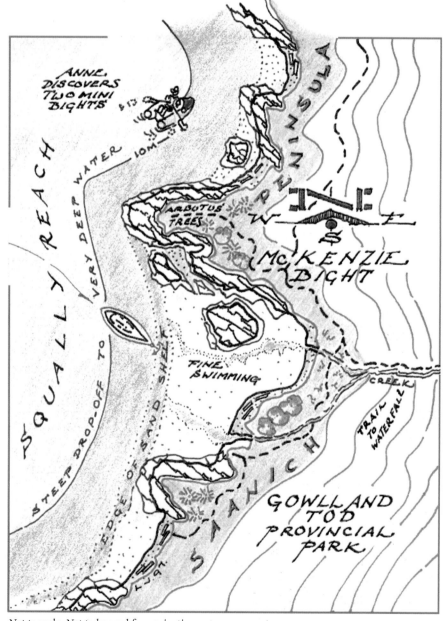

Not to scale. Not to be used for navigation.

Surrounded by steep cliffs, this small bight provides an excellent swimming and snorkelling spot. Access to Gowlland Tod Provincial Park and Mount Work Regional Park, with their numerous trails, is also possible from the head of the bight. As the tide begins to cover the sun-warmed sand, fine swimming can be found in the bight. Two delightful miniature bights are waiting to be explored N of the arbutus tree point. Keep in mind that this is only a temporary, fair-weather stop.

Finding this picnic spot may be the big challenge.

CHARTS

3441. 3313, page 13. SCN Map B2.

APPROACH

From the N, leaving Sawluctus Island to port. Extensive mud flats deposited by the Goldstream River extend out from the head of the arm.

ANCHOR

N of the marina.

DEPTHS

4 - 8 m (13 - 26 ft). Holding good in mud.

MARINA

GOLDSTREAM BOATHOUSE (250-478-4407) has visitor moorage and a complete haul-out and boat repair facility, as well as a store.

BOAT LAUNCH

At marina.

FUEL

At marina (gas only).

48°31'N 123°33'W

The trip down from McKenzie Bight is truly awe-inspiring, much like the scenery from an epic motion picture. Seals, bald eagles and the occasional pod of killer whales frequent the fjordlike arm of Saanich Inlet, and an eerie peacefulness hangs over this quiet stretch of water. GOLDSTREAM BOATHOUSE, situated at the delta of the Goldstream River, has transient moorage available for boats up to 15 m (49 ft). They also have a complete haul-out and boat repair facility. The popular GOLDSTREAM PROVINCIAL PARK, with its preserved rainforest, is within easy walking distance from the marina. GOLDSTREAM RIVER is now a nature sanctuary.

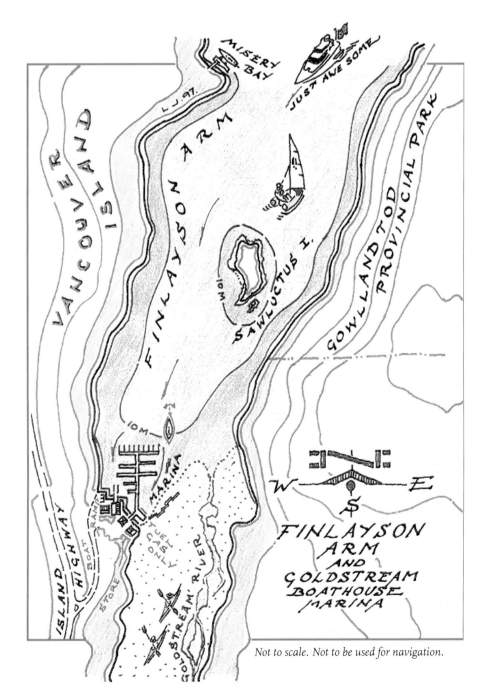

Not to scale. Not to be used for navigation.

Goldstream Boathouse beyond Sawluctus Island.

6.7 GOWLLAND TOD PROVINCIAL PARK & MOUNT WORK REGIONAL PARK

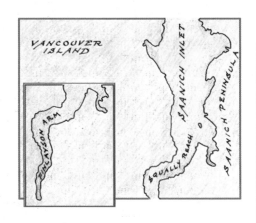

Looking south into Squally Reach.

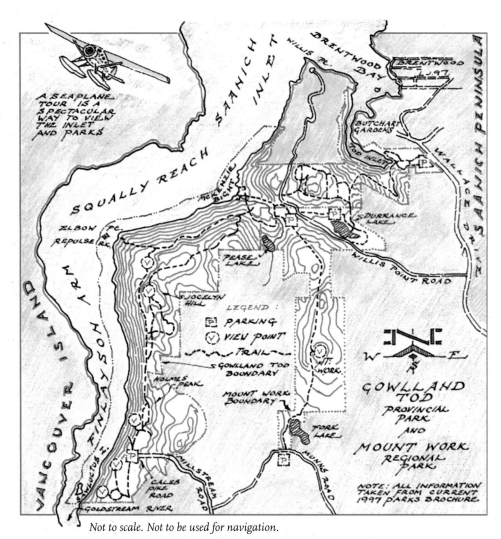

Not to scale. Not to be used for navigation.

Established in 1994, the large Gowlland Tod Provincial Park protects a significant portion of the Gowlland Range, one of the last remaining natural areas in Greater Victoria. The park also includes a portion of the natural shoreline and uplands of Tod Inlet. Visitors are asked to stay on marked trails and to show respect for the cultural and natural environment. This area is home to dozens of rare and threatened plant species, and the diverse wildlife includes the Peale's peregrine falcon, river otter and red squirrel. The hike to the summit of MOUNT WORK takes a good 2 hours but affords spectacular views on arrival. DURRANCE and PEASE LAKES can be reached in about 45 minutes. Change rooms are provided at Durrance Lake, should you feel inclined to swim. A short, pleasant walk from McKenzie Bight will take you to CASCADE FALLS. (Call 250-391-2300 or 250-478-3344 for information.)

Note: For an extensive day hike or overnight stay, Tod Inlet provides the only secure all-weather anchorage with access to both parks.

Chapter 7
PLUMPER SOUND

Powering up to enter Winter Cove via Boat Passage.

At anchor off Saturna Beach 7.6

Chapter 7
PLUMPER SOUND

TIDES

Reference Port: Fulford Harbour

Secondary Ports: Bedwell Harbour & Samuel Island, S shore

Reference Port: Point Atkinson

Secondary Ports: Tumbo Channel & Samuel Island, N shore

CURRENTS

Reference Station: Active Pass

Secondary Stations: Boat Passage & Georgeson Passage

WEATHER

Area: Strait of Georgia (South), Haro Strait

Reporting Stations: Active Pass, Saturna, East Point

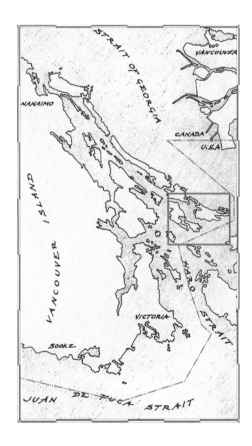

CAUTIONARY NOTES

Keep well clear of Minx Reef.

Slack water has a relatively short window of time in both Boat and Georgeson Passages. The current in Boat Passage can become extremely strong in a very short time, making punctuality essential.

The captivating eastern Gulf Islands offer the visiting boater a variety of irresistible coves, bays and harbours, as well as a chance to "get back to nature" without straying too far from urban comforts. Steeped in natural beauty, these islands offer serene pastoral settings and a less hurried pace of life. Their close proximity to one another makes Plumper Sound an attractive destination for a leisurely one- or two-week cruise.

Plumper Sound is encompassed by the shorelines of Pender, Saturna and Mayne Islands, which offer an exciting assortment of anchorages and picnic stops that include two popular marine parks and two marinas. A quick diversion can be made to Tumbo Island and Cabbage Island Marine Park in the southeast.

Bedwell Harbour, on the western shore of South Pender Island, is the most popular port of entry for U.S. boats heading into Canadian waters and a natural starting-off point for a cruise in the Gulf Islands. Popular Beaumont Marine Park is conveniently situated nearby. It is the perfect spot to unwind with a gentle stroll along its white shell beaches. Alternative and less crowded anchorages are offered at Medicine Beach and Shark Cove further north, where a shortcut can be taken through Pender Canal if your boat fits within the bridge height restrictions. Tranquil Port Browning has a mini shopping centre that is conveniently situated near the marina and anchorage, making this a perfect provisioning stop. Further north, the eclectic village of Hope Bay will take care of your cultural needs.

Over on the western shores of Saturna Island you will find a delightful picnic stop nestled behind Saturna Beach. Lyall Harbour is a good pick-up and drop-off point, as it has the only B.C. Ferries terminal on the island. Alternative anchorage is possible in quiet Boot Cove. Winter Point, in beautiful Winter Cove Marine Park, overlooks narrow Boat Passage and provides an exciting spot to watch boats buck the tide and pop like bottle corks into the cove. Further north, Irish Bay provides a well-protected anchorage, but with no public access ashore.

The southeastern bays of Mayne Island offer a selection of peaceful and less crowded anchorages. Turning southeast, a trip to Tumbo Island and Cabbage Island Marine Park should not be missed. Here you can enjoy south-facing sandy beaches, expansive views and solitude.

FEATURED DESTINATIONS

7.1 Bedwell Harbour & Beaumont Marine Park,
S Pender Island   80

7.2 Medicine Beach, Bedwell Harbour,
N Pender Island   82

7.3 Pender Canal & Shark Cove, Pender Island   83

7.4 Port Browning, N Pender Island   84

7.5 Hope Bay & Village, N Pender Island   86

7.6 Saturna Beach, Saturna Island   87

7.7 Lyall Harbour Public Wharf, Saturna Island   88

7.8 Boot Cove, Saturna Island   89

7.9 Winter Cove Marine Park, Saturna Island   90

7.10 Irish Bay, Samuel Island   92

7.11 Horton Bay Public Wharf, Mayne Island   93

7.12 Curlew Island Bight, Curlew Island   94

7.13 Bennett Bay, Mayne Island   95

7.14 Reef Harbour, Cabbage Island Marine Park
& Tumbo Island   96

Reproduced portion of CHS Chart 3462 for passage planning only. Not to be used for navigation.

7.1　BEDWELL HARBOUR & BEAUMONT MARINE PARK, S PENDER ISLAND

48°45'N　123°14'W

Approach to Bedwell Harbour Marina and public wharf.

An extensive public wharf lies tucked behind Hay Point in Egeria Bay. Each year from May 1 until September 30 the public wharf also serves as a Canada Customs port of entry, which makes the entrance to BEDWELL HARBOUR exceedingly busy.

This convenient location also serves as a marina and island resort, with shower facilities you would sail a few extra hours for. (We recommend using them outside of peak hours.) Their grocery store carries a varied supply of basics as well as locally baked goods and a nice selection of deli meats and cheeses. You can grab a special coffee at the SAILAWAY CAFÉ or sit on the deck of the MARINE BAR & BISTRO and enjoy freshly caught fish with a basket of home-style chips. There is also THE RESTAURANT for fine dining and special occasions.

Because this is a family resort and marina, kids will want for nothing. Try out the heated outdoor pool, the activity centre or the supervised 'kids' movie night, which gives you two hours to relax and enjoy your freedom.

BEAUMONT MARINE PARK is a large, popular anchorage with numerous public buoys and room to anchor, but arrive early as both fill up fast. The most coveted single buoy is opposite the small cove and beach to the W of the anchorage – strategic planning is required to obtain this gem. Access to the E end of the park is gained via relatively steep stairs. Then it's an easy 10-minute walk to the campground and water pump. You can picnic along the shoreline trail or on the shell beaches, and if you walk out to the point at the end of the narrow isthmus you will

Beaumont Marine Park.

be rewarded with a refreshing breeze, a view over the bay and a wooden picnic table for dining alfresco. A popular spot for beaching kayaks and small boats is on the white shell beach inside Skull Islet, but keep a lookout for rocks and a reef near the entrance. To really stretch your legs, hike the new trail from the marine park to the top of Mount Norman, which on average will take about an hour. The view is well worth the climb, so take binoculars and enjoy feeling on top of the world.

CHARTS

3477. 3313, page 11. SCN Map B5.

APPROACH

The harbour is entered from the W between Tilly and Wallace Points. The marina and public wharf lie in Egeria Bay. Beaumont Marine Park lies along the N shore of the harbour.

ANCHOR

Anchor or moor to a buoy below the cliffs to the E of Skull Islet.

DEPTHS

6 - 10 m (19.5 - 33 ft). Holding good in stiff mud.

PUBLIC WHARF

Extensive floats are located at the head of Egeria Bay. The floats to the S are used for customs clearance.

CUSTOMS

A staffed Canada Customs entry port is operational between May 1 and September 30 each year.

MARINA

BEDWELL HARBOUR ISLAND RESORT & MARINA (250-629-3212) offers transient moorage, ice and resort facilities. Monitors VHF channel 68.

FUEL

At marina.

Note: On a busy day Canada Customs often commandeers the public wharf. However, boats are free to tie up after 8:00 p.m. on the NE wharf.

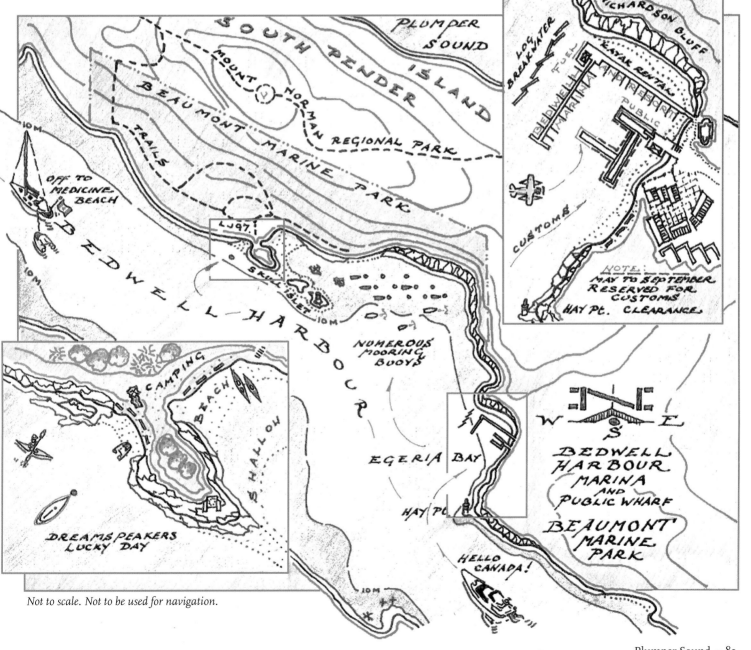

Not to scale. Not to be used for navigation.

7.2 MEDICINE BEACH, BEDWELL HARBOUR, N PENDER ISLAND

48°46'N 123°16'W

CHARTS
3477. 3313, page 11. SCN Map B5.

APPROACH
Medicine Beach lies in the NW at the head of Bedwell Harbour.

ANCHOR
Off beach.

DEPTHS
4 - 6 m (13 - 19.5 ft). Holding good in mud and gravel.

Note: Drew Rock, near the head of the harbour, has 2.1 m (7 ft) over it. Several rocks with less than 2 m (6.5 ft) over them lie between Drew Rock and the head of the harbour.

Not to scale. Not to be used for navigation.

This remarkably serene location forms a natural contrast to the boating hustle and bustle of its neighbours. The shell midden above the beach is the site of a First Nations settlement, established thousands of years ago. The endangered wetland and bird sanctuary, fed by the salt marsh lagoon, is now owned by the Pender Island Conservancy Association. It contains rare plant and bird life that need our protection. Look out for ospreys diving into the sea for their supper – a truly spectacular sight.

A quiet stroll along the gravel beach takes you to unique sandstone formations under the cliffs. A longer hike on the main road will take you to Magic Lake (officially Pender Lake), the local warm-water swimming hole.

Medicine Beach from the east.

CHARTS

3477. 3313, pages II & I2 (inset). SCN Map B5.

PENDER CANAL

APPROACH

Pender Canal leads from the head of Bedwell Harbour into Shark Cove and Port Browning. The canal has a least depth of 2.2 m (7.2 ft). The highway bridge has a vertical clearance of 8.5 m (28 ft) and a width between the piers of I2.2 m (40 ft). Approach is best made near to slack water, as tidal streams attain 3 to 4 knots on a large tide.

SHARK COVE

APPROACH

Either from the S via the canal or from the N, leaving Mortimer Spit to port.

ANCHOR

In the W of the cove, off the local floats and out of the canal's main channel.

DEPTHS

4 m (I3 ft). Holding good in mud.

Note: Sailboats and powerboats that require a vertical clearance of more than 8.5 m (28 ft) should not attempt to transit the canal.

48°46'N 123°15'W

I f you need a flat-water anchorage with good all-around protection, Shark Cove is hard to beat, but it holds only 2 or 3 small boats comfortably. Now and then you will be rocked by the wash of passing boats breaking the low speed limit, which is imposed for safety reasons and to protect the midden beside the bridge from further erosion. Mortimer Spit on S Pender Island provides a clean sand-and-gravel beach for stretching your legs. It has become a favourite local picnic spot, as car access extends close to the head of the spit. From here you can take a shortcut through the Pender Canal if your boat fits within the bridge height restrictions.

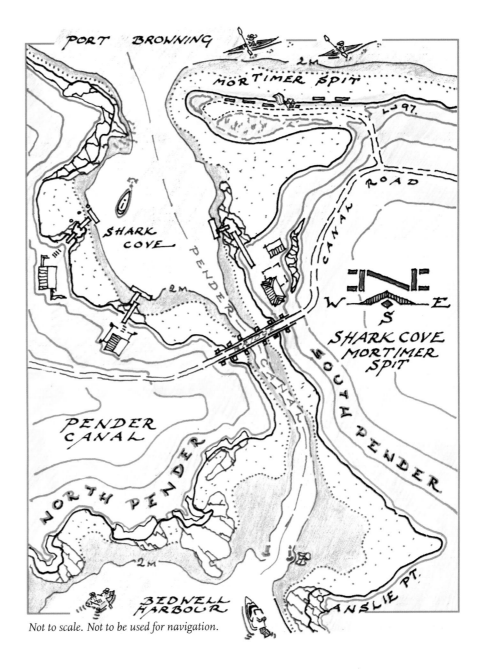

Shark Cove and Pender Canal from Port Browning.

Not to scale. Not to be used for navigation.

7.4   PORT BROWNING, N PENDER ISLAND

48°46'N   123°16'W

Approach to Port Browning.

From the water the foreshore of Port Browning Harbour has a friendly, well-used look. PORT BROWNING MARINA & RESORT and the anchorage off Hamilton Beach are within easy walking distance of the DRIFTWOOD CENTRE, making this a perfect provisioning stop. A public wharf is also situated in the NE anchorage, with road access into town. The Driftwood Centre is a very comprehensive small-scale mall serving as Pender's main hub of commerce and communication. The village bakery provides fresh bread daily, and the owners take pride in other imaginative and delicious baked goods. Other services include a bank (no cash machine), post office, grocery store, liquor store, bistro, laundry facilities and hairdresser. Every Saturday morning from Victoria Day weekend until Labour Day, the colourful FARMERS' MARKET sets up its stands in the open courtyard, with wonderful displays of local fruit, vegetables and preserves. Keep an empty carton on hand so that, in season, you can pick the juicy blackberries along the roadside.

PORT BROWNING MARINA & RESORT has a general store, cold beer and wine store, showers and laundry facilities. Extras include a pool and tennis court. Don't leave without having at least one drink on the sundeck of the SH-QU-ALA INN & CAFÉ, where views out to Mount Norman across the quiet harbour create a tranquil setting so typical of many Gulf Island havens. Hamilton Beach is backed by tall grass and is ideal for a peaceful stroll while offering a variety of beachcombing treasures.

For the pot! If you can entice one into your trap.

CHARTS

3477. 3313, page 11. SCN Map B5.

APPROACH

Either S of Razor Point or via the Pender Canal.

ANCHOR

Off Hamilton Beach in the SW or to the E of the public wharf. Exposed to the SE.

DEPTHS

6 - 8 m (19.5 - 26 ft). Holding good in mud.

PUBLIC WHARF

15 m (49 ft) long. Generally used by local boaters.

MARINA

Port Browning Marina (250-629-3493) has a customs phone-in line and resort facilities. Enter close to the breakwater.

BOAT LAUNCH

On the beach at the foot of Hamilton Road.

Note: Reduce speed and observe "No Wake" signs.

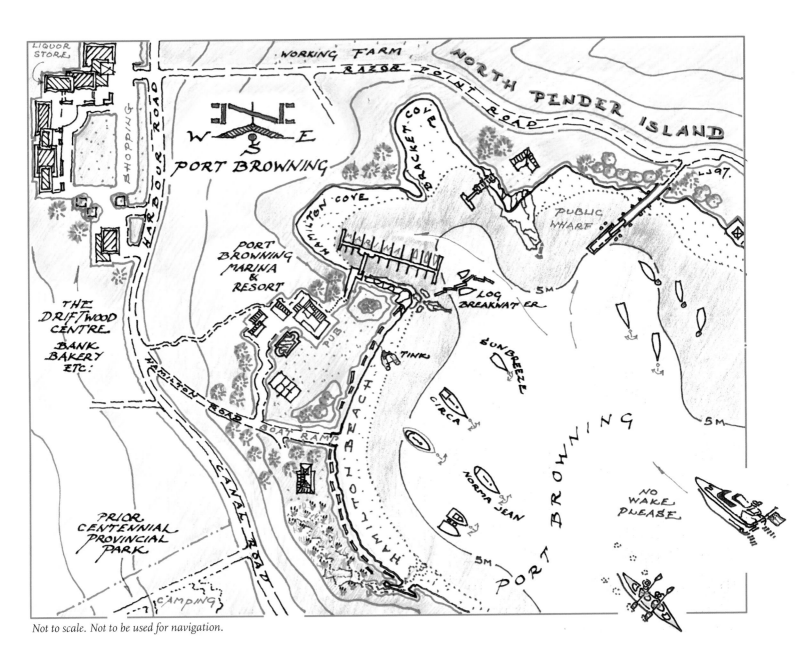

Not to scale. Not to be used for navigation.

7.5   HOPE BAY & VILLAGE, N PENDER ISLAND

48°48'N   123°16'W

CHARTS

3477. 3313, page 11. SCN Map B5.

APPROACH

From the E and to the S of Fane Island. The buildings at the wharfhead become conspicuous landmarks just N of Auchterlonie Point.

PUBLIC WHARF

Relatively extensive floats lie below the wharfhead. However, they are exposed to Plumper Sound chop and the wake of passing boats.

Approach to Hope Bay public wharf.

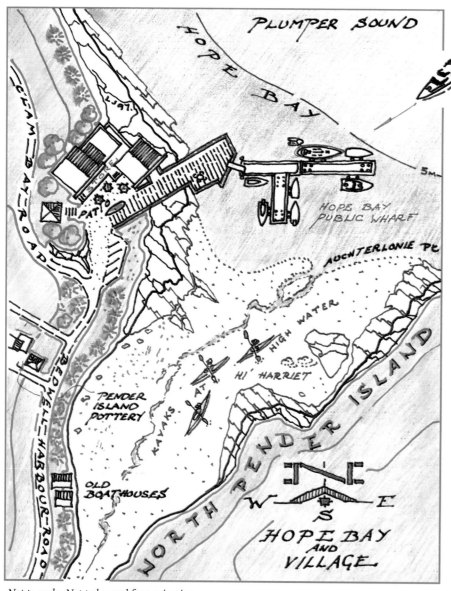

Not to scale. Not to be used for navigation.

This eclectic little bay and village provides an enjoyable cultural stop for the cockpit-weary boater. Tie up alongside the public wharf and, if overnighting, check in with the owners of the HOPE BAY STORE, who double as wharf managers. This funky gift and bookstore with cappuccino bar is a heritage building, dating back to 1912. Also for sale are basic groceries, ice cream, soft drinks and tasty baked goodies. The store has always been a local meeting place and is packed with island character and intriguing personalities. Browse through the bookshelves, visit the art gallery or sit in wicker chairs on the front patio with a freshly made cappuccino. Opposite is a goldsmith's workshop, and the run-down wharf shed below the store – which houses galleries displaying local arts, crafts and clothing – is well worth a visit.

A short walk down Bedwell Harbour Road brings you to PENDER ISLAND POTTERY, where Harriet and Roger Stribley create fine classical and humorous pieces that have become collector's items. Continue your walk a little further and enjoy the nostalgia of Pender's English-style countryside.

CHARTS

3477. 3313, page 11. SCN Map B5.

APPROACH

From the SW. The beach lies in a bight in the SE of Breezy Bay and N of Croker Point.

ANCHOR

Off the beach. Temporary anchorage, open to the NW.

DEPTHS

2 - 4 m (6.5 - 13 ft). Holding good in sand.

Note: Give Croker Point a wide berth, as two submerged rocks with less than 2 m (6.5 ft) over them are close to the W of the light.

48°46'N 123°12'W

It was an unexpected surprise to discover THOMSON PARK, tucked in behind Saturna Beach. With its open meadow and leafy trees, it's the perfect day stop for walking, picnicking or just lazing on the grass for a quiet nap. A couple of wooden benches have been perfectly placed to provide the visitor with a lovely view over Plumper Sound. The property surrounding the park is private, and waterfront lots are now for sale along Croker Point.

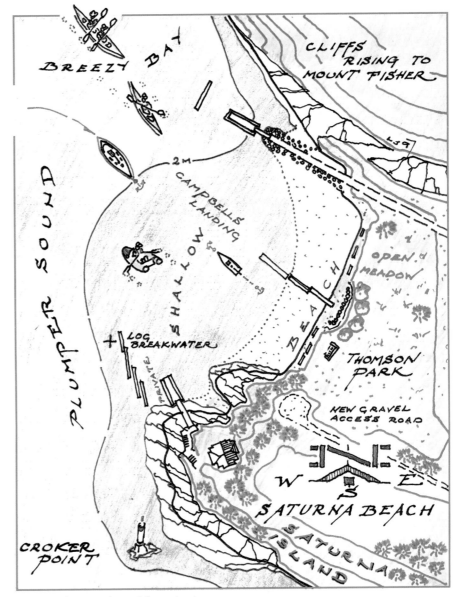

Not to scale. Not to be used for navigation.

The tranquility of Saturna Beach.

7.7 Lyall Harbour Public Wharf, Saturna Island

48°48'N 123°12'W

CHARTS

3477. 3313, page 12. SCN Map B5.

APPROACH

The public wharf lies adjacent to and E of the B.C. Ferries terminal on Saturna Point. The terminal, wharfhead and pub on the point create conspicuous landmarks.

PUBLIC WHARF

Has a 30-m-long (98-ft) float, the outside of which is frequented by visiting boats. No power or water is available.

FUEL

At the public wharf.

Note: Temporary anchorage, open to the W, is possible to the E of the public wharf and at the head of Lyall Harbour.

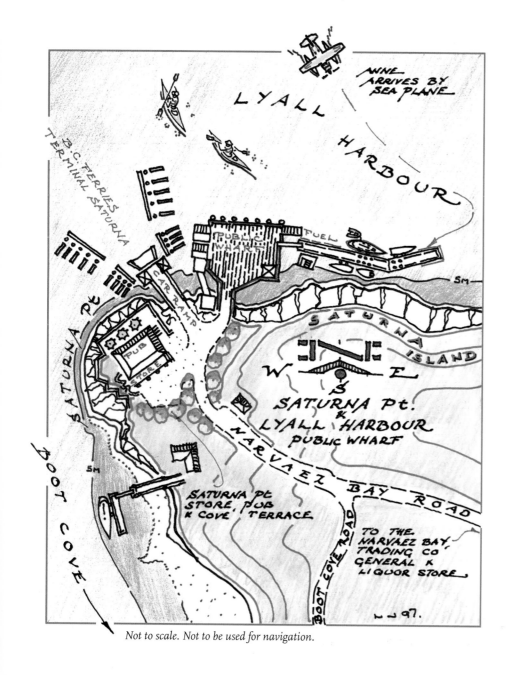

Not to scale. Not to be used for navigation.

Saturna Island is wonderful to explore, but it has no marinas, overnight camping facilites or banks. The only public wharf is in Lyall Harbour, which is a good pick-up and drop-off point, as the B.C. Ferries terminal is directly opposite and floatplanes tie up for a quick transfer at the end of the dock. Diesel and gas pumps on the dock are operated by Saturna Point Store where you can collect an information map of the island as well as purchase groceries, ice and hardware. They also keep delicious organic bread and baked goods produced by Haggis Farms. On Saturdays the Community Hall up the road sells fresh produce, preserves and local crafts. To get to the main shopping centre, continue up the hill and along the road for approximately 2 km (1 mi) until you reach Narvaez Bay Trading Company. This is the island's main grocery store, which also has a B.C. Liquor Store outlet, a post office and a selection of books and hardware.

If you decide to overnight at the public wharf, take a stroll to the Lighthouse Pub or treat yourself to a memorable meal at Saturna Lodge. They offer a shuttle service to and from the public wharf (250-539-2254).

BOOT COVE, SATURNA ISLAND

CHARTS

3477. 3313, page 12. SCN Map B5.

APPROACH

From the NW. The entrance lies S of Saturna Point. Favour the W side when entering to avoid a rock with 0.6 m (2 ft) over it.

ANCHOR

To the SE or N of the fish farm.

DEPTHS

2 - 4 m (6.5 - 13 ft). Holding good in dense mud.

Note: Winds from both the N and S tend to funnel through the cove and accelerate to strong gusts.

48°48'N 123°12'W

In the summer months Boot Cove is an alternative anchorage to Lyall Harbour. This is a quiet spot with all the features of a natural harbour, but be prepared for strong wind gusts that can funnel between the cliffs. These gusts are more common in the autumn, winter and spring months. There is no public access to the foreshore, as it is all privately owned. Access to SATURNA LODGE through one of the private gardens can be arranged if organized ahead of time.

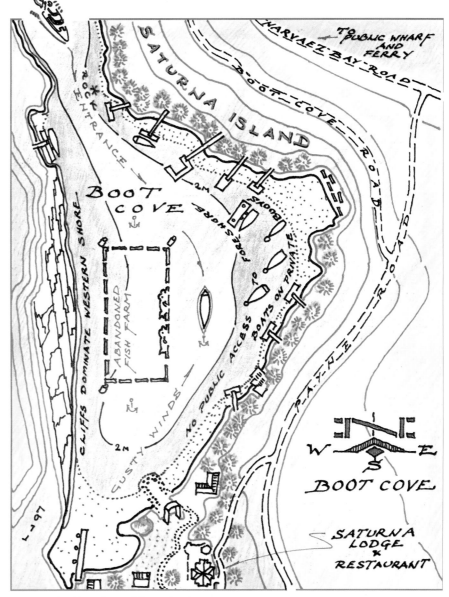

Approach to Lyall Harbour public wharf.

Not to scale. Not to be used for navigation.

7.9 WINTER COVE MARINE PARK, SATURNA ISLAND

48°48'N 123°11'W

Boat Passage to Winter Cove.

This popular anchorage has 2 possible entrances. Boat Passage, a very narrow entrance between Ralph Grey Point and Winter Point, can be safely navigated by small boats at slack water. Look out for a premature flooding current that can take you by surprise when strong winds in Plumper Sound push the tide up into the islands. Rocks E of Ralph Grey Point are sometimes hidden under murky water. The most popular entrance is between Samuel and Saturna Islands. At HW take care to avoid Minx Reef, which extends beyond Digby Point.

Once you are inside, Winter Cove is a large and very pleasant anchorage. However, it is quite shallow in places, so reconnaissance beforehand is advisable. Most boats anchor off the marine park's small boat launch, where reasonable depths can be found. At LW it is fun to walk along the park beaches, where jagged reefs extend out into the anchorage, and then join the trail to Winter Point, which overlooks Boat Passage and the Strait of Georgia. This is also an exciting spot to sit and watch the tide, and boats, rushing through the passage. The trail takes you E along the point, then back through forests and swamps to the park picnic area. Boardwalks take you over the outlets of 2 lagoons covered by bullrushes and a plentiful supply of fresh sea asparagus.

Park facilities include a small boat and kayak launch, water, picnic tables and an emergency helicopter landing area. Take your dinghy into Church Cove, the site of SAINT CHRISTOPHER'S CHURCH, rebuilt over 70 years ago from an original Japanese boathouse.

Winter Cove looking from Plumper Sound.

CHARTS

3477. 3313, page 12. SCN Map B5.

APPROACH

Either from Plumper Sound, giving adequate clearance to Minx Reef, or from the Strait of Georgia via Boat Passage at slack water, avoiding the rocks off Ralph Grey Point.

ANCHOR

Good all-weather anchorage may be found in Winter Cove. However, the cove is shallow, and care and diligence to tide tables must be exercised prior to anchoring.

DEPTHS

2 - 4 m (6.5 - 13 ft). Holding good in mud.

Note: Reefs extend out from both the Saturna and Samuel Island shores. Boat Passage between Ralph Grey Point and Winter Point has a least depth of 2.1 m (7 ft). Tidal streams in Boat Passage may attain 8 knots. Refer to secondary station "Boat Passage" before attempting a transit.

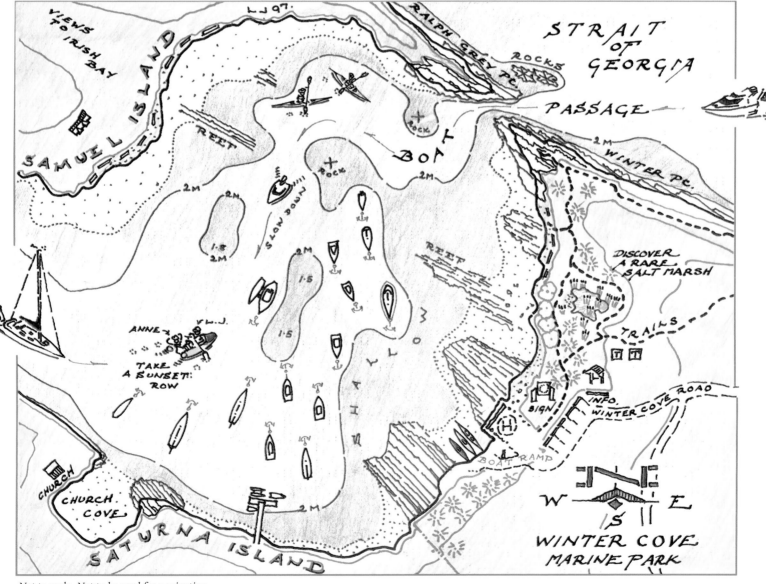

Not to scale. Not to be used for navigation.

48°49'N 123°12'W

CHARTS

3477. 3313, page 12. SCN Map B5.

APPROACH

From the SW out of Plumper Sound, giving adequate clearance to Minx Reef.

ANCHOR

This bay is a natural anchorage. The SE portion is less exposed to winds from the SW and the wash of passing boats than the rest of the anchorage.

DEPTHS

2 - 10 m (6.5 - 33 ft). Holding good in mud.

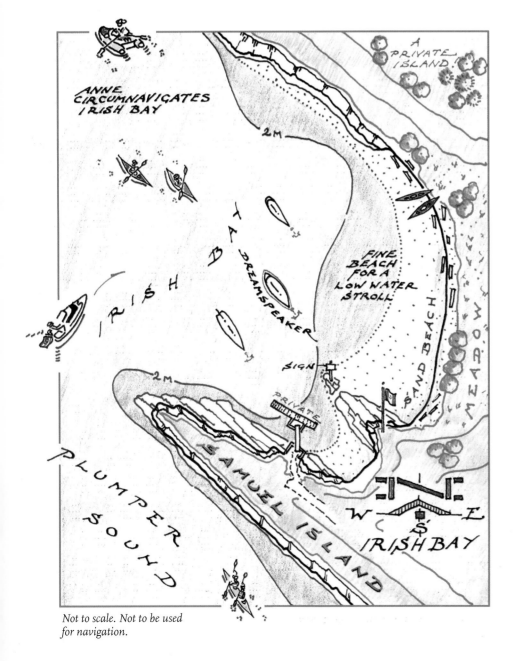

Not to scale. Not to be used for navigation.

Samuel Island is *seriously* private beyond the HW mark; one of the signs reads: RATTLESNAKES BEYOND THIS POINT! Don't be alarmed by the very conscientious caretaker who patrols the grounds and warns those he sees on the beach against trespassing past the HW point. The owners are determined to discourage visitors and preserve their property and its wildlife, especially against the threat of fire. The SE corner of the bay provides well-protected anchorage, while the N part is suitable only for a temporary stop.

Approach to Irish Bay.

CHARTS

3477. 3313, page 12. SCN Map B5.

APPROACH

Either from the E via Robson Channel or from the N passage between Curlew and Mayne Islands.

ANCHOR

Good protected anchorage may be found N and W of the public wharf.

DEPTHS

4 - 8 m (13 - 26 ft).

PUBLIC WHARF

L-shaped with 24 m (80 ft) of moorage and an additional 12 m (40 ft) of loading zone. The wharf is generally jam-packed with local craft.

Note: Approaching from Robson Channel is best done at slack water. A rock with less than 2 m (6.5 ft) over it lies in the E entrance.

48°50'N 123°15'W

The fairly swift tidal streams between the neighbouring islands should be taken into account when transiting Robson Channel or Georgeson Passage. In the summer months the public wharf at Horton Bay is usually filled to capacity with local boats. Anchorage in the W part of the bay is well protected and peaceful. Once ashore, you can take a leisurely walk along Horton Bay Road and turn onto Beachwood. Here you will find ARBUTUS BAY DEER FARMS, which produces organic fallow deer venison. If you wish to purchase their products, call first (250-539-2301). There is a public phone just up from the wharf.

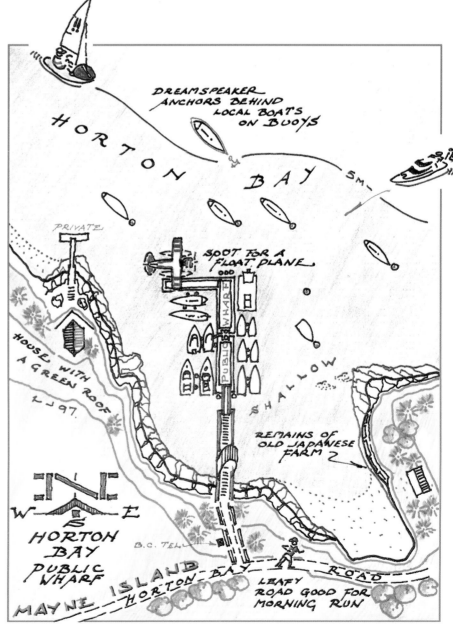

Not to scale. Not to be used for navigation.

Approach to Horton Bay public wharf.

7.12 Curlew Island Bight, Curlew Island

48°50'N 123°14'W

CHARTS

3477. 3313, page 12. SCN Map B5.

APPROACH

Either from the S via Horton Bay or from the N via Bennett Bay.

ANCHOR

Good protected anchorage is found within the channel that separates Curlew and Mayne Islands. Best to anchor off the Curlew Island side.

DEPTHS

4 - 8 m (13 - 26 ft). Holding good in sand and gravel.

BOAT LAUNCH

Public at Aitken Point.

Note: Give Aitken Point a wide berth, as piles extend out from the shore.

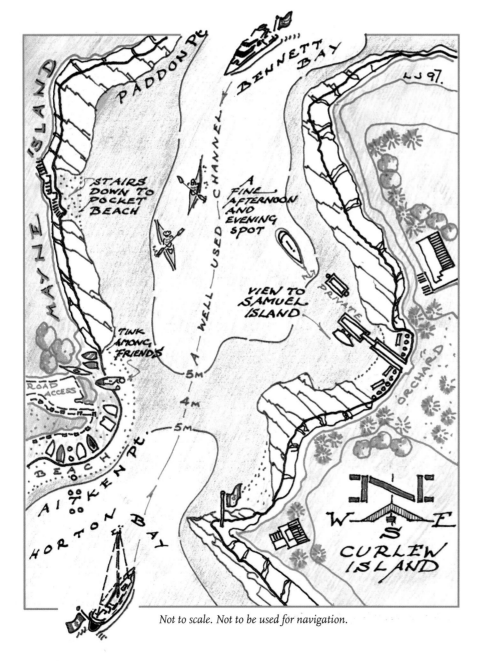

Not to scale. Not to be used for navigation.

The channel that runs between Curlew and Mayne Islands is well used by boats going on to Bennett Bay from Horton Bay. Good anchorage for 2 or 3 small boats can be found in the bight, W of the private dock. In fine weather the anchorage affords good afternoon and evening sunshine. We rowed to a lovely shell beach at Aitken Point, which was piled high with local skiffs of all descriptions. Another small beach, with private stairs leading up the cliff, can be found to the N of Aitken Point.

Curlew Island from Aitken Point, Mayne Island.

CHARTS

3477. 3313, page 12. SCN Map B5.

APPROACH

From the SE. The white structure of the MAYNE INN HOTEL and its long jetty are the most conspicuous landmarks.

ANCHOR

Temporary anchorage can be found off the beach.

DEPTHS

2 - 6 m (6.5 - 19.5 ft). Holding good in sand and gravel.

BOAT LAUNCH

Public off Arbutus Drive.

48°51'N 123°15'W

Be sure to keep a sharp lookout for crab traps and mooring buoys when anchoring off the beach in Bennett Bay, reputed to be one of the busiest and best bathing spots on Mayne Island. The land backing the beach, and including Campbell Point, is now a Parks Protected Area, allowing public access to the old homestead. The MAYNE INN HOTEL sits majestically to the S of the long jetty which, we are pleased to report, has been rebuilt, making a visit to the inn no longer life threatening. A dinghy launch and grassy picnic spot are situated further S of the jetty, off Arbutus Drive.

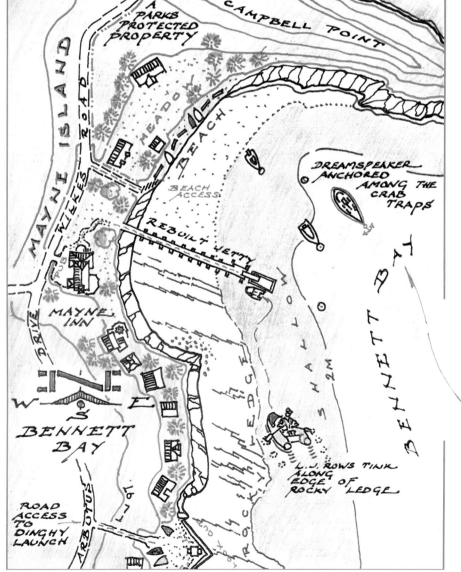

Not to scale. Not to be used for navigation.

Beach and jetty to the Mayne Inn Hotel.

7.14   REEF HARBOUR, CABBAGE ISLAND MARINE PARK & TUMBO ISLAND

48°48'N 123°05'W

Approach to Reef Harbour.

When entering REEF HARBOUR from Tumbo Channel, be sure to give the point a wide berth. Once inside, pick up a public buoy S of Cabbage Island Marine Park. When protection, otherwise given by the reefs, disappears, this anchorage is open to the NW, especially if the tide is up.

Ashore there are minimal park facilities with pit toilets, and no water is available on the island. The main attractions for visiting boaters are the south-facing sandy beaches, the prolific tidal pools in Reef Harbour that are crammed with sea life and the solitude. As low tide approaches, stretch your legs with a 20-minute walk around the island. On the N shore you can enjoy expansive views across the Strait of Georgia while indulging in some fascinating beachcombing. Campers usually pitch their tents above the sandy beaches or in the nearby woods.

In all, Cabbage Island Marine Park is a popular but delightful spot to spend a few days at anchor.

It is now possible to enjoy the natural beauty of TUMBO ISLAND, which was established as a Parks Protected Area in 1997. Two small private lots still remain within the protected area, and their boundaries should be respected. Tumbo Island has a significant freshwater marsh and natural upland, making it one of the last relatively intact landscapes remaining within the Gulf Islands biotic region. Its name is derived from "Tombolo," the sand, shingle and driftwood bar that connects the N and S fingers. This tombolo formed a fresh-water marsh on its western side and helped create the well-protected anchorage in Reef Harbour. There are numerous trails to explore around the island, leading to three magnificent look-out points, and the marsh is home to migratory birds, waterfowl and a family of otters.

The popular sandy beach at Cabbage Island Marine Park.

CHARTS

3441. 3313, page 24. SCN Map B6.

APPROACH

Reef Harbour from Tumbo Channel. It is wise to enter at LW slack, with the rock that extends out from the westernmost tip of Tumbo Island visible. Currents tend to rip strangely SW around this point between tides.

ANCHOR

Within Reef Harbour, between Cabbage Island Marine Park and Tumbo Island (as indicated), or pick up a park mooring buoy.

DEPTHS

2 - 8 m (6.5 - 26 ft). Holding good in sand and gravel.

Note: Reef Harbour is exposed to the NW. Occasionally northwesterly winds and swell will reach this far S. Tumbo Channel is a secondary port for tidal differences referenced on Point Atkinson. There is a dramatic difference between LW and HW in this area.

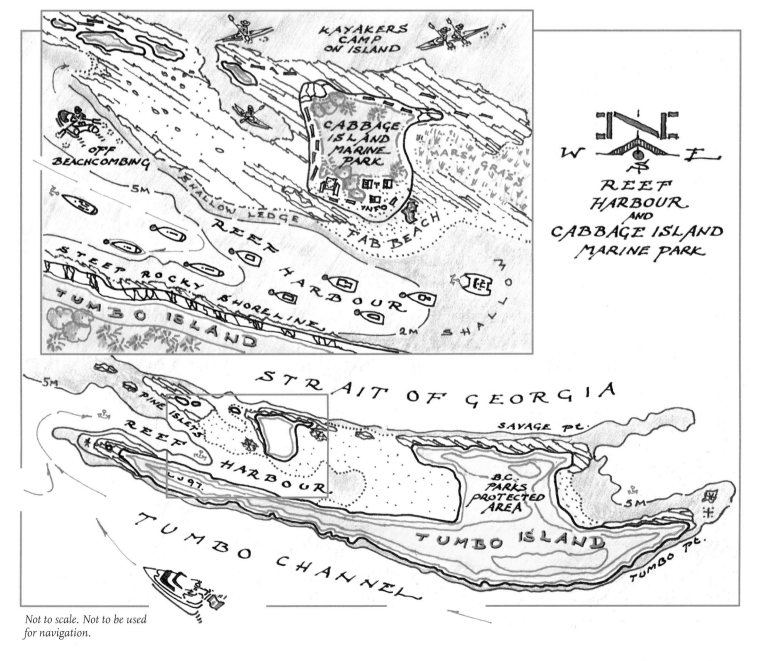

Not to scale. Not to be used for navigation.

Chapter 8
ACTIVE PASS

TIDES

Reference Port: Point Atkinson

Secondary Ports: Miners Bay & Whaler Bay

CURRENTS

Reference Station: Active Pass

WEATHER

Area: Strait of Georgia (South), Haro Strait

Reporting Stations: Active Pass, Saturna Island, East Point

BC Ferries and commercial shipping constantly ply the waters of Active Pass.

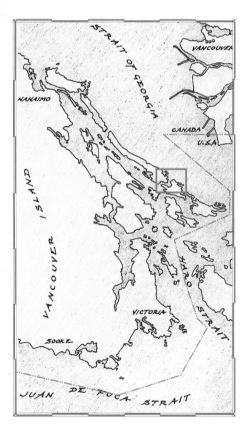

The deep-water passage of Active Pass is famous for its steady flow of ferry traffic, large commercial vessels, fishing boats and pleasure craft. It presents the added challenge of extremely strong tidal currents and hazardous tidal rips. To top it all, the narrow entrance from the Strait of Georgia that runs between the islands of Galiano and Mayne is often crowded with fishing craft out for a day's catch.

Active Pass provides a convenient passage between the outer islands for boaters en route to or from Victoria, Sidney and the more southerly Gulf Islands. Before entering the pass you would be best advised to study the *Canadian Tide and Current Tables* carefully, stay out of the main fairway whenever possible and keep a close and constant watch for large commercial traffic and scheduled ferries that have very limited room to manoeuvre. Bear in mind that if there is potential danger or the possibility of collision, large vessels will give four or more short blasts as prior warning.

The pass is certainly not a place to hang about while taking in the sights, but the abundance of wildlife affords enjoyable observation. Bald eagles nest in the tall trees on the southern shores of Mayne Island, and Helen Point is favoured by Steller's sea lions, porpoises and seasonal pods of orcas.

Included in this short chapter are two destinations worth visiting, both just off the bustling waterway. Miners Bay on Mayne Island provides the only fuelling stop in Active Pass and is well worth an overnight stay. It also offers convenient provisioning in a historic seaside village setting.

Sturdies Bay and Village on Galiano Island makes a good pick-up or drop-off point, as Gulf Island ferries from both Tsawwassen and Swartz Bay stop here. It also serves as a convenient day stop if you need to provision or wish to explore the island. An energetic bike ride to Bluffs Park will be well rewarded with panoramic views over Active Pass.

CAUTIONARY NOTES

Transiting Active Pass under sail or in limited visibility is not recommended.

A serious look at International Regulations for Preventing Collisions at Sea *prior to crossing the pass is highly recommended.*

It is also recommended that Chart 3473 be used to supplement SCN Map Set B and Chart 3442.

FEATURED DESTINATIONS

8.1 Miners Bay & Village, Mayne Island   100

8.2 Sturdies Bay & Village, Galiano Island   102

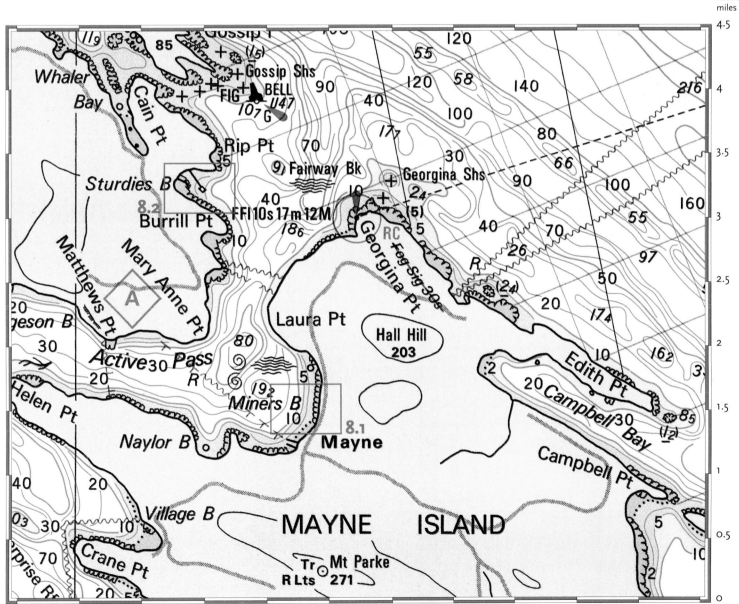

Reproduced portion of CHS Chart 3462 for passage planning only. Not to be used for navigation.

8.1 Miners Bay & Village, Mayne Island

48°51'N   123°18'W

Approaching the public wharf and fuel float.

Miners Bay and its friendly community still welcome visitors to Mayne Island today as they did more than a century ago. A walk around the historic village is well worthwhile, with shops for provisioning and decks for lazing just up from the public wharf. Georgina Point Road will take you to the handsome SAINT MARY MAGDALENE ANGLICAN CHURCH, which was built in 1898 and hosts the annual July Country Fair. Don't overlook the "cemetery with a view," which accommodates headstones of many famous island pioneers. At the head of the dock SPRINGWATER LODGE sits comfortably overlooking the bay. The wooden deck, shaded by colourful umbrellas, provides a perfect spot to while away a warm summer's afternoon. Built in the 1890s, this is the oldest continuously operating hotel in British Columbia. The tiny MAYNE MUSEUM was once the local lockup and is crammed with intriguing pieces of history, including fossils 70 million years old. The AGRICULTURAL HALL, built in the early 1900s, is home to the Quilts Exhibition in July and the Fall Fair on the third Saturday in August. RENAISSANCE BOOKS, housed in an original Arts and Crafts-style building, carries a good selection of secondhand books and local artists' work. Indulge in an ice cream at the MINERS BAY DELI, which also has outside seating. The well-stocked MINERS BAY TRADING POST provides one-stop shopping, with groceries, fresh produce and a B.C. LIQUOR STORE. Across the way, on Village Bay Road, are two places of interest. THE ROOT SELLER INN welcomes explorers on a budget to a relaxing heritage home and offers group rates for kayakers, cyclists and hikers. MANNA BAKERY CAFÉ has a cappuccino bar and carries a fine selection of freshly baked breads and pastries (their cinnamon buns are heavenly). MAYNE OPEN MARKET ("MOM'S") is located in the middle of the island, between Miners Bay and Bennett Bay, but it is worth a visit if you have transportation. They carry local organic produce, delicious Haggis Farms bread and other tasty baked goods, and they will deliver groceries to your boat after 6:00 p.m. (250-539-5024). The island's post office is also housed here.

Miners Bay Trading Post on Fernhill Road.

CHARTS

3473. 3313, page 9. SCN Map B5.

APPROACH

Miners Bay lies to the centre and E within Active Pass. The white structure of the SPRINGWATER LODGE behind the wharfhead is the most conspicuous landmark.

ANCHOR

As close inshore as possible, within the vicinity of the public wharf and mooring buoys.

DEPTHS

6 - 8 m (19.5 - 26 ft). Holding good in mud.

PUBLIC WHARF

Floats extend out from the wharfhead both to the N and S. Transient moorage is available on the S float.

FUEL

There is a fuel float at the wharfhead run by ACTIVE PASS AUTO MARINE LTD.

Note: Back eddies counter to the tidal stream whirl off the public wharf. Ferry wash makes the anchorage more than a little rolly.

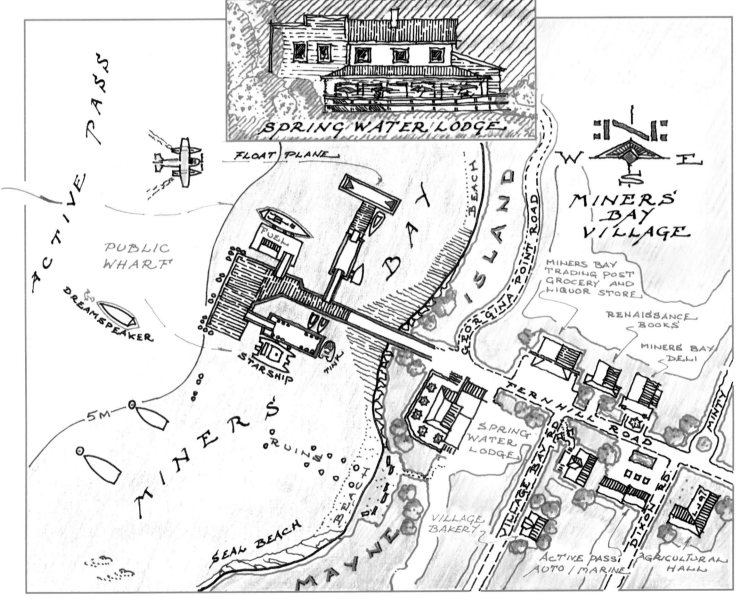

Not to scale. Not to be used for navigation.

8.2 STURDIES BAY & VILLAGE, GALIANO ISLAND

48°53'N 123°19'W

On approach leave the floating lead to starboard.

Sturdies Bay is a convenient day stop with easy access to grocery stores, cafés and galleries. The ferries from Tsawwassen and Swartz Bay stop here, making it a good pick-up and drop-off point. GALIANO LODGE & RESORT and many private homes line the W shore, with public access to the beaches from the ferry parking lot. Here you will also find the notable MAX & MORITZ SPICY ISLAND FOOD HOUSE, serving German hot dogs and Indonesian fare. This eclectic blend of edibles is housed in a red caravan, with outside seating under bright umbrellas. There is a tourist information stand across from Madrona Road where you can pick up the *Galiano Visitors Guide and Map* as well as brochures on island attractions and events. The DANDELION GALLERY on Madrona Road has become a well-respected artists' co-op, representing a wealth of island talent. HOME COMFORT ZONE stocks desirable home and garden treasures. Galiano's first bookstore plans to open in 1998 and will include the works of a variety of local (Gulf Island) and Canadian authors. On a more practical note, propane tanks can be filled at WELLS SERVICES, located just behind STURDIES BAY GAS & GROCERIES, where a good selection of food items and fresh produce can be purchased. A short walk up Sturdies Bay Road takes you to the TRINCOMALI CENTRE, where art, fresh coffee and tasty treats await the weary shopper. Look out for a bargain at DÉJÀ VU, a recycled clothing trailer, situated just past the centre. If serious shopping and provisioning is your quest, or a liquor store is vital, then a 2-km (1-mi) trip is required to take you to THE CORNER STORE/LIQUOR AGENCY, the DAYSTAR MARKET and the IXCHEL CRAFT SHOP (a second location operates from May through October at the MONTAGUE MARINA). This might be the perfect opportunity to rent a bike and combine shopping with a bit of island touring. GALIANO BICYCLE RENTAL & REPAIR on Burrill Road will fill all your needs, down to an "add on" bike for the kids (250-539-9906). Alternatively, call GO GALIANO ISLAND SHUTTLE taxi service (250-539-0202). If you have time, drop into the legendary HUMMINGBIRD PUB to experience local island flavour and great pub food.

BELLHOUSE PROVINCIAL PARK has fine picnicking rocks, and BLUFFS PARK offers wonderful views of Active Pass and the lighthouse on Mayne Island. On a clear day, Mount Baker appears majestically to the E.

Herons can often be spied in the majestic trees of Galiano Island.

CHARTS

3473. 3313, page 9. SCN Map B4.

APPROACH

Sturdies Bay lies to the W within the Strait of Georgia entrance to Active Pass. The long jetty and the B.C. Ferries terminal form the most conspicuous landmarks.

ANCHOR

Temporary anchorage can be found off the public wharf, behind the floating lead.

DEPTHS

4 m (13 ft). Holding dubious over a gravel/rocky bottom.

PUBLIC WHARF

Relatively small with little room for transient moorage. A short stop at the loading zone may be all that is available.

Note: Sturdies Bay is exposed to the SE and it occasionally becomes unsafe for the ferries to dock here, due to a very strong southeasterly. Although sheltered from NW winds, swells from the N curl around Rip Point and enter the bay. An overnight stay is not recommended.

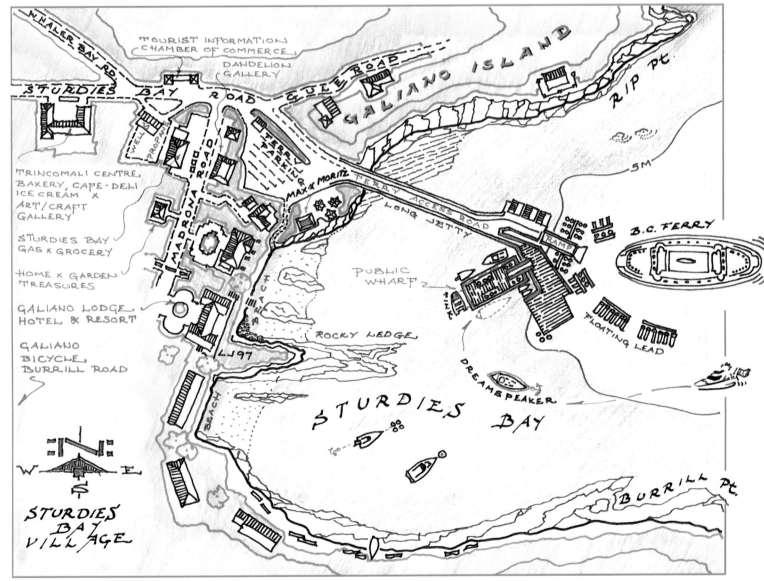

Not to scale. Not to be used for navigation.

Chapter 9
TRINCOMALI CHANNEL

TIDES

Reference Port: Fulford Harbour

Secondary Ports: Ganges Harbour &
Montague Harbour

CURRENTS

Reference Station: Race Passage

Secondary Stations: Swanson Channel &
Trincomali Channel

WEATHER

Area: Strait of Georgia (South), Haro Strait

Reporting Stations: Active Pass, Saturna
Island & East Point

Small boat basin at Ganges   9.1

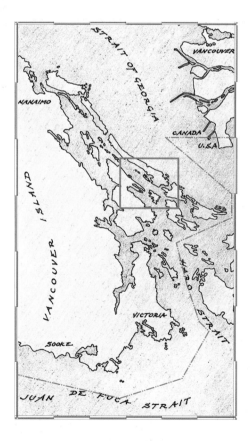

The enjoyable cruising waters in this chapter offer a medley of inviting anchorages and picnic stops rich in natural charm. So much so that in the busy months of July and August, you would be best advised to arrive early in the day to guarantee moorage or decent anchorage.

Trincomali Channel is the predominant body of water in this sector of the Gulf Islands, forming junctions at its southern end with Captain Passage, Swanson Channel, Navy Channel and Active Pass. These waterways all contribute to creating an extensive and varied shoreline that includes Prevost, portions of Saltspring, Galiano and North Pender Islands. Most of the area is easily accessible by boat or ferry from the mainland, and there are numerous launching and camping spots for kayakers and canoeists.

Saltspring Island provides an excellent provisioning base in the mini-metropolis of Ganges Village. Most boat-related services can also be found here, along with an urban fix complete with fine dining for those boat-bound souls. Long Harbour offers good shelter and an ample length of protected water. Walker Hook is a wonderful picnic spot, with a fine sand-and-shell beach that invites you to run barefoot.

Southwestern Galiano Island offers the boater a delightful marine park in Montague Harbour. This was British Columbia's first marine park and is still one of the most popular in the Gulf Islands. Safe anchorage for numerous boats is possible, and sunsets from the northern shore are spectacular. Montague Harbour Marina provides easy access to transportation on the island.

Prevost Island, a pastoral hideaway surrounded by water, is perfect for circumnavigation and has seven scenic anchorages as well as a natural Parks Protected Area in James Bay, with woods, meadows and an apple orchard.

North Pender Island is easily accessible from the public wharf in sleepy Port Washington or the well-managed marina in Hyashi Cove. The island has excellent walking and cycling roads. It supports an active artist community and has a varied choice of good restaurants.

CAUTIONARY NOTES

Trincomali Channel is a crossroads for pleasure craft from all points of the compass. The sheer volume of boats, especially in August, presents a potential hazard to navigation.

This area is especially popular with kayakers and canoeists. Power-driven craft of all descriptions need to slow down and reduce wake to a minimum.

FEATURED DESTINATIONS

9.1 Ganges Harbour & Madrona Bay,
      Saltspring Island   106

9.2 Long Harbour & Welbury Bay,
      Saltspring Island   108

9.3 Walker Hook, Saltspring Island   110

9.4 Montague Harbour Marine Park,
      Galiano Island   112

9.5 Montague Harbour Public Wharf & Marina,
      Galiano Island   114

9.6 Richardson Bay, SE Prevost Island   115

9.7 Glenthorne Passage, Ellen & Diver Bays,
      SE Prevost Island   116

9.8 James Bay, Selby Cove & Annette Inlet,
      NW Prevost Island   118

9.9 Port Washington, Grimmer Bay,
      N Pender Island   120

9.10 Hyashi Cove & Otter Bay Marina,
      N Pender Island   121

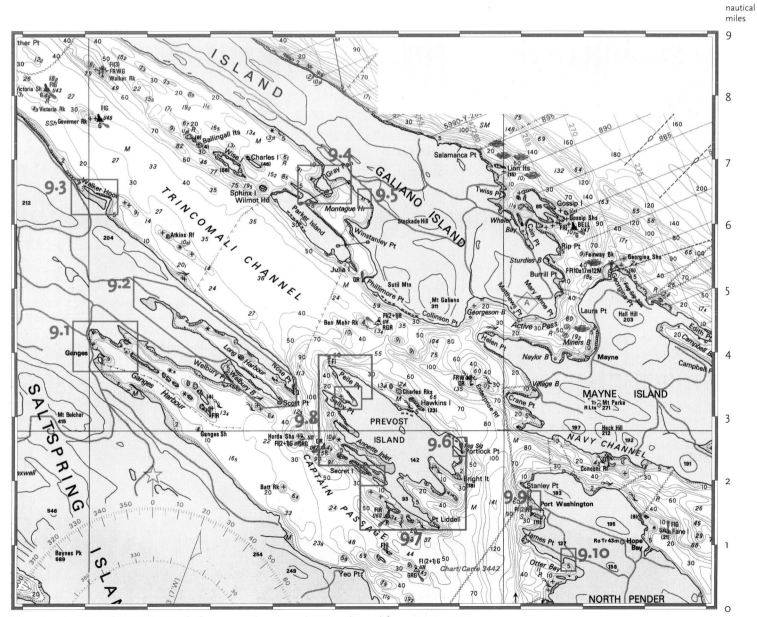

nautical miles

Reproduced portion of CHS Chart 3462 for passage planning only. Not to be used for navigation.

9.1 GANGES HARBOUR & MADRONA BAY, SALTSPRING ISLAND

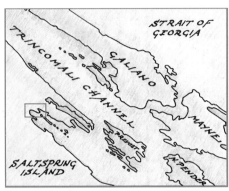

Ganges Harbour: 48°51'N 123°28'W
Madrona Bay: 48°51'N 123°29'W

CHARTS

3478. 3313, page 10. SCN Map B4.

MADRONA BAY

APPROACH

Madrona Bay either N and E of Chain Islands or from Ganges Harbour between Powder Islet and Goat Island.

ANCHOR

In centre of bay. Temporary anchorage open to the SE.

DEPTHS

4 - 6 m (13 - 19.5 ft). Holding good in sticky black mud and shell.

Note: Although open to the SE, the Chain Islands provide adequate shelter in light to moderate winds.

Approach to Madrona Bay.

Ganges is a fun stop with full provisioning facilities. Although it is an urban centre, it presents itself to the visitor as a pedestrian seaside village. If you have been island-hopping for too long, this is the perfect spot to get your urban fix. It has great shopping and a large selection of places to buy and eat good food. You can also enjoy leisurely promenades along the sections of boardwalk from CENTENNIAL PARK in the S to MOBY'S MARINE PUB at the SALTSPRING MARINA in the N.

Centennial Park hosts the SATURDAY MARKET, where local arts, crafts and food go hand in hand. This varied and colourful event takes place every Saturday in the summer months and is well worth a visit. From here you can continue your provisioning spree through the downtown core. Pick up a current edition of the Saltspring map at the tourist information centre, as this lists retail shops and island events. THRIFTY FOODS is the largest supermarket in the Gulf Islands and MOUAT'S MALL, the landmark green-and-white building, provides an eclectic shopping experience. THE FISHERY, which is owned and operated by commercial fishers, is a must for local Dungeness crab, smoked fish and the catch of the day. Treat yourself to HARLAN'S CHOCOLATES, handmade on Saltspring and very more-ish.

Ganges has a wonderful selection of restaurants to choose from, but for an imaginative Sunday brunch, splash out and reserve a table at HASTINGS HOUSE. The food is delicious and you can finish off with a gentle stroll through the beautiful grounds and herb garden.

There are two public wharves, one being the small boat basin to the W of Grace Islet, which is mainly commercial with limited transient moorage available. The other is W of the seaplane terminal and coast guard station and is free of charge from 8:00 a.m. to 4:00 p.m. daily. SALTSPRING MARINA and GANGES MARINA provide necessary amenities and marine supplies for the visiting boater. Although there is temporary anchorage in Ganges Harbour, there is an alternative and quieter temporary anchorage on the harbour's E side (E of Goat Island) and in Madrona Bay.

Approach to Ganges Harbour.

GANGES HARBOUR

APPROACH

Ganges Harbour from the S and W of the Chain Islands. Ganges Village lies at the head of Ganges Harbour.

ANCHOR

E of Money Makers Rock and the marinas. Temporary anchorage open to the SE.

DEPTHS

4 - 6 m (13 - 19.5 ft). Holding good in mud.

PUBLIC WHARF

The small boat basin W of Grace Islet is reserved mainly for local and commercial craft. Dedicated transient moorage is available at the public wharf S of the marinas.

MARINAS

SALTSPRING MARINA (250-537-5810) and GANGES MARINA (250-537-5242). Both marinas offer transient moorage and monitor VHF channel 68. Prebooking is advisable.

BOAT LAUNCH

At public wharf and at Saltspring Marina.

FUEL

At Ganges Marina.

Note: Money Makers Rock lies close off the Ganges Marina breakwater.

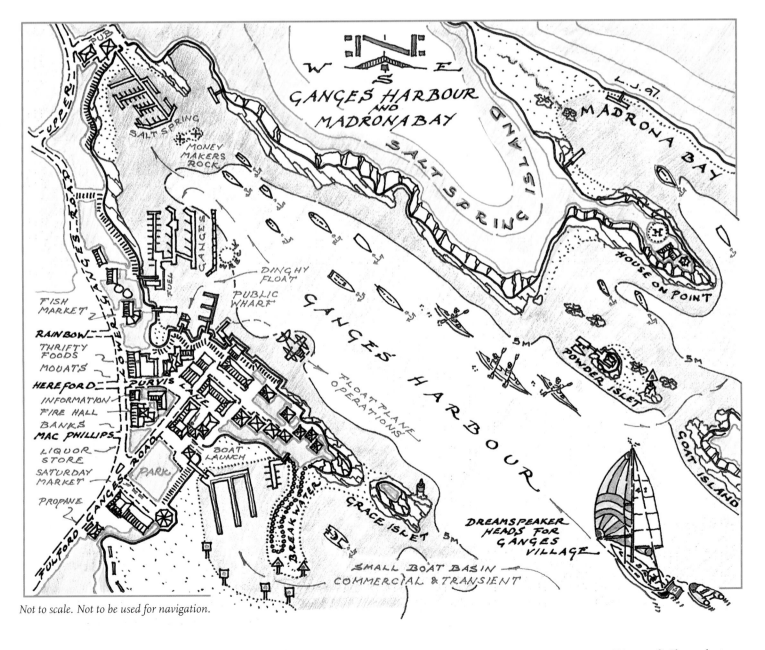

Not to scale. Not to be used for navigation.

9.2 LONG HARBOUR & WELBURY BAY, SALTSPRING ISLAND

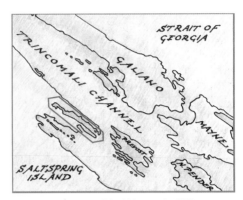

Long Harbour: 48°51'N   123°26'W
Welbury Bay: 48°51'N   123°27'W

Approach to Long Harbour between Scott and Nose Points.

There is clearly nothing short about LONG HARBOUR, as it stretches approximately 5 km (3 mi) from Nose Point to the head of the inlet. Long Harbour is protected from all winds except southeasterlies. The wind and swell begin to die off around Clamshell Islet, and good protection can be found beyond this point, especially close to shore. There is a varied selection of quiet hideaway anchorages to enjoy, with the convenience of Ganges close by for provisioning. Because nothing is ever quite perfect in paradise, expect the occasional ferry wash in the S portion of the harbour. The B.C. Ferries terminal on the S shore of Long Harbour connects Saltspring Island twice daily with Pender, Mayne and Galiano Islands, as well as Tsawwassen on the mainland. A launch ramp for kayaks, canoes and small boats lies alongside the ferry wharf.

ANCHORAGES

A: A temporary anchorage recommended by local sailors. Anchor in the centre of the bight and tie a stern line ashore.

B: A good lunch stop with protection from southeasterlies and great for exploring the islets and beaches toward Nose Point.

C & D: Beautifully quiet and enjoy the longest evening light.

E: We can vouch for this anchorage being cosy, quiet and, in favourable weather, glassy smooth. It is an excellent spot for exploring the inlet and lagoon by dinghy or kayak at HW. We passed lush paddocks with horses grazing tranquilly in the morning sun. Take care not to be caught on a falling tide on your return journey.

WELBURY BAY is an alternative temporary anchorage but is open to southeasterlies. The NE corner is conveniently situated a few metres from the Long Harbour B.C. Ferries terminal, should you be picking up or dropping off visitors.

Antique craft moored at the head of Long Harbour.

CHARTS

3478. 3313, page 10. SCN Map B4.

LONG HARBOUR

APPROACH

Long Harbour from Captain Passage and enter between Scott and Nose Points.

ANCHOR

As indicated. Spots C, D and E provide good all-weather shelter.

DEPTHS

2 - 4 m (6.5 - 13 ft). Holding good in mud.

Note: Spots A and B are considered temporary anchorages only. Ferries use Long Harbour at frequent intervals.

WELBURY BAY

APPROACH

Welbury Bay from Captain Passage between Scott and Welbury Points.

ANCHOR

In centre of bay.

DEPTHS

Holding and bottom condition unrecorded.

Note: Rocky patch NW of buoy U49.

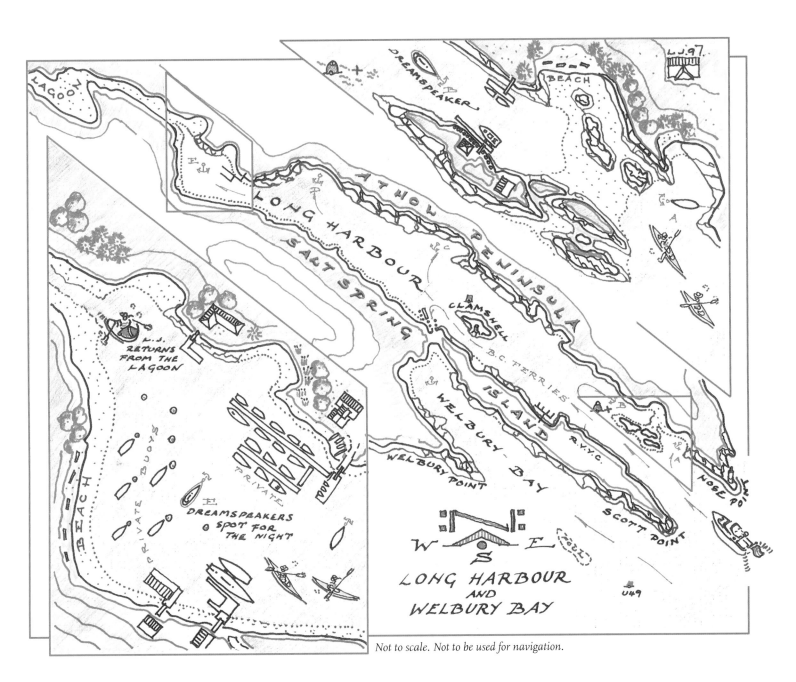

Not to scale. Not to be used for navigation.

9.3   WALKER HOOK, SALTSPRING ISLAND

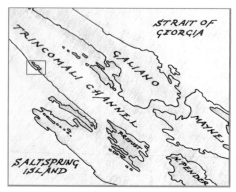

48°53'N   123°30'W

The beach stretches westward from the rocky tip of Walker Hook.

On a sunny day this is a magical spot to drop your anchor, stretch your legs and dig your toes into the clean sand. We anchored in the centre of the bight formed by the hook, just a boat's length (at LW) off the beach.

The hook is formed by a sandy isthmus that connects to a wooded, rocky peninsula. The length of the beach and the width of the isthmus come as quite a surprise. The fine sand-and-shell beach shelves gently from the HW line, then drops off quite quickly, allowing you to anchor well in. The hook also gives some shelter from light northwesterly breezes.

There is good swimming and clam digging off the SE corner of the beach, with flat rocks near the point for spreading out your picnic lunch. We met kayakers who had explored the drying lagoon behind the beach at HW and were delighted with their new discovery. Land beyond the HW mark is privately owned, so due respect should be given to property boundaries.

Colourful kayaks line the beach at low water.

CHARTS

3442. 3313, page 17. SCN Map C2.

APPROACH

From the SW of Atkins Reef or from the NW by clearing the NE tip of Walker Hook.

ANCHOR

Off-beach, temporary anchorage with no real overnight shelter.

DEPTHS

2 - 4 m (6.5 - 13 ft). Holding good in sand.

BOAT LAUNCH

N of lagoon, where road meets shoreline.

Note: The drying lagoon is good territory for exploration by dinghy, canoe or kayak.

Good swimming off the southeast corner of the beach.

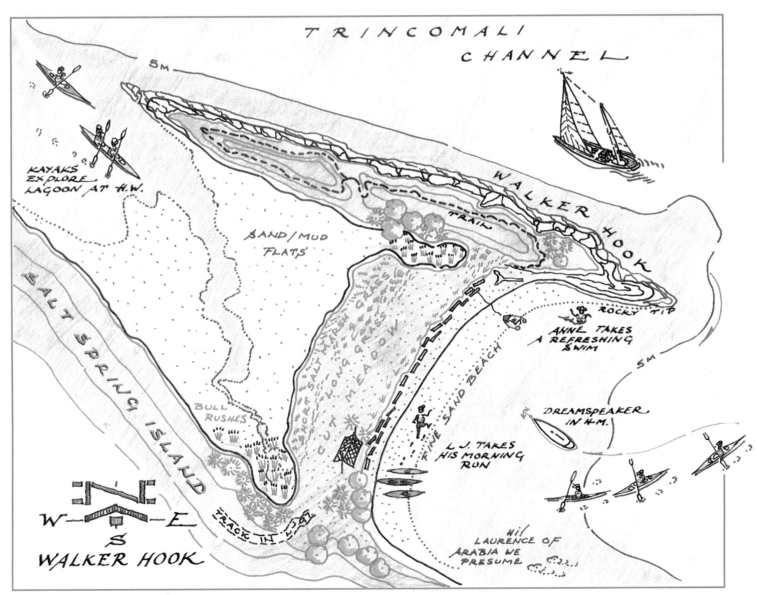

Not to scale. Not to be used for navigation.

9.4   MONTAGUE HARBOUR MARINE PARK, GALIANO ISLAND

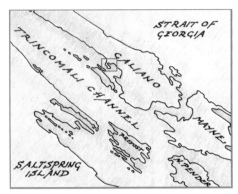

48°54'N 123°24'W

Approach to Montague Harbour's western entrance.

Sunset from the shell beach.

As the first marine park established in British Columbia, Montague Harbour ranks as a superstar and is always a delight to visit. It is an added bonus to find a vacant mooring buoy or anchorage in the summer months, as this is a popular destination. Seasoned boaters arrive well before 2:00 p.m. to claim their favourite spot. In the western entrance keep clear of the rocks off Gray Peninsula, which are well covered at high tide and extend further than you think.

The park, which has walk-in and drive-in camping, occupies the former site of an ancient Coast Salish settlement. In the early morning, sit at the midden site and try to imagine 3,000 years of culture that have left no scars and very little evidence, save for the telltale white shell that spills out onto the beach.

At the head of the harbour a float for small boats and dinghies leads you to the marine park information rack and NATURE HOUSE, which in July and August hosts a display of touchy-feely sea life for kids young and old. From here you can join the 8-km (5-mi) trail that winds through fir and hemlock forests, along white shell-and-sand beaches and into a tidal lagoon inhabited by interesting marshland flora.

Montague Harbour is still a good spot for crabbing: drop your trap NW of the launch ramp and relax on the beach while dreaming of exotic crab feasts. In stable summer conditions, the temporary anchorage off the N shore is a perfect location for sunset picnics, as nature provides a spectacular display of glowing colour from burnt orange to hazy pink. This is a great way to celebrate the end to a perfect West Coast day. A fun alternative would be to hop aboard the local pub bus and enjoy great food at the HUMMINGBIRD PUB. The bus transports customers daily from the marine park gate as well as from MONTAGUE HARBOUR MARINA, and it runs every hour from 6:00 p.m. to 11:00 p.m., May to September (call 250-539-5472).

Looking north to the marine park.

CHARTS

3473. 3313, pages 9 (insert) & 17. SCN Maps B6 & C2.

APPROACH

From the NW, entering between Gray Peninsula and Parker Island, or from the SE, entering between Phillimore Point and Julia Island.

ANCHOR

Sheltered anchorage can be found throughout the harbour. Alternatively, pick up one of the numerous mooring buoys within the park boundary.

DEPTHS

6 - 12 m (19.5 - 39 ft). Holding good in mud and shell.

PUBLIC WHARF

The marine park has extensive moorage for vessels under 7 m (23 ft).

Note: Care should be taken to avoid anchoring in the approach to the alternative ferry terminal. The anchorage N of Gray Peninsula is only temporary.

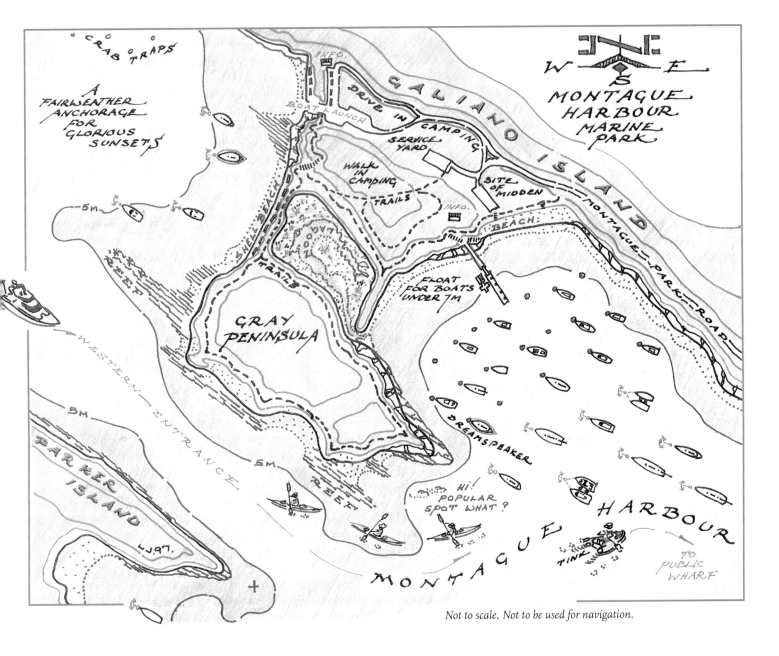

Not to scale. Not to be used for navigation.

9.5 MONTAGUE HARBOUR PUBLIC WHARF & MARINA, GALIANO ISLAND

48°53'N 123°24'W

CHARTS

3473. 3313, pages 9 & 17. SCN Maps B6 & C2.

APPROACH

The public wharf and marina lie central along the NE shore of Montague Harbour, adjacent to the ferry terminal. This terminal is only used when strong southeasterlies make berthing at Sturdies Bay precarious.

PUBLIC WHARF

Although the floats are quite extensive, local boats rafted 2 - 3 deep leave little room for visitors. Kayaks also launch from the floats, and the floatplane berth is in frequent use.

MARINA

MONTAGUE HARBOUR MARINA (250-539-5733) has extensive transient moorage, fuel and a marina store and sundeck.

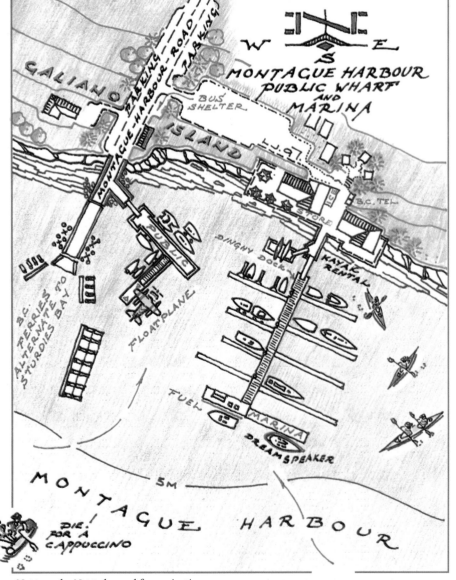

Not to scale. Not to be used for navigation.

The waters of Montague Harbour are bustling with boaters, floatplanes and kayakers. We rowed in from the marine park to top up our provisions and tied up to the dinghy dock alongside the ramp at MONTAGUE HARBOUR MARINA. The small marina store sells a good selection of basic groceries and books and has a well-stocked deli section. Outside, on the cosy sundeck, you can enjoy a cappuccino, ice cream or a light lunch. Beer and wine are served with meals only. The GO GALIANO ISLAND SHUTTLE taxi service (250-539-0202) will take you to any location on the island and also connects with the ferry at Sturdies Bay.

Approach to the public wharf and marina.

CHARTS

3442. 3313, page 8. SCN Map B4.

APPROACH

From Swanson Channel, the lighthouse on Portlock Point being a very conspicuous landmark.

ANCHOR

In centre of bay, below the automated light. Temporary anchorage for 1 - 2 boats, exposed to the SE.

DEPTHS

4 m (13 ft) abeam of the light. This rapidly shallows toward the beach. Holding good in mud and shell.

Note: Watch out for deadheads. The bay is exposed to ferry wash.

48°49'N   123°21'W

This temporary anchorage has all the essential ingredients to rank high among the best picnic anchorages in the Gulf Islands. Take a sedate row or paddle to explore the shoreline before deciding on the perfect spot. You can choose between a grassy patch that sits above the cliffs to the S of the bay or the soft, mossy hump a little further N. Alternatively, the three small islets named by us, "Crabtree Islets," have tidal shell beaches to enjoy, and the smooth, rounded rocks in front of the old lighthouse foundation provide a lovely picnic setting.

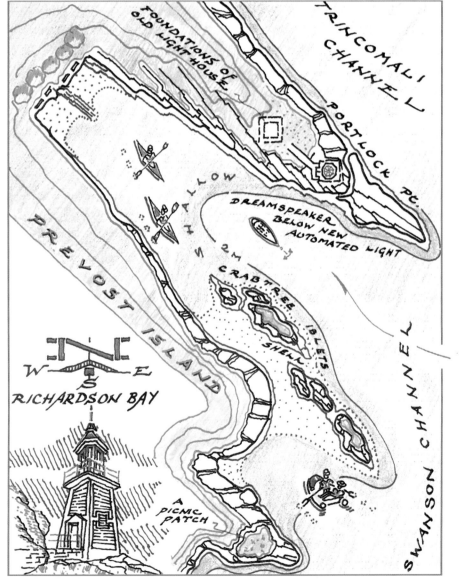

Not to scale. Not to be used for navigation.

A perfect picnic spot.

9.7 GLENTHORNE PASSAGE, ELLEN & DIVER BAYS, SE PREVOST ISLAND

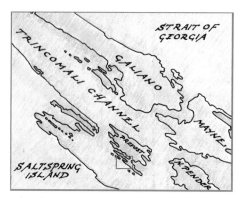

Glenthorne Passage: 48°49'N   123°23'W
Ellen & Diver Bays: 48°49'N   123°22'W

Approach to Glenthorne Passage looking southeast over Owl Island.

Evening at the head of Glenthorne Passage.

Prevost Island is a cruising area in its own right, with 7 anchorages to choose from. Local boaters from Saltspring Island often lose themselves in one of the bays or coves for a quiet weekend getaway. The SE side of the island provides sunny morning anchorages, while the NW side is great for sunsets. The island is privately owned, with the exception of James Bay and the connecting waterfront land on adjacent Selby Cove. This is now maintained by B.C. Parks and is accessible by boat only. Any park services will remain minimal, as it is the natural scenery of this parkland that the Marine Heritage Legacy is striving to preserve. The island is moderately high in parts and thickly wooded with large expanses of meadow between, giving it a certain pastoral charm. If you are game for some fun daytime coastal exploration around the island, begin with Glenthorne Passage and end with Annette Inlet (see pages 118 & 119).

After giving a wide berth to Point Liddell, cruise down Captain Passage into GLENTHORNE PASSAGE. This snug and picturesque all-weather haven is without question the most popular anchorage on Prevost Island. When we anchored for the night we had a wonderful view out to the sunset, with the evening light penetrating deep into the passage. Secret Island on the W side has a large cabin community and is private. The small boat pass between Secret Island and Glenthorne Point is considered a dinghy pass only.

The small boat pass into Glenthorne Passage.

Both ELLEN and DIVER Bays provide good shelter from northwesterlies but are exposed to southeasterlies and the effect of ferry wash (this, however, is not too uncomfortable, due to the depth of the bays). You couldn't wish for more pristine surroundings or better holding. We had fun sailing our dinghy *Tink* in these bays, as there is plenty of room to tack and no obstructions.

CHARTS

3478. 3442. 3313, pages 8 & 10. SCN Map B4.

Note: For Richardson Bay see page 115.

GLENTHORNE PASSAGE

APPROACH

Glenthorne Passage from Captain Passage and enter from the NW, leaving Owl Island to starboard, or between Owl Island and Secret Island.

ANCHOR

Good all-weather anchorage can be found throughout the passage.

DEPTHS

4 - 6 m (13 - 19.5 ft). Holding good in mud.

ELLEN & DIVER BAYS

APPROACH

Ellen and Diver Bays from Swanson Channel.

ANCHOR

At the head of the bays. Temporary anchorage, open to the SE.

DEPTHS

Holding and bottom condition unrecorded.

Note: The small boat pass from Captain Passage into Glenthorne Passage should only be used with prior knowledge.

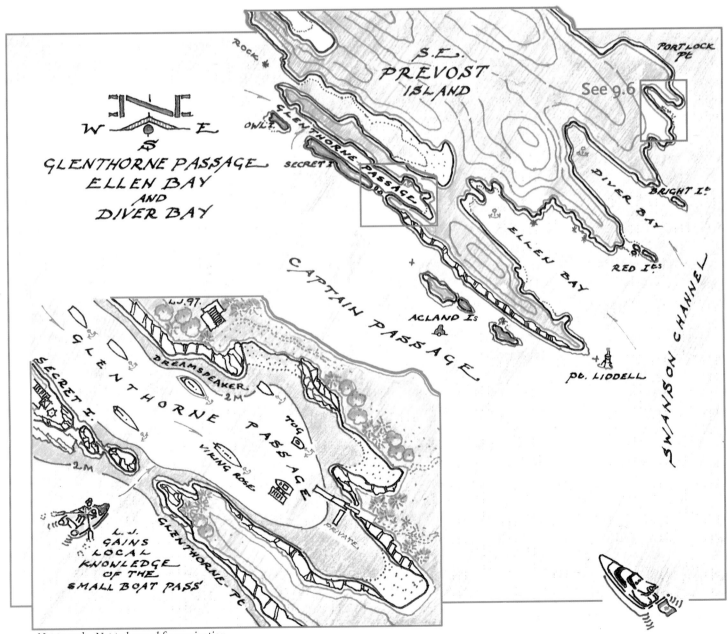

Not to scale. Not to be used for navigation.

9.8 James Bay, Selby Cove & Annette Inlet, NW Prevost Island

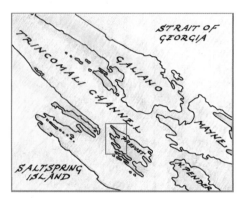

James Bay: 48°51'N 123°24'W
Selby Cove: 48°50'N 123°24'W
Annette Inlet: 48°50'N 123°24'W

Approach to James Bay. O'Reilly Beach is to port.

Boats at anchor in Selby Cove.

James Bay, in the NW corner of Prevost Island, is home to a B.C. Parks Protected Area. Its natural charm is enhanced by a small apple orchard and a valley that leads inland. At the head of the bay there are two gravel beaches. O'Reilly Beach fronts a pasture where you might be confronted by grazing cows. A sheep trail takes you to Peile Point, which offers inspiring views over Trincomali Channel. Foundations of original homestead dwellings can be found in the orchard behind the smaller beach. This is also a perfect spot for picnicking and warm-water swimming, with a hiking trail along the ridge. As an anchorage, James Bay is open to the full fetch of Trincomali Channel to the NW. It does, however, offer good protection from southeasterlies, as well as great sunsets.

Selby Cove affords good protection from all winds if you anchor in 4 - 6 m (13 - 19.5 ft), tuck into the nook along the NE shore and tie a stern line to the nearest tree. The middle portion of this shoreline is now part of the Parks Protected Area that connects to James Bay, making access to its natural beauty easily available.

On entering Annette Inlet take care to avoid the rock in the middle of the bight that forms the entrance. All-weather shelter can be found within. Annette Inlet is quite different from its neighbours, as it is shallow in parts. Pay close attention to your depth sounder. The pastoral woodland setting makes you feel content to just laze in the cockpit with a good book in one hand and a glass of wine in the other.

Approach to Annette Inlet.

CHARTS

3478. 3313, pages 8 & 10. SCN Map B4.

JAMES BAY

APPROACH

James Bay from Captain Passage and enter between Peile and Selby Points.

ANCHOR

Off O'Reilly Beach, clear of reef that extends from tip of escarpment. Temporary anchorage, exposed to the N and the full fetch of Trincomali Channel.

DEPTHS

2 - 6 m (6.5 - 19.5 ft). Holding good in mud.

SELBY COVE

APPROACH

Selby Cove from Captain Passage and enter to the N of Annette Point.

ANCHOR

Temporary anchorage may be found in the centre of the cove.

ANNETTE INLET

APPROACH

Annette Inlet from Captain Passage, taking care to avoid the rocky, shallow patch to the W of the entrance.

ANCHOR

Good all-around shelter may be found in the inlet.

Note: Depths, holding and bottom condition were not recorded in Selby Cove and Annette Inlet.

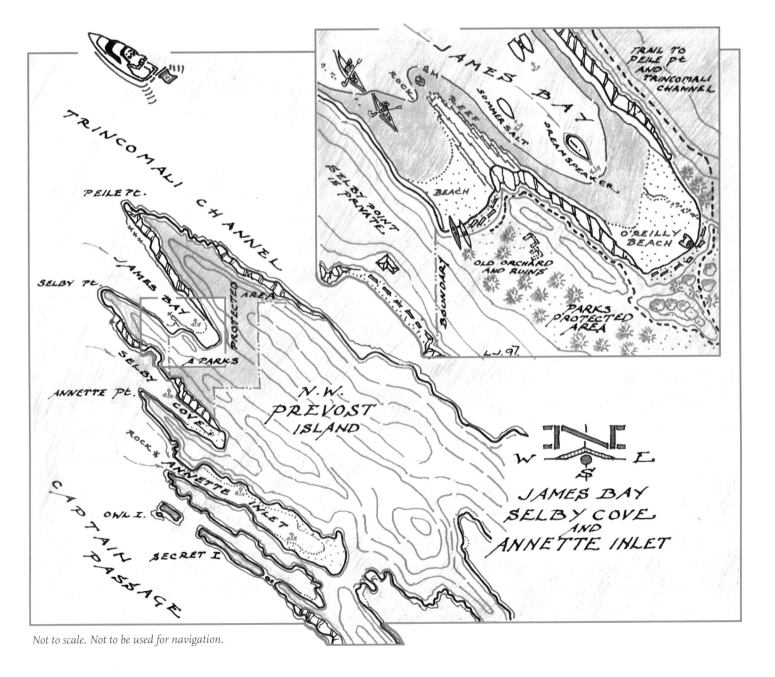

Not to scale. Not to be used for navigation.

9.9 PORT WASHINGTON, GRIMMER BAY, N PENDER ISLAND

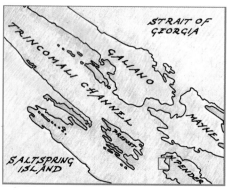

48°49'N 123°19'W

CHARTS

3442. 3313, page 8. SCN Map B4.

APPROACH

From Swanson Channel, N of Boat Islet. A warehouse-like structure above the wharfhead makes a conspicuous landmark.

ANCHOR

Anchorage is possible in the SE of Grimmer Bay. However, it is exposed to the NW and to frequent ferry wash.

Depths, holding and bottom condition unrecorded.

PUBLIC WHARF

The public wharf services the small community of Port Washington. There is 46 m (150 ft) of float on the N side of the wharfhead. The N portion is a loading zone.

Note: A rock with less than 1.8 m (6 ft) over it lies about 45 m (148 ft) S of the SE end of the public wharf.

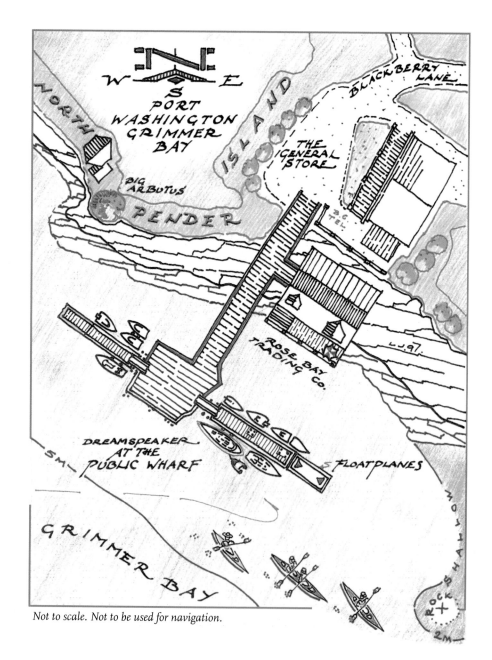

Not to scale. Not to be used for navigation.

The charm of this pretty bay lies in its quiet repose. It is also a good spot to stretch your legs with a leisurely walk along Blackberry Lane. You will pass the old GENERAL STORE, which now houses artist studios, and in season, you can gather up some of Pender's famous blackberries. About 2 km (1 mi) or so along the lane you will find the ARMSTRONG GALLERY, which specializes in bird and marine paintings, and next door, THE PARLOUR, which offers local crafts and workshops. The OLD ORCHARD FARM, located at the Port Washington Road intersection, has recently been restored to its former Victorian glory. In season, fruit and flowers are sold from the stand at the gate. The public wharf is used by the occasional floatplane and water taxi.

Approaching the public wharf.

CHARTS

3442. 3313, page 8. SCN Map B4.

APPROACH

Otter Bay from Swanson Channel and enter Hyashi Cove by leaving to port the U57 port-hand buoy and the flag-decked breakwater of the marina.

ANCHOR

E of the marina, off the small beach. Temporary anchorage open to the SW.

DEPTHS

4 - 6 m (13 - 19.5 ft). Holding good in mud.

MARINA

OTTER BAY MARINA (250-629-3579). In summer the outer float is dedicated to transient moorage. The marina monitors VHF channel 68 and has well-managed shore facilities.

BOAT LAUNCH

At marina.

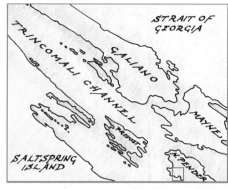

48°48'N 123°18'W

H yashi Cove is the only sheltered spot in the region that is relatively protected from ferry wash and prevailing winds. As you enter the cove from Otter Bay you will find OTTER BAY MARINA, which is tucked neatly behind the breakwater and sports a deck of colourful flags. This well-managed family marina offers moorage, kayak rentals, a store with basic provisions, a cappuccino bar, swimming pool and a shower/laundry cabin that is one of the best this side of the border. You will also find a kids' playhouse equipped with toys and a small play area. For the best burgers on the island, walk out of the marina to THE STAND, which is situated right next to the ferry terminal.

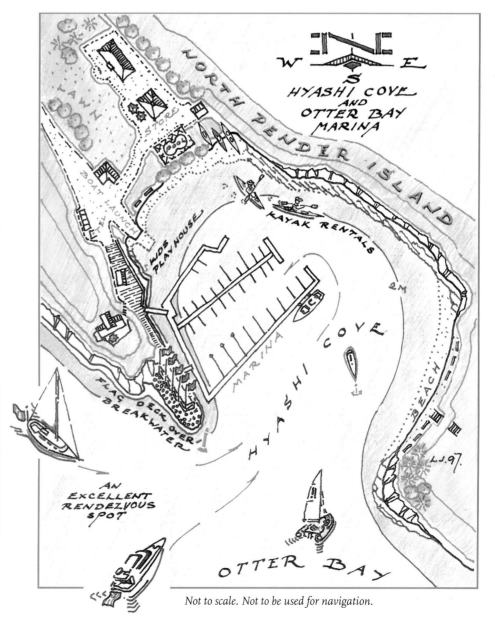

Not to scale. Not to be used for navigation.

Approach to Hyashi Cove.

Montague Harbour can accommodate many visiting boats.

A Little Harbour sailboat cautiously exits Conover Cove, Wallace Island Marine Park.

A family takes an evening stroll beside the lagoon at Montague Harbour Marine Park.

Chapter 10
PORLIER PASS

Looking northeast over the islet off Reid Island to Porlier Pass.

Chapter 10
PORLIER PASS

TIDES
Reference Port: Fulford Harbour
Secondary Port: Porlier Pass
Reference Port: Point Atkinson
Secondary Port: Dionisio Point

CURRENTS
Reference Station: Race Passage
Secondary Station: Trincomali Channel
Reference Station: Porlier Pass

WEATHER
Area: Strait of Georgia (South)
Reporting Stations: Entrance Island, Sand Heads, Active Pass

Heading out to Porlier Pass after a long day.

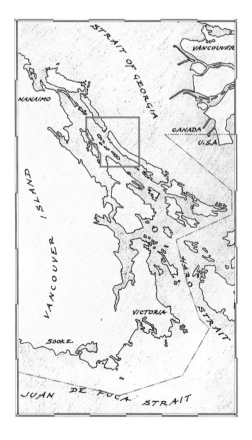

Porlier Pass, the busy thoroughfare between Valdes and Galiano Islands, provides handy access into or out of Trincomali Channel and the central Gulf Islands.

The safest and often the only time to enter the pass is at slack water. The cruising boater should be aware of ferocious tidal rips and extremely dangerous tidal currents of up to nine knots that can occur in the pass. It should also be noted that strong winds can be blowing on the outside of the pass when all is calm within. Wind over tide can then create standing waves large enough to enter and fill your cockpit. Although the pass has its fair share of dangerous rocks, they are clearly marked and most are found on the Valdes Island side of the pass. Porlier Pass is also frequented by working tugs, so don't be surprised to find yourself in the company of one or two of them pulling laden barges or extensive log booms.

This chapter shows how the simple delights of northern Trincomali Channel and Houstoun Passage can easily be explored for a week-long holiday. There is no large provisioning stop, but Fernwood Point on Saltspring Island in the south provides basic provisions. Peaceful Retreat Cove is a good place to stretch your legs while visiting the fascinating sandstone galleries at "Bramel Point" (local name).

Most of Wallace Island is now a charming marine park with protected anchorages in Conover Cove and "Princess Bay" (local name). It is popular with kayakers and boaters alike and well worth an extended visit. Allow yourself time to picnic in the lovely old orchard and to explore the shady trails that meander through the entire length of the island.

Semi-protected anchorage and a tidal beach can be found between North and South Secretary Islands, while Clam Bay on Kuper Island provides space, comfort and, sometimes, solitude.

If the tides through Porlier Pass are against you, anchor off the southern tip of Reid Island and explore the small recreational reserve, or tie up at North Galiano public wharf and picnic in the pocket park. Dionisio Point Marine Park on the northern tip of Galiano Island has a beautiful white sandy beach – perfect for a day's visit.

CAUTIONARY NOTES

Northwesterly winds associated with a high-pressure ridge frequently penetrate this cruising area, building overnight to attain 15 - 20 knots by mid-morning.

Tide and tidal current information needs to be carefully consulted prior to transiting Porlier Pass.

Featured Destinations

10.1 Fernwood Point & Public Wharf,
      Saltspring Island   126

10.2 Retreat Cove & Public Wharf,
      Galiano Island   127

10.3 Conover Cove, Wallace Island Marine Park   128

10.4 Princess Bay, Wallace Island Marine Park   130

10.5 Secretary Islands   131

10.6 Clam Bay, Thetis & Kuper Islands   132

10.7 Reid Island   134

10.8 North Galiano Public Wharf,
      Galiano Island   135

10.9 Dionisio Point Marine Park,
      Galiano Island   136

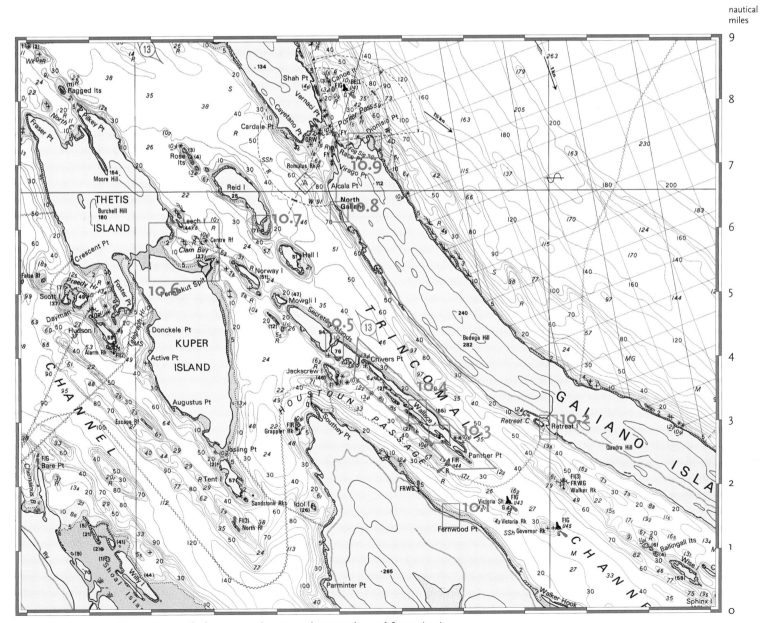

Reproduced portion of CHS Chart 3463 for passage planning only. Not to be used for navigation.

10.1 FERNWOOD POINT & PUBLIC WHARF, SALTSPRING ISLAND

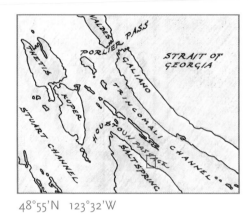

48°55'N 123°32'W

CHARTS

3442. 3313, page 17. SCN Map C2.

APPROACH

The public wharf from the NE or NW. The long jetty extending out from the shoreline is the most conspicuous landmark.

PUBLIC WHARF

Minimal float space for temporary, short visits. The wharf is exposed to any wind, swell or wash from Trincomali Channel.

Note: In calm conditions it is possible to anchor for a short period just E of the public wharf. Depths, holding and bottom condition unrecorded.

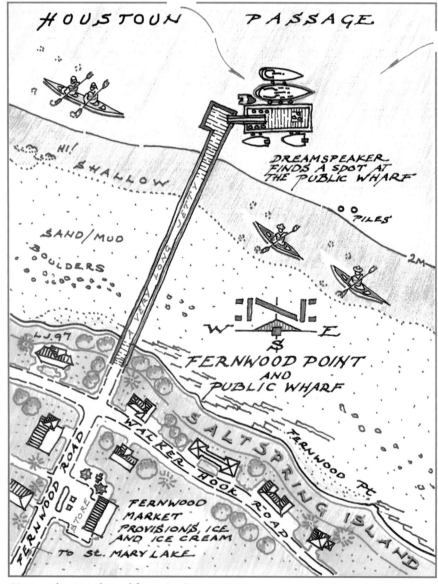

Not to scale. Not to be used for navigation.

The public wharf at Fernwood Point provides limited docking space, with a very long jetty crossing the mud flats en route to FERNWOOD MARKET. At the market you will find ice, gas, basic provisions and a mouthwatering selection of local ice cream. If you like the idea of a freshwater swim, take the 2-km (1-mi) hike to ST. MARY LAKE, the largest in the southern Gulf Islands. The only public access to the lake is along North End Road, where there is a small swimming beach and kayak and canoe launch is also possible. Note that the rest of the lake's shoreline is private property, and public foreshore rights do not apply on lakes.

Public wharf at Fernwood Point.

RETREAT COVE & PUBLIC WHARF, GALIANO ISLAND 10.2

CHARTS

3442. 3313, page 17. SCN Map C2.

APPROACH

From the SW and enter between the southern tip of Retreat Island and "Bramel Point."

ANCHOR

Off the public wharf to the NW. Good shelter from all winds except westerlies.

DEPTHS

2 - 3 m (6.5 - 10 ft). Holding good in mud.

PUBLIC WHARF

The outside of the wharf has moorage for 2 - 3 boats.

Note: At LW Retreat Island connects to the Galiano shore just NW of the private float.

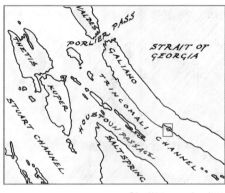

48°56'N   123°30'W

There is enough room for 2 to 3 boats on the outside of the public wharf. The inside, being shallow, is used mainly by small local runabouts. Anchorage in the middle of the cove is comfortable for 1 boat only. Retreat Cove is a good place to stretch your legs with a walk, run or cycle to the local fire hall, which often hosts interesting local events in the summer months. There are fascinating sandstone galleries at "Bramel Point," with public access from the road or shoreline. When things are very quiet, the otter family that lives below the public wharf comes out to play, making this peaceful retreat complete. Retreat Island to the W is privately owned.

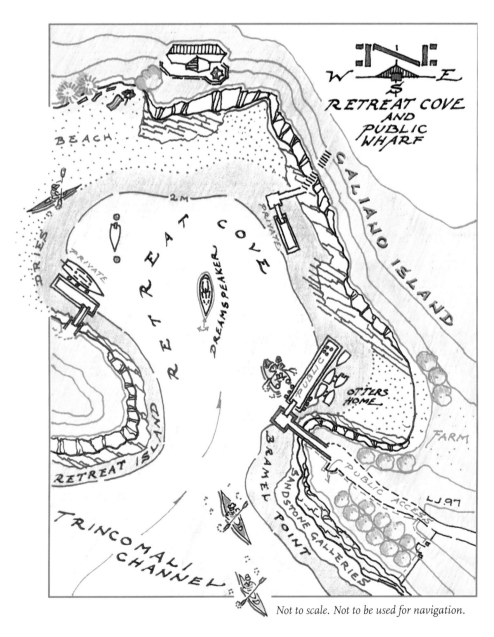

Not to scale. Not to be used for navigation.

Approach to Retreat Cove.

10.3   CONOVER COVE, WALLACE ISLAND MARINE PARK

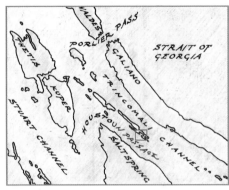

48°56'N   123°33'W

Entrance to Conover Cove. Note the rocky ledge that extends from the northwest side.

Stern line to a ring or tree is a must.

Conover Cove is extremely popular in the summer months.

The lovely old orchards in Conover Cove were planted by the industrious Jeremiah Chivers, Wallace Island's first owner. The Conover family then bought the island and turned it into a successful resort. Some of the original buildings still stand today. David Conover's books, *Once Upon an Island* and *One Man's Island,* are worth reading and provide insight into island life in the 1940s. The island is now a marine park, except for several private properties whose boundaries should be respected.

CONOVER COVE provides a well-protected shoal anchorage with a tricky entrance that we experienced firsthand. The NW point has an underwater ledge extending further into the entrance than we initially estimated. Note that the deepest part of the anchorage is between 1.8 - 3 m (6 - 10 ft) at zero tide, making careful depth calculation essential.

The park operators take great pride in maintaining Wallace Island Marine Park to the highest standard. The grassy orchard with picnic tables and resort cabins no longer in use provides a shady, homely spot for kayakers and campers to pitch their tents. Fresh water can be taken from the pump in the old farm meadow, where good trails lead you NW to "Princess Bay" or N to "Cabin Bay" (both local names) and Chivers Point, about 4 km (2.5 mi) away. Shady trails lead S to "Picnic Point" (also a local name) and Panther Point, named after HMS Panther, which ran aground here in 1874.

Swinging is not recommended in this somewhat narrow anchorage, and yellow-painted metal hooks on shoreline rocks are provided for your stern line. A visitors' float for approximately 6 boats is also available. Because this is an ex-tremely popular anchorage in the summer months, it has been designated as a quiet zone between 9:00 p.m. and 9:00 a.m. Watch for river otters slinking between the rocks or sliding down the grassy slopes.

CHARTS

3442. 3313, page 17. SCN Map C2.

APPROACH

Conover Cove with extreme caution, keeping a watchful eye on the depth sounder at the tricky entrance. Favour the S side of the entrance, as an underwater ledge extends from the NW side.

ANCHOR

Perpendicular to a ring on the shore, attaching a stern line back to the ring.

DEPTHS

1.8 - 3 m (6 - 10 ft). Holding good in mud.

PUBLIC WHARF

A marine park float can accommodate 6 - 8 boats.

Note: Calculate your time of departure carefully, as the bar at the entrance to the cove is shallower than the waters within. Do not attempt to swing at anchor, as this would restrict the use of the anchorage by other craft.

Snug in Conover Cove.

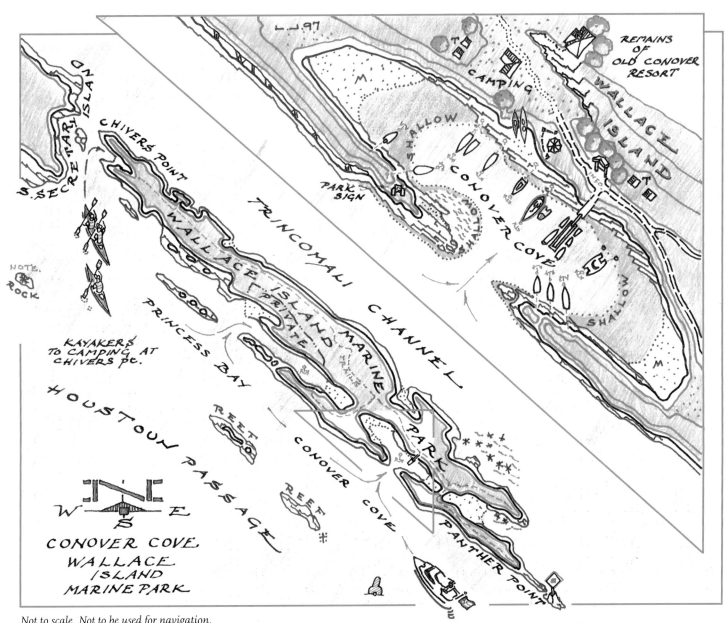

Not to scale. Not to be used for navigation.

10.4   PRINCESS BAY, WALLACE ISLAND MARINE PARK

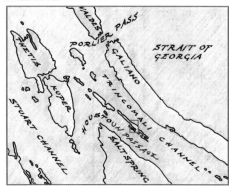

48°56'N   123°33'W

CHARTS

3442. 3313, page 17. SCN Map C2.

APPROACH

The small islet at the bay's entrance and enter by rounding, with adequate clearance, its northern tip.

ANCHOR

Perpendicular to the rocky peninsula, attaching a stern line back to the ring or tree onshore. Good shelter, but exposed to the NW.

DEPTHS

5 - 7 m (16 - 23 ft). Holding good in mud.

Note: Angle the bow toward the NW prior to attaching a stern line ashore, as this will help counter a northwesterly that tends to build overnight.

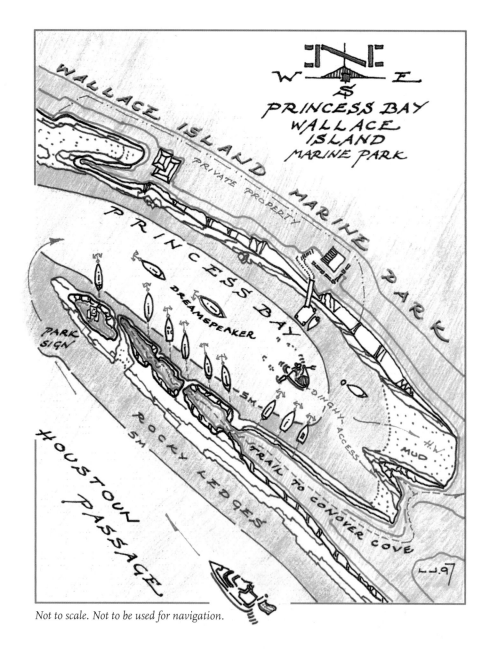

Not to scale. Not to be used for navigation.

This is an alternative, deep-water anchorage that can easily accommodate 50 or more boats on a busy summer weekend. A long, narrow sandstone peninsula gives the bay a feeling of privacy. Boats usually anchor along the peninsula, attaching a stern line to trees or to the metal rings provided. Anchorage is also possible in the centre of the bay, along the northern shore (which is partly private), or in the more exposed entrance area. Convenient dinghy access to the island trails is available on the southeastern shore of the bay. It is also fun to explore the Houstoun Passage side of the peninsula, with its rocky ledges and tidal pools that, at certain times, provide warm-water swimming.

"Princess Bay" looking northwest.

CHARTS

3442. 3313, page 17. SCN Map C2.

APPROACH

The drying gap between N and S Secretary Islands from the N. Deep water lies in the centre of the bay.

ANCHOR

As far in as your draft and the tide will allow. Sheltered anchorage for 3 - 4 boats. Exposed to the N and the wash of passing boats.

DEPTHS

2 - 4 m (6.5 - 13 ft). Holding good in mud and sand.

Note: A rocky ledge extends out from the NE tip of S Secretary Island.

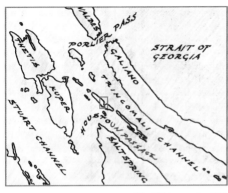

48°58'N   123°35'W

S urprisingly good anchorage can be found between these two islands, just in from Trincomali Channel. When entering, keep a look-out for the rocky ledge just off the NE shore. The tree-fringed cove narrows to a sand-and-shell beach that joins the two islands at LW. At HW it is possible for dinghies and kayaks to pass between the N and S Secretaries to Jackscrew Island in Houstoun Passage. The Secretary Islands are private, with bold signs indicating this fact.

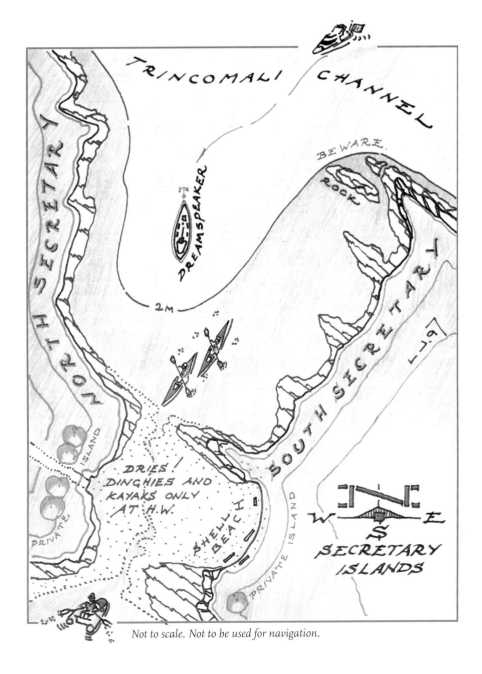

The gap between North and South Secretary Islands.

Not to scale. Not to be used for navigation.

10.6   CLAM BAY,
THETIS & KUPER ISLANDS

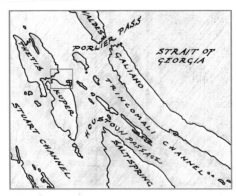

48°59'N 123°39'W

Looking northwest over Penelakut Spit into Clam Bay.

Kuper Island is a First Nations reserve that is owned by the Penelakut Band and has an active, thriving community. A tidy village with a tall church spire fringes the shoreline, and houses on the hill overlook the lagoon. There is a busy private wharf at the entrance to the lagoon.

Although it feels quite open, good shelter can be found in Clam Bay off both Thetis and Kuper Islands, depending on the direction of the wind. Keep a careful watch out for Centre Reef and Rocket Shoal when entering between Leech Island and Penelakut Spit. The long sandy spit connects to a small, tree-covered private island, which forms an effective breakwater to southeasterly winds. This is a large, comfortable anchorage where it is possible to find your own patch of solitude without encroaching on the privacy of the island.

You are never too young to start paddling.

CHARTS

3477. 3313, pages 15 & 16. SCN Maps C1 & C4.

APPROACH

From the E, between the red conical buoy and the tip of Penelakut Spit.

ANCHOR

In the NW or SE, depending on forecast conditions. NW winds may reach this far S, building overnight.

DEPTHS

5 - 8 m (16 - 26 ft). Holding good in mud and sand.

Note: Although marked by day marks, The Cut, a HW small boat passage to Telegraph Harbour, should only be navigated with prior knowledge of the area.

The Cut at low water.

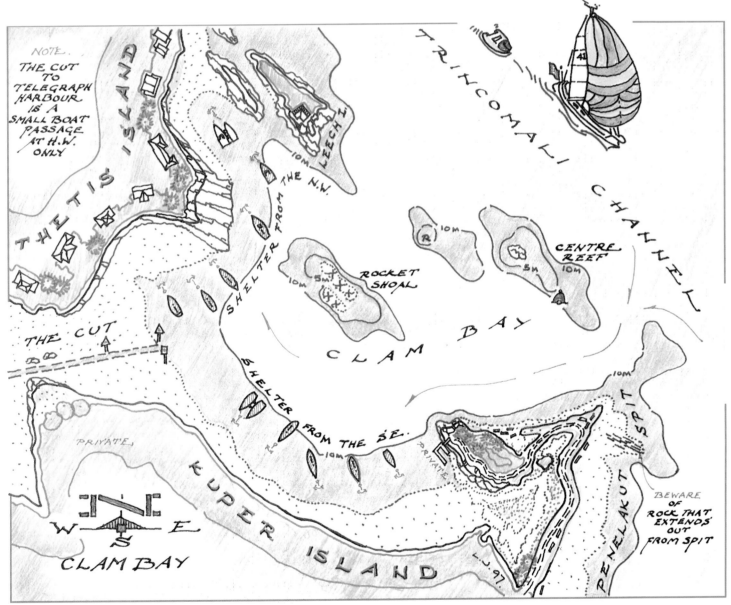

Not to scale. Not to be used for navigation.

10.7   REID ISLAND

49°00'N   123°38'W

CHARTS

3442. 3313, page 15. SCN Map C1.

APPROACH

With extreme caution at LW, when the surrounding reef is clearly visible. The entrance pass from the NE is the wider channel.

ANCHOR

Off the rocky foreshore of Reid Island and to the E of the islet, within the reef. Temporary anchorage, exposed to the SE.

DEPTHS

2 - 6 m (6.5 - 19.5 ft). Holding and bottom condition unrecorded.

Note: Reef covers completely at HW, leaving the anchorage exposed to any wind or swell in Trincomali Channel.

Not to scale. Not to be used for navigation.

On the southern tip of Reid Island lies an unexpected picnic stop that is protected by a drying reef and an enchanting islet. What we call "Little Reid Islet" is a recreational reserve and an ideal camping spot for kayakers and canoeists who don't mind a rocky landing. Head for the S side of the islet, where you will find exposed flat-rock ledges below and a small grassy area above that is ideal for pitching a few tents. The view is spectacular and the entire islet is dotted with beautiful arbutus trees. Please note that no fires are permitted on the reserve. The anchorage holds only 1 to 2 boats comfortably, and wonderfully clean water entices you to take a quick dip before lunch.

Looking northeast over Reid Island and "Little Reid Islet."

CHARTS

3443. 3313, page 16. SCN Map C4.

APPROACH

The public wharf from the W. The red roof of the store over the wharfhead is a conspicuous landmark.

PUBLIC WHARF

Minimal float space, restricted to the outside of the wharf for loading and short visits. The inside is used by small local boats.

Note: Temporary anchorage is possible just W of the public wharf. However, it is totally exposed to winds and currents in Trincomali Channel.

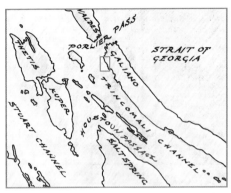

49°00'N 123°35'W

This is a convenient stop if you are waiting for the tide to turn in Porlier Pass. The wharf is set in a bight along low sandstone cliffs. Perched on these cliffs is the SPANISH HILLS GENERAL STORE (for sale when we visited [1997]), which may offer groceries, hamburgers, ice and hardware. DIONISIO POINT PARK EXPRESS/GALIANO DIVING operates from the public wharf. Trips to Dionisio Point Marine Park leave at 12:00 p.m. and 5:00 p.m. daily, and return trips to the dock are available at around 12:15 p.m. and 5:15 p.m. respectively. Diving charters can also be arranged (call Martin at 250-539-3109). A small craft launch for kayaks and canoes is possible from the pocket park on the NW shore.

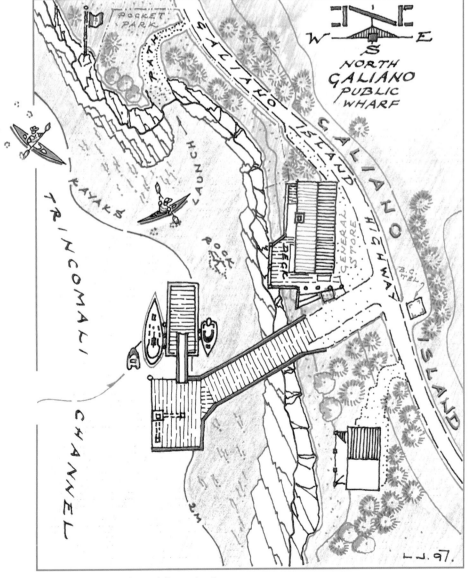

North Galiano public wharf.

Not to scale. Not to be used for navigation.

10.9   DIONISIO POINT MARINE PARK, GALIANO ISLAND

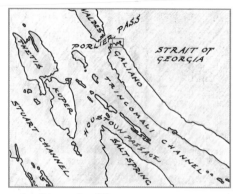

49°01'N   123°34'W

Rocky Dionisio Point and "First Beach" at low water.

When the forecast calls for sunny skies and light to moderate southeasterlies, Dionisio Point Marine Park is the perfect picnic stop. You can also anchor overnight off one of the 3 beaches, although the swell that curves around Dionisio Point makes "First Beach" an uncomfortable anchorage. Better protection can be found off "Second" or "Third Beach." ("First," "Second" and "Third" are names given to the beaches by us.)

Dionisio Point has a wonderfully classic sandy beach ("First Beach"), backed by a grassy isthmus. Honeycombed flat rocks and sandstone sculptured into alien-like shapes flank the points on either side. Swimming is great at HW off the rocks below the lookout point and also in the warm waters of Coon Bay, when the tide begins to cover the sun-baked sand. Coon Bay at HW offers easy kayak and canoe access to the shoreline campsites. Walking trails go out to both the lookout point and Dionisio Point, and they also follow the shoreline W.

Camping boundaries in the park are strictly enforced to preserve the sensitive ecosystem. If a tent is pitched out of bounds, the park ranger will request its immediate removal. There are numerous walk-in/paddle-in campsites, and a freshwater pump and information shelter are located S of the isthmus.

During the summer months this is a popular family destination for both locals and off-islanders. It also serves as a convenient stop for boaters waiting for the tide to turn in Porlier Pass.

Note: At present (1997) land access to the park is prohibited and water access is the only available alternative.

Porlier Pass from the Strait of Georgia.

CHARTS

3473. 3313, page 16. SCN Map C4.

APPROACH

With extreme caution from the Strait of Georgia. Dionisio Point and adjacent sand isthmus are the most conspicuous landmarks.

ANCHOR

Three bays, all temporary and exposed to the NW. If anchoring overnight, the spots off "Second" and "Third Beach,"

as we call them, are more sheltered from the swell curling around Dionisio Point.

DEPTHS

2 - 5 m (6.5 - 16 ft). Holding good in sand and gravel.

Note: Beware of the rock to the NW of the lookout point.

At anchor below the lookout point.

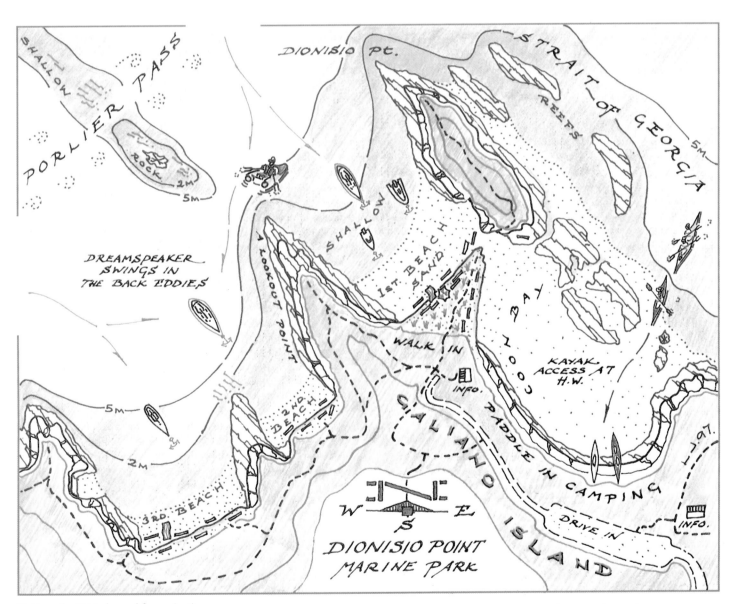

Not to scale. Not to be used for navigation.

Chapter 11
SANSUM NARROWS

TIDES
Reference Port: Fulford Harbour

Secondary Ports: Cowichan Bay, Maple Bay & Crofton

CURRENTS
Reference Station: Active Pass

Secondary Station: Sansum Narrows

WEATHER
No specific reference or reporting stations. However, if strong winds are forecast in the Strait of Georgia or Haro Strait, both direction and strength of wind in the narrows tend to follow suit.

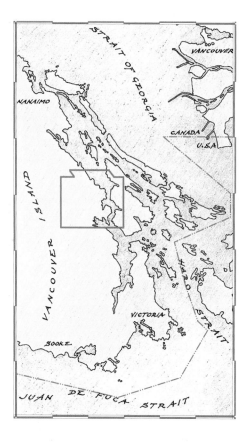

The public wharf at Musgrave Landing 11.3

A very pleasant and popular cruising ground has been established over the years between Cowichan and Vesuvius Bays, attracting fishermen, pleasure boaters and kayakers who use Maple Bay as their favoured rendezvous centre.

The southeastern shores of Vancouver Island and the western shoreline of Saltspring Island parallel each other in a serpentine fashion between Separation and Maxwell Points, forming the imposing Sansum Narrows. This sinuous channel of water experiences its own unique wind patterns and strong tidal currents that make navigation a little more difficult but provide excellent fishing opportunities, if you feel so inclined.

On the Vancouver Island shore, the charming waterside village of Cowichan Bay extends a friendly welcome to visiting boaters. At first the bay resembles an unfathomable maze, but after careful reconnaissance all will become clear. Don't miss the irresistible charm of Genoa Bay and The Grape-vine Café, with its hearty West Coast/French cuisine.

Musgrave Landing, once home to the celebrated Brigadier Miles and Beryl Smeeton, lies in a sheltered cove on the western shores of Saltspring Island. Protected from southerlies, this pocket cove is a pleasant spot for either a day stop or an overnight stay.

Back on the shores of Vancouver Island, the halfway rendezvous stop at Maple Bay presents a choice of two marinas, a public wharf, a virtually all-weather anchorage and a good selection of sociable pubs and restaurants.

From Maple Bay, a trip east takes you to the peaceful western shores of Saltspring Island, where you can enjoy the delights of Maxwell Creek, Booth Bay and Vesuvius Village. Here you will still find clean sandy beaches, a tidal inlet with an abundance of wildlife, heavenly loaves of freshly baked bread and a languid sunset or two.

By travelling further north you can provision and relax in neat and quiet Crofton. Try to be in town to celebrate the annual salmon barbecue and summer fair, which takes place on the second weekend in July.

CAUTIONARY NOTES

Winds tend to funnel along the axis of the narrows and are inclined to be directionally erratic.

Whirlpools and tidal rips occur around Burial Islet and between Sansum and Bold Bluff Points. In a wind-over-tide situation these can be hazardous to small craft.

FEATURED DESTINATIONS

11.1 Cowichan Bay & Village 140

11.2 Genoa Bay & Marina 142

11.3 Musgrave Landing, Saltspring Island 143

11.4 Maple Bay Public Wharf & Village 144

11.5 Birds Eye Cove, Maple Bay 145

11.6 Osborn Bay & Crofton Town 146

11.7 Maxwell Creek & Arbutus Beach, Saltspring Island ... 148

11.8 Booth Bay & Inlet, Saltspring Island 149

11.9 Vesuvius Bay & Village, Saltspring Island ... 150

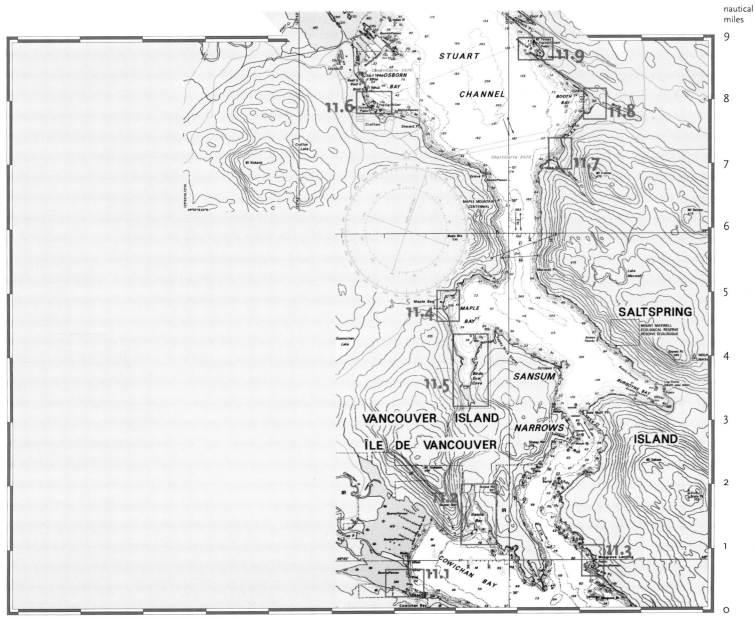

Reproduced portion of CHS Chart 3313, page 14, for passage planning only. Not to be used for navigation.

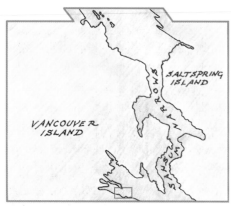

48°44'N 123°37'W

Approach to public wharf should be made close to the breakwater.

Dreamspeaker at anchor off the maritime centre. Mount Tzuhalem in the background.

Known locally as "Cow Bay," the friendly waterside village of Cowichan Bay is a charming maze of floats, houseboats and stilt houses. Reminscent of a Victorian seaport, the village hugs the water's edge and provides plenty to see and do, making it well worth a visit. You can either anchor, tie up at the public wharf or reserve a mooring at one of the many marinas. The MASTHEAD MARINA and THE INN AT THE WATER offer complimentary overnight mooring at their visitors' floats for boaters dining at either of their restaurants. The BLUENOSE MARINA provides 4 mooring buoys for visitors if the marina is full, or you can book marina space with the office in advance of your arrival. There is also a designated dinghy dock at the head of the marina, giving visitors easy access to the BLUENOSE BISTRO/CAFÉ with its outdoor patio and colourful umbrellas. A large percentage of the community lives and works within this floating village, which provides a fascinating walking tour.

THE COWICHAN BAY MARITIME CENTRE houses the MARITIME MUSEUM and a boat-building school. This unique centre is fascinating to explore with its mix of boat-building exhibits and maritime paraphernalia. At the MARINE ECOLOGY STATION (250-748-4522) you can explore tidal pools without going to the beach. Their exhibit includes 12 aquariums, a touch pool and a display of several miniature habitats under microscopes. Pop into THE RED DOOR STUDIO to watch textile and jewellry artists at work.

There is no shortage of good fish-and-chip shops in town, and the COWICHAN BAY FISH MARKET sells fish fresh off the boat at affordable prices. Live crab and seafood are also available. COW BAY CAFÉ serves home-style cooking for hearty appetites and is excellent value. The historic white-and-green MASTHEAD RESTAURANT was a store in pioneering days. Their specialty is seafood, and the large patio overlooking the water is the perfect venue for a romantic sunset dinner.

Basic provisions and ice can be purchased at BELLE'S MARKET BY THE BAY, and the beer-and-wine store at THE INN AT THE WATER has an excellent selection of local Cowichan Valley wine. Authentic Cowichan sweaters are available from the NATIVE HERITAGE CENTRE in Duncan, which is well worth a visit. (For information on vineyards and wine tours, see Chapter 6, Mill Bay, page 68.)

CHARTS

3478. 3313, page 14. SCN Map B3.

APPROACH

From the NE. The most conspicuous landmark is the modern INN AT THE WATER, located behind the timber breakwater that protects the public wharf.

ANCHOR

Temporary anchorage off and parallel to the complex of marinas. Reasonable shelter from prevailing summer winds.

DEPTHS

4 - 6 m (13 - 19.5 ft). Holding good in mud.

PUBLIC WHARF

E – extensive behind the breakwater. W – commercial fishing boats only.

MARINAS

From E to W: THE INN AT THE WATER (250-748-6222). MASTHEAD MARINA (250-748-5368). ANCHOR MARINA (250-748-8801). PIER 66 MARINA (250-748-8444). BLUENOSE MARINA (250-748-2222). Boat repairs: COWICHAN SHIPYARD (250-748-7285) and COASTAL SHIPYARD (250-746-4705).

BOAT LAUNCH

Public at Hecate Park.

FUEL

At PIER 66 MARINA.

Note: THE COWICHAN BAY MARITIME CENTRE (250-746-4955) has a day float, and the BLUENOSE MARINA has 4 mooring buoys for visitors.

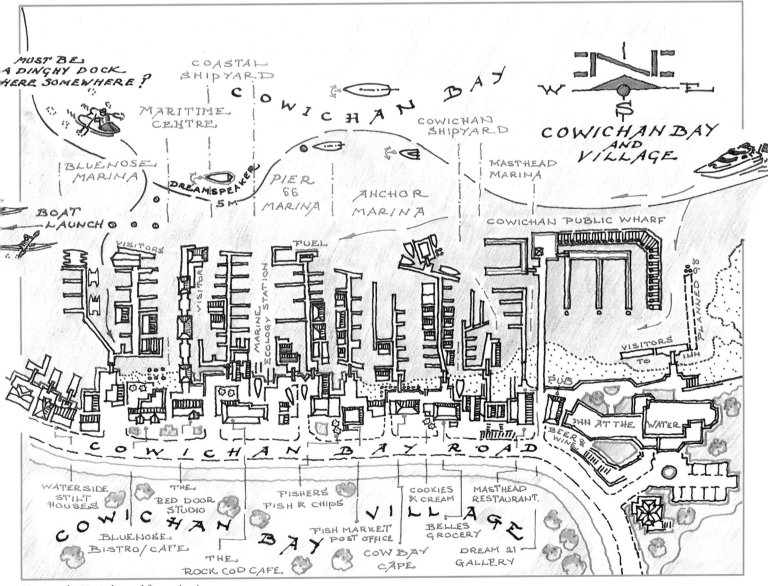

Not to scale. Not to be used for navigation.

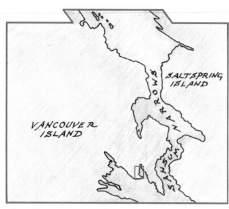

48°46'N 123°36'W

CHARTS

3478. 3313, page 14. SCN Map B3.

APPROACH

From the S and enter the bay between the starboard-hand day mark and the port-hand buoy.

ANCHOR

Good temporary anchorage for numerous boats. Exposed to the S.

DEPTHS

6 - 10 m (19.5 - 33 ft). Holding good in black, dense mud.

MARINA

GENOA BAY MARINA (250-746-7621) welcomes transient visitors and provides designated moorage.

Note: Wind from the SE out of Satellite Channel and from the W out of Cowichan Bay will bend and funnel N through the bay.

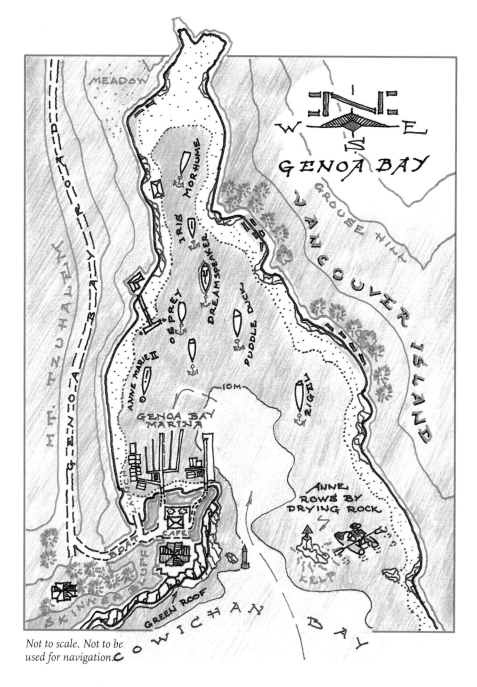

Not to scale. Not to be used for navigation.

Mount Tzuhalem rises steeply to the W of Genoa Bay, a charming, sheltered spot favoured by cruising boaters, kayakers and fishermen. THE GRAPEVINE CAFÉ at GENOA BAY MARINA is a popular rendezvous spot, with its hearty West Coast/French cuisine and homey atmosphere. (Reservations required in the summer months, 250-746-0797). The chef is well known for his adventurous spirit and original ostrich burgers. The small marina store stocks basic groceries, local crafts, clothing and knickknacks. There is good exploring ashore, with scenic walks along Genoa Bay Road or more energetic hikes up Skinner Bluff to Mount Tzuhalem. A trail can be found between the private homes on Skinner Point. The route is steep, but the 1-hour hike is made worthwhile by the stunning views of the Gulf Islands.

Approach to Genoa Bay.

CHARTS

3478. 3313, page 14. SCN Map B3.

APPROACH

Musgrave Landing lies in a cove just to the N of Musgrave Point. Approach from the W, giving clearance to the log breakwater that extends out from the S shore.

PUBLIC WHARF

Has 46 m (150 ft) of float that extends out from the N shore, used almost exclusively by visiting boats.

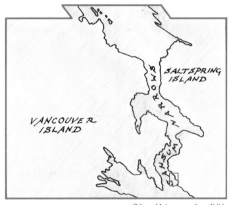

48°45'N 123°33'W

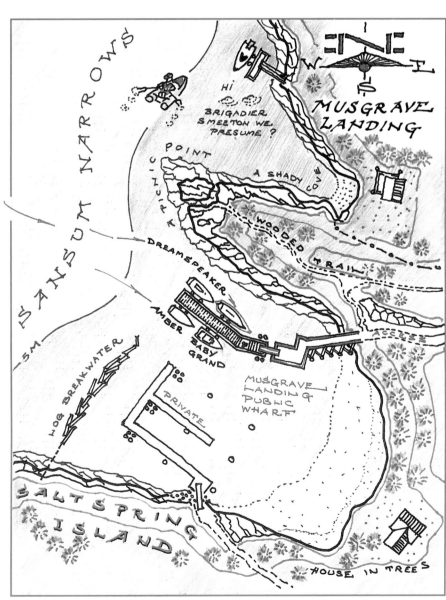

Tranquil Musgrave Landing is protected from southerlies in a pleasant little pocket cove on Saltspring Island.

A public wharf runs parallel to the N shore, accommodating 4 to 6 boats and providing access to roads and trails leading to Bruce Peak in MOUNT BRUCE PROVINCIAL PARK. En route you will pass MUSGRAVE FARM, the former home of Brigadier Miles and Beryl Smeeton, celebrated sailors, adventurers and pioneers. Miles Smeeton's books, including *Once Is Enough*, *A Change of Jungles* and *The Sea Was Our Village*, make fascinating reading, as does *High Endeavours*, written by both Miles and Beryl Smeeton.

Approach to Musgrave Landing.

Not to scale. Not to be used for navigation.

11.4 MAPLE BAY PUBLIC WHARF & VILLAGE

48°49'N 123°36'W

CHARTS

3478. 3313, page 14. SCN Map B3.

APPROACH

The public wharf and village lie in the NW corner of Maple Bay.

PUBLIC WHARF

Has a total of 76 m (250 ft) of alongside moorage, used in summer almost exclusively by visiting boats.

BOAT LAUNCH

Public off Beaumont Road.

Note: A rock with less than 2 m (6.5 ft) over it and a shoal patch with 2.1 m (7 ft) over it lie to the SE of the public wharf. Beware of strong crosscurrents. We ob-served boats at anchor off the public wharf.

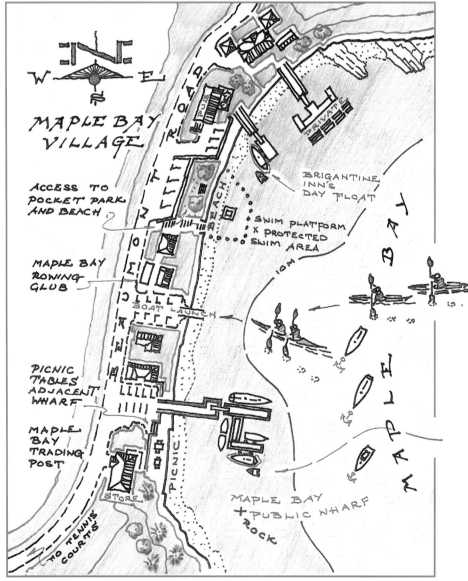

Not to scale. Not to be used for navigation.

The well-maintained MAPLE BAY PUBLIC WHARF can accommodate 4 to 6 larger boats and provides access to the small village. The anchorage is a little exposed but fine in stable summer conditions, and the public boat launch is a favourite with kayakers off to explore Sansum Narrows. The MAPLE BAY TRADING POST has a good selection of basic provisions, including ice. The beach N of the public wharf, a popular swimming and water-skiing spot, is backed by a shady green park, dotted with picnic tables. The relaxed BRIGANTINE INN PUB serves local draft beer and provides a float for guests. If you're game for tennis, public courts are available at the top of the hill on Beaumont Road.

Maple Bay public wharf.

CHARTS

3478. 3313, page 14. SCN Map B3.

APPROACH

Birds Eye Cove lies in the S portion of Maple Bay.

ANCHOR

In the centre of the cove. Good all-weather protection.

DEPTHS

6 - 12 m (19.5 - 39 ft). Holding good in mud.

MARINAS

BIRDS EYE COVE MARINA (250-748-4255) has some transient moorage. MAPLE BAY MARINA (250-746-8482) has propane and ample designated visitor moorage; monitors VHF channel 68. Boat repairs: COVE YACHTS LTD. (250-748-8136). Fuel available at both marinas.

Note: 4.3-knot speed limit in bay and cove. Reciprocal moorage, if available, at MAPLE BAY YACHT CLUB.

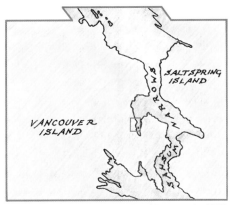

48°48'N   123°36'W

A ll-weather anchorage can be found in most parts of the cove, which is also home to the MAPLE BAY YACHT CLUB, BIRDS EYE COVE MARINA and the popular MAPLE BAY MARINA. The latter marina offers extensive transient moorage and is a favoured rendezvous spot for cruising boaters. The sociable pub and restaurant serve tasty West Coast food with a good selection of local wines and draft beer. An alternative is the notable QUAMICHAN INN, frequented for years by galley-weary boaters. They will transport you from Birds Eye Cove, Maple Bay or Genoa Bay to a beautifully converted Tudor-style home, which is now a restaurant with bed-and-breakfast facilities (call Clive or Pam at 250-746-7028).

The tidal lagoon S of Chisholm Island offers a peaceful setting for a quiet row or paddle.

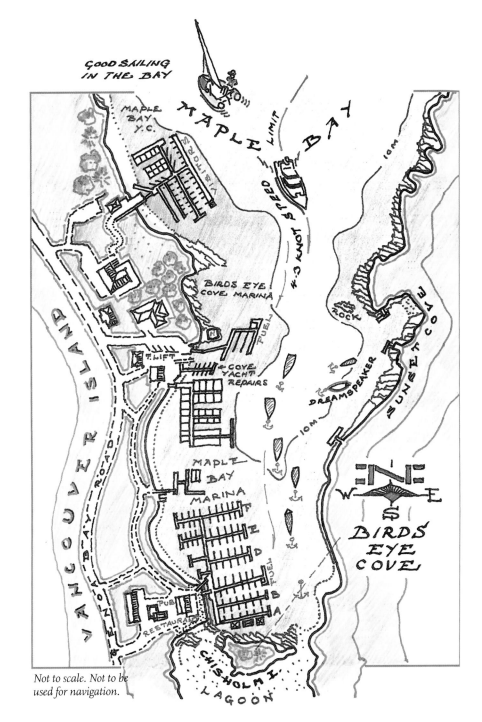

Not to scale. Not to be used for navigation.

Approach to Birds Eye Cove from Maple Bay.

48°52'N   123°38'W

Approach to Crofton's small craft basin and public wharf from Osborn Bay.

Crofton is a neat, quiet town with a great sense of community spirit. This was one of Canada's first "instant towns," created in 1902 to accommodate a copper smelter, and then, in 1957, a pulp and paper mill. The well-kept public wharf leads up to the OLD SCHOOL MUSEUM, which doubles as an information centre. The original one-room schoolhouse, built in 1905, was transported to this site from Edmund Street in 1971. Shower facilities are available below the centre (a key can be obtained from the B.C. Ferries ticket office at the foot of Chaplin Street). Handy laundry facilities can be found at the TWIN GABLES MOTEL.

A walk up Joan Avenue will satisfy most of your provisioning needs, as both the supermarket and bakery have a good choice of fresh products. The well-stocked hardware store also sells fishing licences. A visit to CAROL'S PLACE is a must for anyone in need of a really thick milk shake fix.

Crofton's annual salmon barbecue and summer fair takes place on the second weekend in July, and during July and August tours of the old pulp mill are offered to visitors, with special emphasis on new environmental improvements.

Surprisingly clean, warm-water swimming can be found in Osborn Bay, S of the gravel spit, where a lovely sand-and-gravel beach is backed by a community park. This is also an ideal spot for kayakers, as the OSBORN BAY RESORT offers campground facilities with waterfront sites and log cottages for rent year-round (1-800-567-7275). You can hike along the trails to Maple Mountain or take in a game of tennis at the COMMUNITY CENTRE, which also has an outdoor pool and a fully equipped playground.

The one-room schoolhouse, now a museum and information centre.

CHARTS

3475. 3313, page 14. SCN Map B3.

APPROACH

CROFTON PUBLIC WHARF from the E. The ferry terminal and the stone breakwater protecting the small craft basin are the most conspicuous landmarks. Enter the small craft basin close to the end of the breakwater.

PUBLIC WHARF

Extensive public floats lie within the basin, which was dredged to 2.1 m (7 ft) in 1976.

Note: Power is available on the floats, and water at the wharfhead.

Sailing north from Sansum Narrows.

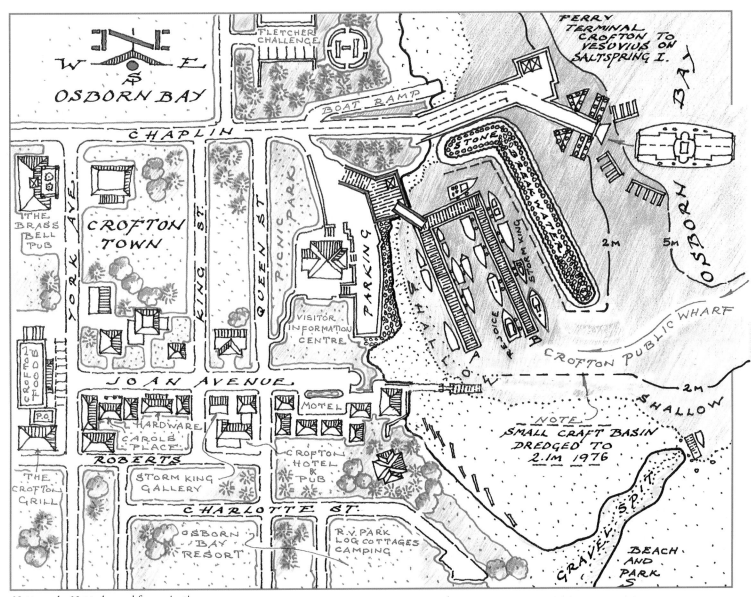

Not to scale. Not to be used for navigation.

11.7 MAXWELL CREEK & ARBUTUS BEACH, SALTSPRING ISLAND

48°51'N 123°34'W

CHARTS

3478. 3313, page 14. SCN Map B3.

APPROACH

"Arbutus Beach" (local name) lies in a bight just N of Erskine Point on Saltspring Island. Approach with caution, as depths decrease rapidly toward the beach.

ANCHOR

Off the delta formed by the sands deposited by Maxwell Creek. Temporary, exposed to the N and W.

DEPTHS

8 - 10 m (26 - 33 ft). Holding good over sand.

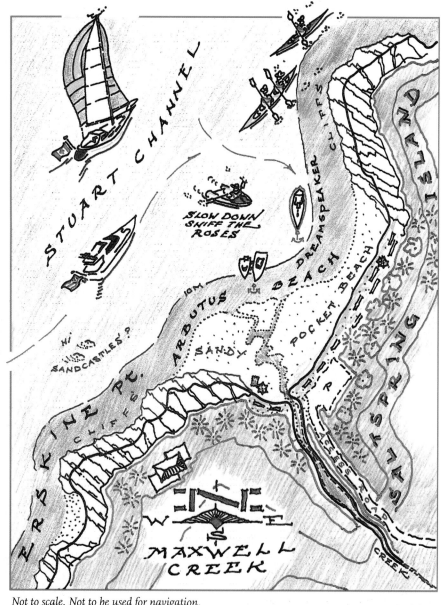

Not to scale. Not to be used for navigation.

"Arbutus Beach" (local name) has a generous expanse of tightly packed sand and gravel, from which excellent sand sculptures can be shaped. The beach lies at the delta of Maxwell Creek and makes a perfect picnic stop for kayakers and boaters en route to Vesuvius or Maple Bays. Its size and convenient road access also make it a popular spot with the locals. Note that the anchorage shallows quite quickly after the 10-m (33-ft) mark, due to the deposits of silt built up from the creek. It's easy to simply pass Erskine Point and continue northbound, but on a hot, sunny day, "Arbutus Beach" may be just the ticket for the family.

Approach to "Arbutus Beach."

CHARTS

3442. 3313, page 14. SCN Map B3.

APPROACH

Booth Bay lies in the SE reaches of Stuart Channel. Approach from the W. A house with a red oriental-style roof is the most conspicuous landmark.

ANCHOR

S of the fish farm. Temporary anchorage, open to the N and W.

DEPTHS

4 - 6 m (13 - 19.5 ft). Holding good over a sand-and-gravel bottom.

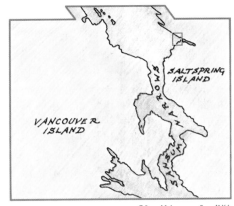

48°52'N 123°33'W

Clean water, a delightful sandy beach and a peaceful tidal inlet make Booth Bay a special place. When the tide is out you can walk the N shoreline or explore Booth Inlet in your wellie boots. At HW it's fun to row or paddle up the inlet to the bridge, where the waters are calm and the wildlife engrossing. For a cheap thrill, enter the inlet on a flooding tide and allow yourself to be swept along for a few hundred metres. This is a popular destination for kayakers paddling from Maple or Vesuvius Bays. In fair weather an overnight stay will have the added bonus of a fine sunset.

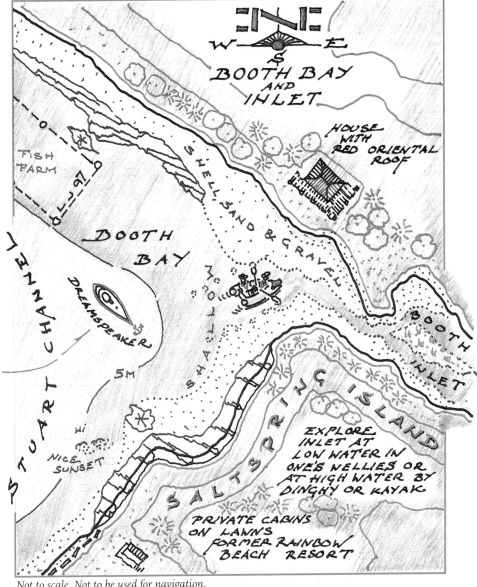

Not to scale. Not to be used for navigation.

Booth Bay and Inlet.

11.9   VESUVIUS BAY & VILLAGE, SALTSPRING ISLAND

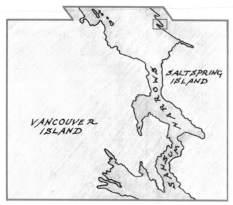

48°53'N 123°34'W

Approach to Vesuvius Bay.

If you are ever taken by a foolhardy urge to circumnavigate the globe, then at least be wise enough to begin and end your journey at Vesuvius. This relaxed and unassuming village produces heavenly loaves of freshly baked bread and is a fine spot to watch the sun go down.

The small public wharf is adjacent to the Crofton/Saltspring Island ferry terminal and just down from the delightful VESUVIUS INN NEIGHBOURHOOD PUB. Here you can sample a variety of local beers and scrumptious pub food with a West Coast twist. The pub's flower-filled balcony affords languid views across Stuart Channel to the mountains of Vancouver Island. A walk along Vesuvius Bay Road will take you to the cosy SEASIDE KITCHEN, which serves choice fresh seafood with a view. Hearty breakfasts are also available. The VESUVIUS VILLAGE STORE is jam-packed with goodies – if you need it, they usually stock it. Several varieties of mouthwatering bread are baked each morning, but you should arrive early to avoid disappointment. They also keep daily newspapers. The wooden tables outside give you an opportunity to relax with a freshly made coffee or refreshing gelati. Don't pass by without visiting THE ARK, a tiny studio and gift shop tucked behind a private carport on Vesuvius Bay Road.

The temporary anchorage in Vesuvius Bay is quiet and gives you easy access to the lovely pebble beach, which also boasts a convenient portable toilet. Stunning sunsets can be enjoyed from here or on the "Sunset Rocks" W of the rocky peninsula.

Vesuvius Village Store displays some of those heavenly loaves of freshly baked bread.

CHARTS

3442. 3313, page 14. SCN Map B3.

APPROACH

From the NW. The pub on the bluff overlooking the ferry terminal provides a conspicuous landmark.

ANCHOR

To the SW of the ferry terminal, N of and among boats on mooring buoys. Temporary, open to the NW.

DEPTHS

4 - 8 m (13 - 26 ft). Holding good in mud.

PUBLIC WHARF

To the N of the ferry terminal.

BOAT LAUNCH

Kayaks launch from the beach, reached via steps off Langley Road.

The Vesuvius Inn Neighbourhood Pub is a short walk from the public wharf.

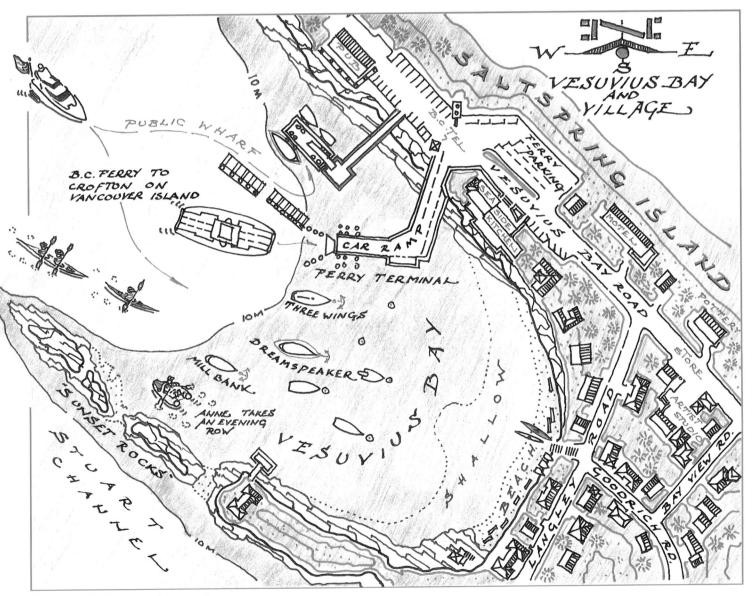

Not to scale. Not to be used for navigation.

Chapter 12
STUART CHANNEL

TIDES

Reference Port: Fulford Harbour

Secondary Ports: Chemainus Bay, Preedy Harbour, Ladysmith Harbour

CURRENTS

Tidal streams in this part of Stuart Channel are weak and not specifically referenced in the *Canadian Tide and Current Tables, Volume 5.*

WEATHER

Stuart Channel is not specifically covered by the marine forecast. However, weather conditions for the channel can be extrapolated from the forecast for the surrounding areas.

A fine sunset over Vancouver Island from Sibell Bay   12.6

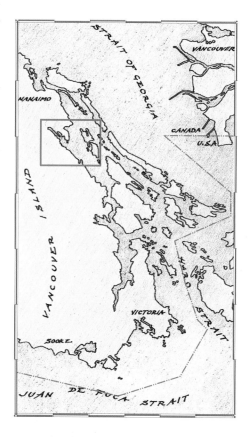

In sharp contrast to many of the waterways covered in previous chapters, peaceful Stuart Channel encompasses a stretch of protected coastline between Chemainus Bay and Ladysmith Harbour on Vancouver Island and is shielded by Thetis, Kuper and Tent Islands to the east. It is blessed with placid winds, minimal tidal currents, a sprinkling of protected anchorages and the occasional warm-water swimming spot. There are also two convenient provisioning stops and some very pleasant small beaches to choose from.

Stuart Channel is easily accessible from the south via Sansum Narrows or from the north via Porlier Pass, weaving your way between the charming islands of Reid, Hall, Norway and Mowgli.

Begin with the enterprising town of Chemainus on Vancouver Island, where choice in provisioning far outweighs that of moorage space. It is well worth taking a little extra time to explore the award-winning murals that grace the outsides of many of the town's buildings.

With its regular ferry service to Chemainus, Preedy Harbour on Thetis Island provides a sensible alternative to finding space at the public wharf in Chemainus Bay. It also offers alternative access to popular Telegraph Harbour, with its craft studios, shops, cafés and pubs. Telegraph Harbour has two reputable marinas with excellent services and amenities.

Petite Tent Island and its inviting sandy beach is a kayaker's haven and also provides the cruising boater with a scenic and comfortable anchorage in stable weather conditions.

The trip west takes you to the 49th Parallel and the sleepy harbour of Ladysmith. With its preserved turn-of-the-century architecture, you can go back in time while stocking up at the local butcher, baker and friendly bookstore.

Sibell Bay affords spectacular sunset vistas, while Evening Cove and Yellow Point provide intimate beaches for picnicking, warm-water swimming and quiet seclusion. When anchoring in North Cove take the opportunity to explore beautiful Cufra Inlet on Thetis Island by dinghy, kayak or canoe.

CAUTIONARY NOTES

Although generally an area of light-wind conditions, listen carefully for strong Qualicum westerly winds forecast for the Strait of Georgia. Strong winds occasionally blow down from the mountains of Vancouver Island and create sea conditions that are quite dangerous for small boats.

FEATURED DESTINATIONS

12.1 Chemainus Bay & Town 154

12.2 Tent Island 156

12.3 Preedy Harbour, Thetis Island 157

12.4 Telegraph Harbour, Thetis & Kuper Islands 158

12.5 Ladysmith Harbour & Town 160

12.6 Sibell Bay, Ladysmith Harbour 162

12.7 Evening Cove 163

12.8 North Cove, Thetis Island 164

12.9 Yellow Point 165

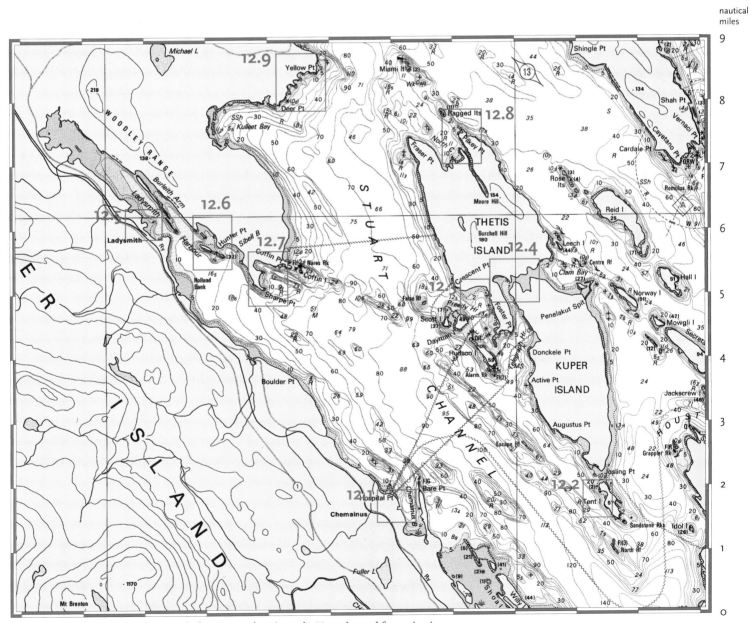

Reproduced portion of CHS Chart 3463 for passage planning only. Not to be used for navigation.

48°55'N   123°42'W

Approach to the ferry terminal and public wharf, Chemainus Bay.

Chemainus's well-preserved heritage charm.

As "The little town that did!" Chemainus is certainly a wonderful example of downtown revitalization and community spirit. For the boater, it is also a primary provisioning stop, with 2 well-stocked supermarkets, a bakery, liquor store, post office and banking centre all within walking distance. The public wharf is extensive, and well used by local boaters; the outer wharf is reserved for visiting boaters. The wharf is adjacent to the Thetis and Kuper Islands ferry terminal and has water if you can get your boat close enough to the hose at the bottom of the access ramps.

It is well worth taking a little extra time to explore this unique town, with its award-winning historical murals painted on the walls of local buildings. In 1982, to keep its heritage alive, Chemainus invited well-known artists to transform the small mill town into the world's largest outdoor gallery, where even the garbage cans are painted! You can pick up a mural map from the visitor information centre, or just follow the yellow footsteps painted along the town's sidewalks for a self-guided tour. There is no shortage of cappuccino bars, ice cream parlours, sidewalk cafés and tearooms in this town, and if you really feel like being a tourist, take a horse-and-buggy ride from the lower to the upper town and back again.

Rafting is the norm at the Chemainus public wharf.

CHARTS

3475. 3313, page 15. SCN Map C1.

APPROACH

From the NE. Enter Chemainus Bay between Bare and Hospital Points. Leave the red starboard-hand buoy to starboard.

PUBLIC WHARF

Lies on the W shore, S of the B.C. Ferries terminal. Moorage for visiting vessels is generally made available on the outside float, and rafting 2 - 3 deep is common.

BOAT LAUNCH

Public, situated at Hospital Point.

Note: Anchoring in the bay is not recommended due to extensive log booming and the activities of a busy harbour. Temporary anchorage is possible between the boat launch and Hospital Rock. Depths, holding and bottom condition unrecorded.

An old railcar is now the visitor information centre.

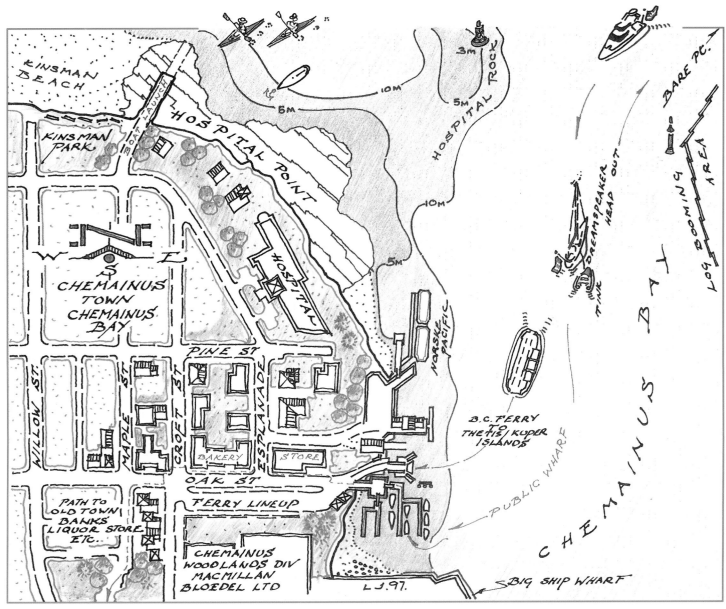

Not to scale. Not to be used for navigation.

12.2   TENT ISLAND

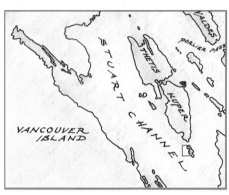

48°56'N   123°38'W

CHARTS

3442. 3313, page 15. SCN Map C1.

APPROACH

From the W. The W side of Tent Island has deep water extending close inshore and then shelves rapidly.

ANCHOR

Temporary anchorage can be found off the sandy crescent beach.

DEPTHS

4 - 6 m (13 - 19.5 ft). Holding good in sand and gravel.

Note: If approaching from the S after rounding Sandstone Rock, beware of an isolated rock off the SW tip of Tent Island.

This scenic island is popular with boaters, who can anchor off the sandy crescent beach in the spacious bay to the W of the island. It is also a favourite of kayakers and canoeists, who are able to camp overnight on the beach or in the arbutus forests above. Tent Island is joined to Kuper Island by a tombolo that is exposed at LW. It belongs to the Penelakut Band and permission to camp on the island should be obtained by contacting the band office (250-246-2321). Please note that no fires are permitted anywhere on the island. All garbage must be taken with you when leaving.

Because the anchorage is totally exposed to the W, overnighting is not recommended.

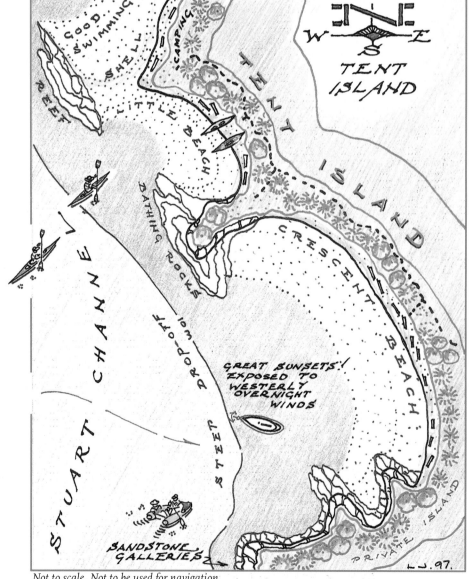

Not to scale. Not to be used for navigation.

Tent Island's crescent beach from the northwest.

PREEDY HARBOUR, THETIS ISLAND
12.3

CHARTS

3477. 3313, page 16. SCN Map C4.

APPROACH

Preedy Harbour has 3 entrance channels. The marked entrance channel between Dayman and Hudson Islands has a least depth of 4.3 m (14 ft), so stay in the centre of this channel.

ANCHOR

Good shelter can be found in the N of the harbour, clear of the Chemainus/Thetis Island ferry route.

DEPTHS

4 - 6 m (13 - 19.5 ft). Holding good in sand and shingle.

PUBLIC WHARF

Has minimal float length. Temporary and reserved for the loading and unloading of local craft. Dinghy tie-up is possible.

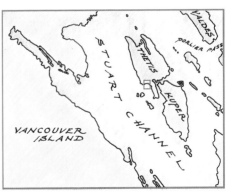

48°58'N 123°41'W

Thetis Island offers regular ferry service to Chemainus from Preedy Harbour, providing a sensible alternative to finding space at the public wharf in Chemainus Bay. Thetis Island is relatively undeveloped, making it popular with cyclists, and most shops and amenities are within walking distance of the ferry terminal or the marinas in Telegraph Harbour (see Telegraph Harbour, page 158, for more details). If you choose to anchor and take the dinghy to the public wharf in Preedy Harbour, then peaceful St. Margaret's Cemetery is well worth a visit. It is situated at the end of St. Margaret's Lane, but beach access is also available on the NW shore. For an intriguing self-guided tour of the cemetery, pick up "The Lives Behind the Headstones" from either of the marina stores.

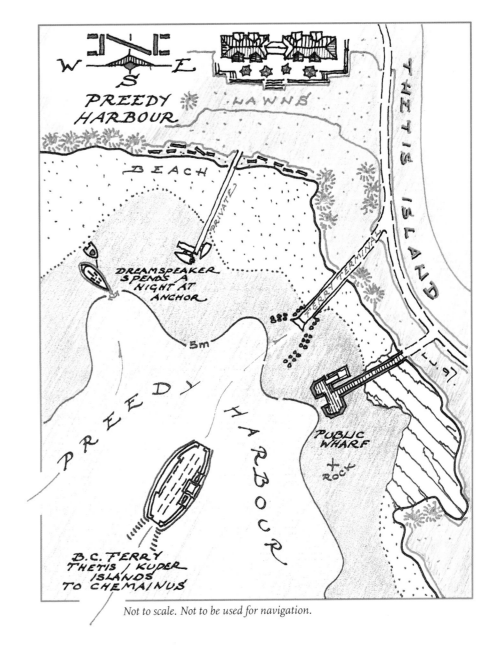

Approach to the anchorage in Preedy Harbour.

Not to scale. Not to be used for navigation.

12.4   TELEGRAPH HARBOUR,
THETIS & KUPER ISLANDS

48°58'N   123°40'W

Channel to Thetis Island Marina and Telegraph Harbour Marina.

Two well-run marinas and good anchorage make Telegraph Harbour a popular destination. Both marinas are worth visiting, as each offers its own specialties. It's fun to take a walking tour of the area, which is reputed for its craft studios, and you can begin at one marina and end at the other. If you start at THETIS ISLAND MARINA & PUB and continue along Harbour Road, you will come to THIS & THAT COTTAGE, which often has freshly baked goods and tasty homemade jams alongside their jewellry and hand-woven crafts. It is worth taking a quick detour up to the community centre on North Cove Road to find out about local events. THETIS ISLAND HANDCRAFTS on Pilkey Point Road carries a variety of local artists' work, including handcrafted "Pots by Nicé." Next, your nose will guide you to the POT OF GOLD COFFEE ROASTING COMPANY, where you can stop for a fresh coffee, purchase a variety of roasted beans or, if you are fortunate, sample their famous roasted peanuts with a distinctive coffee flavour. If you continue your walk to the end of Blue Heron Road, you will be welcomed by a herd of charming alpacas at THE SPINNING WHEEL STUDIO & RANCH. Here the owners produce naturally dyed alpaca and angora wool, which they sell along with their beautiful hand-knit sweaters. Summer hours are Wednesday through Sunday, 11:00 a.m. to 5:00 p.m. A refreshing, old-fashioned milk shake at TELEGRAPH HARBOUR MARINA will be a welcome reward on your return trip. The MARINA STORE & CAFÉ offers light breakfasts and meals on the patio, as well as basic groceries, ice cream, baked goods and local crafts.

THETIS ISLAND MARINA has a pub with a sunny patio and a restaurant that offers excellent food. They also have a post office and a well-stocked grocery store that sells crafts and books. Both marinas have picnic and barbecue facilities ashore.

Telegraph Harbour Marina looking toward The Cut to Clam Bay.

CHARTS

3477. 3313, page 16. SCN Map C4.

APPROACH

From the S and enter between Alarm Rock and Active Point. The sheltered channel that forms the harbour lies between Kuper Island and a peninsula extending S from Thetis Island.

ANCHOR

Good shelter can be found along the E shore of Thetis Island, to the N of THETIS ISLAND MARINA.

DEPTHS

2 - 3 m (6.5 - 10 ft). Holding good in mud.

MARINAS

THETIS ISLAND MARINA (250-246-2464). TELEGRAPH HARBOUR MARINA (250-246-9511). Both marinas have extensive visitor moorage and monitor VHF channel 68.

FUEL

At marinas.

Note: The Kuper Island shoreline is the preferred channel of both small craft and floatplanes intending to dock at Telegraph Harbour Marina. Stay clear.

For more details on the boat passage between Thetis and Kuper Islands, see Chapter 10, Clam Bay, page 133.

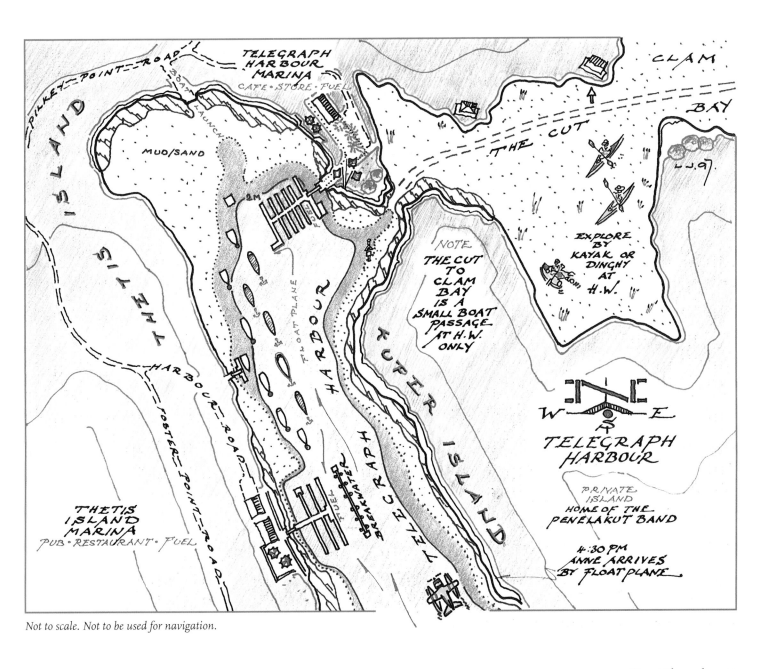

Not to scale. Not to be used for navigation.

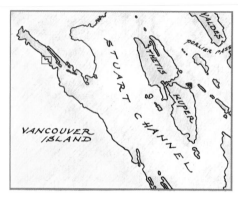

49°00'N 123°48'W

Approach to the Ladysmith Harbour public wharf.

This historic little town, sitting on the 49th Parallel, provides a fun provisioning stop before heading N into Gabriola Passage or S to Stuart Channel. Tie up at the sleepy public wharf and take an energetic walk into town. The timber-stepped trail at the end of the public wharf road crosses the railway line and ends abruptly at Highway 1. If you plan to have an extensive shopping spree, a taxi back to the dock is highly recommended.

Ladysmith's turn-of-the-century architecture has been largely preserved, and a walk along Main Street and down various side streets will take you back in time. You will be rewarded with a local butcher shop, bakery and well-stocked hardware store, as well as a friendly bookstore that sells quality new and used books – the perfect place to top up your boat's library without breaking the bank. The 49TH PARALLEL SUPERMARKET is extremely well stocked and includes a deli and bakery. A B.C. LIQUOR STORE is conveniently situated next door. For a warm saltwater swim, turn left on the trail that takes you into town and walk along it until you reach TRANSFER PARK & BEACH.

If you are short on fuel and need to top up, the MAÑANA LODGE (250-245-2312), just NW of the public wharf, has a fuel float and small marina. If you're also thirsty and need a snack, the lodge serves appetizers and alcohol on their sundeck during the summer months.

The tranquil anchorage of Sibell Bay lies a short distance to the southeast.

CHARTS

3475. 3313, page 15. SCN Map C1.

APPROACH

Between Slag Point and the southernmost tip of Woods Islands. The public wharf lies N of a stone breakwater. Approach the wharf from the NE after rounding the port-hand day beacon.

PUBLIC WHARF

Has extensive floats arranged as 3 fingers. Visitors usually find moorage on the southernmost float.

BOAT LAUNCH

Public, adjacent to the public wharf.

FUEL

At Mañana Lodge & Marina, NW of the public wharf.

Note: The associated anchorage lies to the SE in Sibell Bay (see page 162 for details).

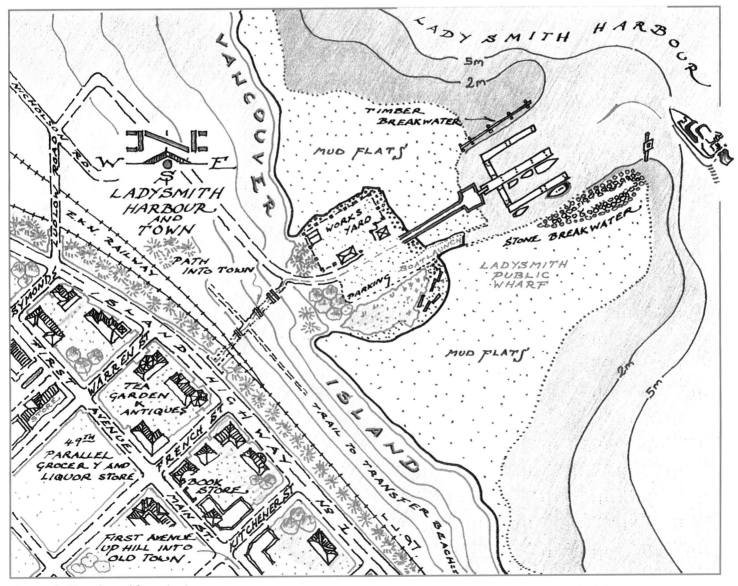

Not to scale. Not to be used for navigation.

12.6 SIBELL BAY, LADYSMITH HARBOUR

48°59'N 123°47'W

CHARTS

3475. 3313, page 15. SCN Map C1.

APPROACH

From the W and enter the anchorage between Bute Island and N Dunsmuir Island.

ANCHOR

Good sheltered anchorage lies between Bute Island and N Dunsmuir Island.

DEPTHS

2 - 6 m (6.5 - 19.5 ft). Holding good in sand and mud.

Note: The anchorage within the main portion of Sibell Bay and to the SE of the Dunsmuir Islands is exposed to wind and swell from the S.

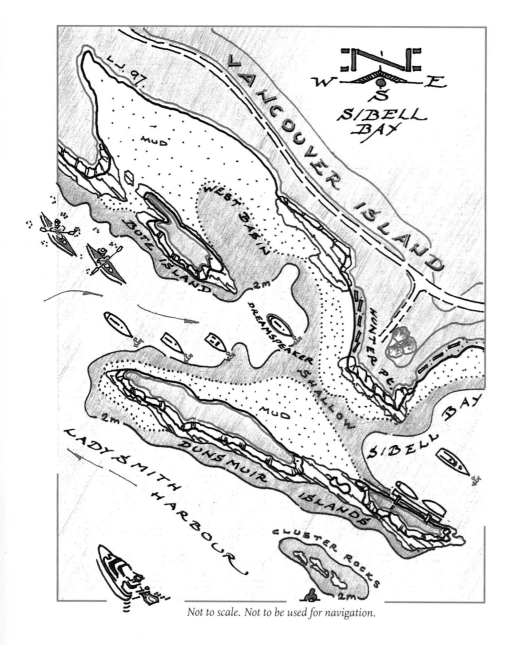

Not to scale. Not to be used for navigation.

Seattle Yacht Club has an outstation on S Dunsmuir Island. The Dunsmuir Islands protect Sibell Bay and the west basin, making this one of the safest anchorages in the immediate Ladysmith area. Conveniently situated just S of Ladysmith Harbour, Sibell Bay affords spectacular sunset vistas over the mountains of Vancouver Island and is extremely popular in the summer months. Note that the Sibell Bay foreshore and Hunter Point are Indian reserves.

The anchorage to the north of the Dunsmuir Islands.

CHARTS

3475. 3313, page 15. SCN Map C1.

APPROACH

From the SE. Evening Cove lies between Coffin and Sharpe Points.

ANCHOR

Temporary anchorage can be found in various locations in the cove, but all are exposed to the SE. The best shelter is found in the NW of the cove.

DEPTHS

4 - 6 m (13 - 19.5 ft). Holding good in sand and gravel.

Note: Pay attention to the depths and position of Collins Shoal.

48°59'N 123°46'W

This is a good picnic stop or temporary anchorage when the wind is not from the S or SE. You can tuck into the northern bay behind Coffin Point, taking care on approach to avoid Nares Rock to the E of the point and Collins Shoal in the centre of the cove. The tiny crescent beach has public access and is great for swimming and picnicking. The western bay provides a good overnight anchorage in favourable weather conditions, as you can anchor close in. The southern bay is fronted by private homes, making the beach feel a little out-of-bounds.

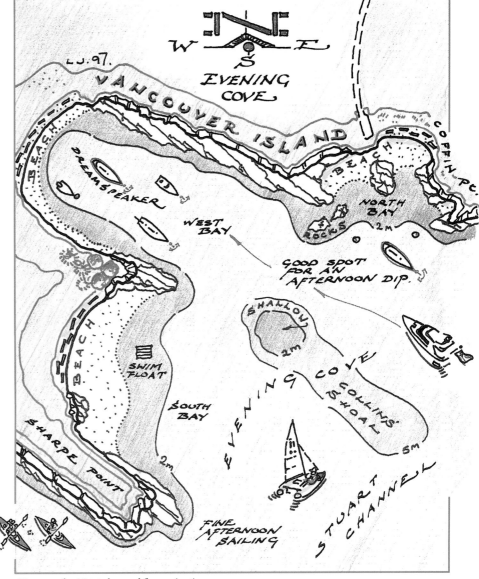

Not to scale. Not to be used for navigation.

Evening Cove, pleasant and peaceful but exposed to the southeast.

49°01'N   123°42'W

CHARTS

3443. 3313, page 15. SCN Map C1.

APPROACH

From Trincomali Channel, between Pilkey Point and the Ragged Islets. Or by rounding Fraser Point from Stuart Channel.

ANCHOR

There are a variety of spots to anchor, but all are exposed to winds from the N and NW.

DEPTHS

4 - 8 m (13 - 26 ft). Holding good in sand.

Note: Cufra Inlet dries completely at LW.

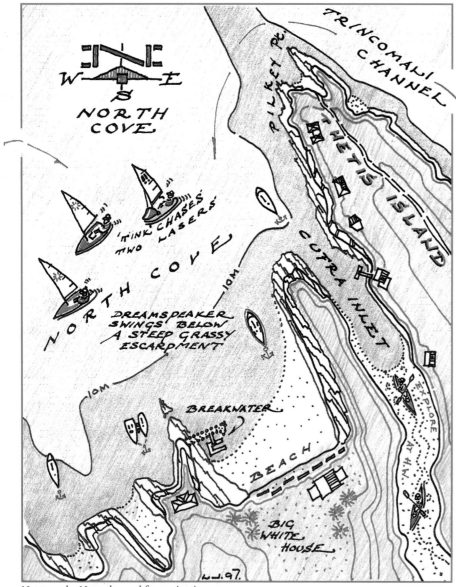

Not to scale. Not to be used for navigation.

If a southeasterly is blowing and you need a well-protected anchorage, then North Cove, Thetis Island, is a good destination. Note that it is completely exposed to the NW. An orderly camp/resort with manicured lawns and private homes lines the shore at the head of the cove. Cufra Inlet, E of the cove, extends for a narrow and beautiful mile into the Thetis Island interior. This inlet can be safely explored by dinghy, kayak or canoe at HW, but tides and distance to be covered should be carefully calculated, or you could find yourself high and dry on the mud. It is not recommended to overnight here if a northwesterly is forecast, or you may find your boat high and dry on the beach.

North Cove looking southeast.

CHARTS

3443. 3313, page 18. SCN Map C3.

APPROACH

From the SE. YELLOW POINT LODGE, perched above a rocky bluff, is a conspicuous landmark.

ANCHOR

Temporary anchorage can be found in one of the tiny coves to the S of Yellow Point.

DEPTHS

2 - 4 m (6.5 - 13 ft). Holding good in mud and sand.

Note: Day picnic stop. Exposed to the S and SE as well as to the swell from Stuart Channel.

49°02'N 123°45'W

You can't miss the gabled YELLOW POINT LODGE perched majestically on the mighty boulders of Yellow Point. There are 3 small but picturesque coves with shell beaches to choose from S of Yellow Point, making this an ideal picnic stop. Only the lunchtime gong at the lodge and the cry of the gulls above could be heard when we anchored in the secluded third cove for a leisurely brunch. The lodge, well known for its cosy accommodation and hearty meals, offers the use of its private dock to boaters taking a room for the night. YELLOW POINT LODGE offers adults-only accommodation; guests must be 16 years or older. It is extremely popular in the summer months, and booking well in advance is advised (250-245-7422).

Yellow Point looking southwest.

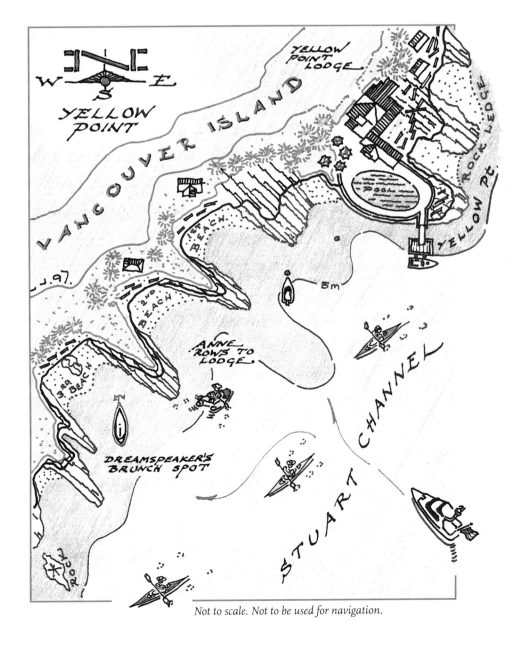

Not to scale. Not to be used for navigation.

*Two young buccaneers make a raft in "Wally's Bay,"
Pirates Cove Marine Park.*

*Dreamspeaker at anchor in Booth Bay. The oriental-
style house and inlet are in the background.*

*Sunset over Cowichan Bay.
The First Nations people called
this place the "warm land."*

Chapter 13
GABRIOLA PASSAGE

Looking west over Rogers Reef to Gabriola Passage.

"Wally's Bay," Pirates Cove Marine Park   13.1

Chapter 13
GABRIOLA PASSAGE

TIDES
Reference Port: Fulford Harbour
Secondary Port: Degnen Bay
Reference Port: Point Atkinson
Secondary Ports: Silva Bay, Valdes Island

CURRENTS
Reference Stations: Gabriola Passage,
Dodd Narrows
Secondary Station: False Narrows

WEATHER
Area: Strait of Georgia (South)
Reporting Stations: Entrance Island,
Thrasher Rock

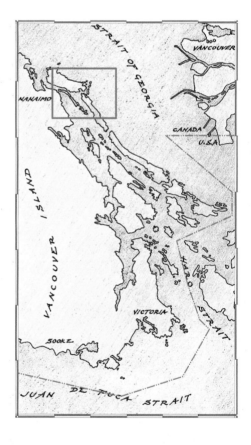

CAUTIONARY NOTES

Tides and timing of currents need careful consideration when transiting Gabriola Passage. (For Cautionary Notes on Dodd Narrows and False Narrows, see Chapter 14, page 178.)

Navigational hazards to be aware of: Danger Reefs, situated N of Thetis Island, and other reefs at the entrances to Pirates Cove and Silva Bay.

Cruising boaters seeking the shortest route from Vancouver to the Gulf Islands regard Gabriola Passage as the gateway to their destinations. It is also the smallest and most popular of the four major passes. Tidal currents run up to eight knots and the pass narrows considerably between Josef and Cordero Points. The safest time to enter is at slack water, but this is not always possible, as the currents change direction so rapidly. If you have to enter the pass with the current, be sure to leave adequate room between vessels, as the eddies and whirlpools can often swing boats around like toys in a bathtub. The pass is also favoured by tugboats, and it is not uncommon to find boat traffic backed up at either end while waiting for a long and very slow log boom to move through.

If cruising from Vancouver, the waters covered in this chapter give boating visitors a wonderful introduction to the traditional Gulf Islands. The beauty of these islands is that they are protected from foul weather in the Strait of Georgia by Gabriola and Valdes Islands, and many of the coves and bays offer well-sheltered anchorages. Although the Gulf Islands are very popular in the summer months, surprisingly enough, quiet and solitude can still be found.

Pirates Cove Marine Park on De Courcy Island is one of the most visited anchorages, but be aware of its very tricky entrance that has surprised even the most experienced of boaters. An enchanting bay and shell beach on its south side provide simple campsites and languid sunsets. Herring Bay on Ruxton Island invites you to anchor while waiting for the delightful "Disappearing Beach" to reappear. Whaleboat Island Marine Park is small and unassuming, often providing a quiet, undisturbed picnic stop.

Cosy and well-protected anchorage is available in Degnen Bay on Gabriola Island, where easy access to many mystical petroglyphs is possible. Don't race by the small anchorage off Drumbeg Provincial Park, as it is a lovely picnic stop with wooded trails, rocky ledges and a clean, inviting beach. Kendrick Island, opposite the park, is perfectly situated to provide convenient anchorage if you are waiting for the tide to turn in Gabriola Passage.

Finally, popular Silva Bay, a favourite rendezvous spot for boaters, offers a choice of marinas. Anchorage space fills up fast toward evening but empties in the morning or as soon as the tide is right to enter Gabriola Passage.

FEATURED DESTINATIONS

13.1 Pirates Cove Marine Park, De Courcy Island   170

13.2 Whaleboat Island Marine Park   172

13.3 Herring Bay, Ruxton Island   173

13.4 Degnen Bay, Gabriola Island   174

13.5 Drumbeg Provincial Park & Kendrick Island, Gabriola Passage   175

13.6 Silva Bay, Gabriola Island   176

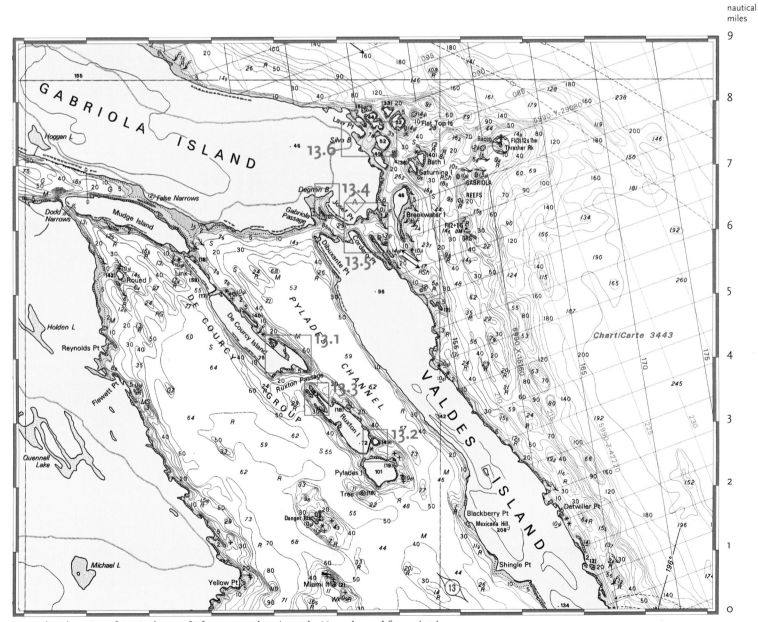

Reproduced portion of CHS Chart 3463 for passage planning only. Not to be used for navigation.

13.1 PIRATES COVE MARINE PARK, DE COURCY ISLAND

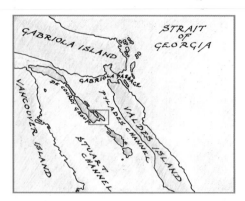

49°05'N 123°43'W

Entrance to Pirates Cove. The reef extends northwest from the day mark.

A picturesque and comfortable anchorage on De Courcy Island awaits the cruising boater once the extensive reef and tricky entrance to the cove have been safely navigated. Pirates Cove is protected from all but northerly winds and is conveniently located at the N end of the Gulf Islands, making it easily accessible from Vancouver, Victoria or Nanaimo.

Because of its location and charm, Pirates Cove Marine Park is extremely popular in the summer months, with up to 70 boats snugly anchored in the cove. Regulars to the cove are well aware of the shallow central depths and poor holding and usually attach a stern line to shore, making use of the many metal hooks provided.

The lovely wooded trails, walk-in campsites and pit toilets can be accessed via the 2 dinghy docks located on either side of the cove. The unique 12-sided design of the docks successfully discourages use by larger boats.

Cove Trail provides the shortest route to the S side of the park, where an enchanting bay and shell beach provide warm-water swimming and washed-up logs to lie back on (named "Wally's Bay" by us). This side of the marine park is popular with kayakers and campers, who can pitch their tents under the arbutus trees, pump fresh water from the well and picnic on the many tables provided. Boaters wishing to get away from the crowds in Pirates Cove or the winds in Herring Bay often slip into unassuming "Wally's Bay," which is protected from all but southerly winds and is well positioned for languid sunsets.

Looking north to "Wally's Bay," Pirates Cove Marine Park.

CHARTS

3475. 3313, page 18. SCN Map C3.

APPROACH

Pirates Cove entrance bar at a suitable tidal depth according to your draft. The bar has a least depth of 0.6 m (2 ft) on a zero tide. Align the leading marks prior to turning to port and enter between the port-hand day mark and starboard-hand buoy.

ANCHOR

Locals advise to attach a stern line to one of the numerous mooring rings that line the rocks around the cove, as anchors have been known to drag in the centre.

DEPTHS

2 - 3 m (6.5 - 10 ft). Holding in centre poor in soft mud.

Note: Don't try to cut the corner at the entrance. The reef extends considerably NW from the position of the day beacon. Alternative anchorage is available in "Wally's Bay" (as named by us), to the S of the park off Ruxton Passage. Exposed to the S.

Dreamspeaker snug in the cove with a stern line ashore.

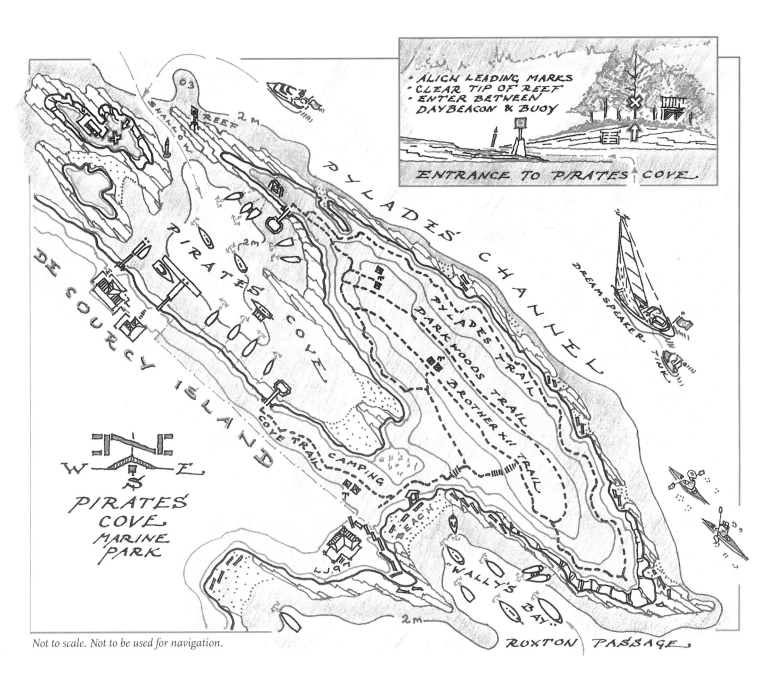

Not to scale. Not to be used for navigation.

13.2   WHALEBOAT ISLAND MARINE PARK

49°04'N 123°42'W

CHARTS

3443. 3313, page 18. SCN Map C3.

APPROACH

From the E via Pylades Channel or from the W via Whaleboat Passage.

ANCHOR

To the SE of Whaleboat Island. Temporary anchorage, open to the SE.

DEPTHS

4 - 6 m (13 - 19.5 ft). Holding good in mud.

Note: Beware of a rock to the SW of Whaleboat Island that dries, but once covered, is hard to spot.

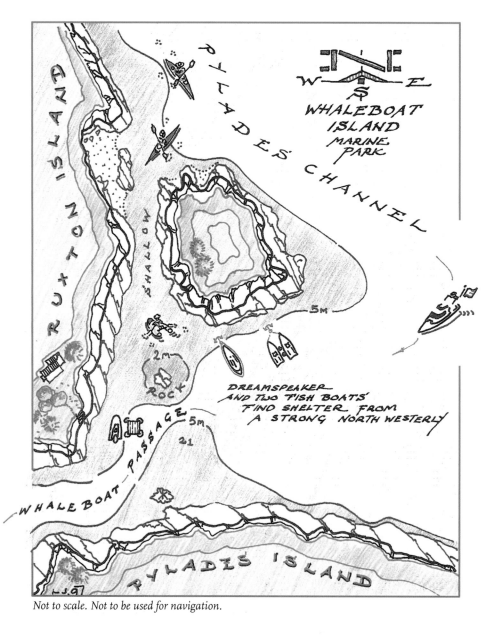

Not to scale. Not to be used for navigation.

Secluded and often undisturbed temporary anchorage can be found E of the drying rock between Ruxton and Whaleboat Islands. Established as a marine park in 1981 and to date undeveloped, Whaleboat Island provides a natural habitat for wildlife and modest shelter for visiting kayakers. The island is easier to access from its northern shores via 2 small rocky bights. From here the view over to Valdes Island is wonderfully uninterrupted.

Looking northwest to the pass between Whaleboat and Ruxton Islands. Note rock in foreground.

CHARTS

3475. 3313, page 18. SCN Map C3.

APPROACH

From Ruxton Passage and enter the channel between the starboard-hand day beacon and the sandstone islets (named "Jim's Islets" by us). Run straight and parallel to the islets prior to entering the bay. Alternatively, approach from Stuart Channel at LW, when the extent of the reef and rocky ledge extending N from Ruxton Island are visible.

ANCHOR

Temporary anchorage, exposed to the NW.

DEPTHS

4 - 6 m (13 - 19.5 ft). Holding good in sand and mud.

Note: Locals warn of an isolated rock that lies to the S of the reef.

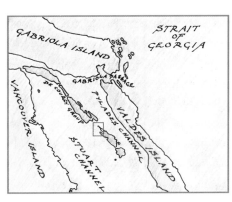

49°05'N 123°43'W

This charming and quite generous bay is somewhat protected to the W by the drying reef but is open to northerly winds. It supports a large variety of wildlife and migrating birds, and "Jim's Islets" (as we've named them) are home to otters and bald eagles. You can spend hours exploring the wonderfully sculpted sandstone ledges or, at low tide, digging for clams on the shell beach between the islets. In the springtime wildflowers abound.

When the tide is down, "Disappearing Beach" (also named by us) to the W of the bay appears, providing a magical, white-shell paradise for just a few short hours. When the tide begins to rise and all is quiet, seals can be found balancing in comical positions on the exposed portions of the reef.

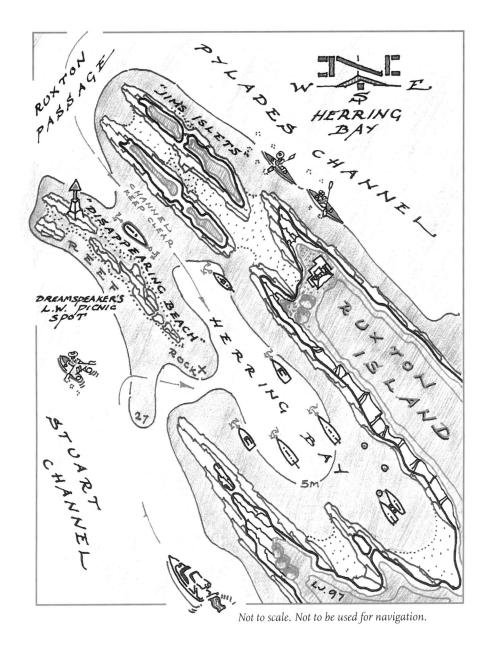

Not to scale. Not to be used for navigation.

The reef at high water disappears completely, leaving just the day mark.

13.4 DEGNEN BAY, GABRIOLA ISLAND

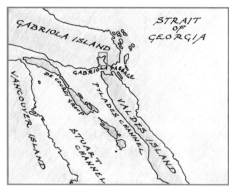

49°08'N 123°43'W

CHARTS

3475. 3313, page 19. SCN Map C3.

APPROACH

From Gabriola Passage, between the unnamed islet and the rock face of the Gabriola shoreline.

ANCHOR

Deep into the bay, off the public wharf for good all-weather shelter.

DEPTHS

5 - 7 m (16 - 23 ft). Holding good in sand and mud.

PUBLIC WHARF

Although relatively extensive, finding room among the local boats can be a problem.

Note: Anchoring N of the islet is an alternative if the bay is crowded.

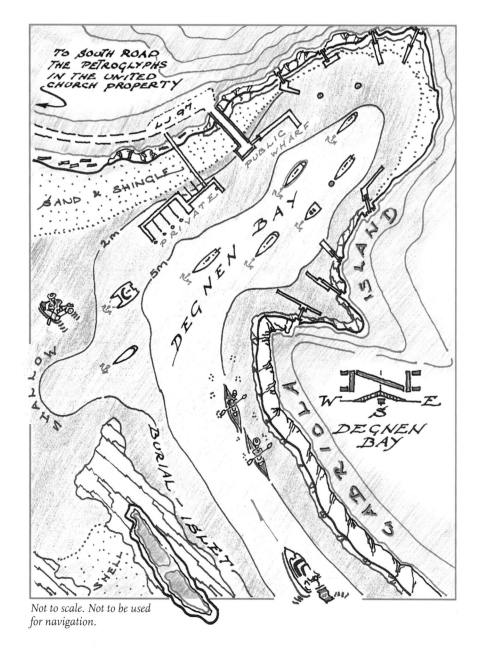

Not to scale. Not to be used for navigation.

The NE end of Degnen Bay provides well-protected, cosy anchorage and is a quieter and less crowded alternative to Silva Bay, but be prepared to anchor between the many private buoys and permanently anchored boats. There is also a large public wharf crowded with local boats that provides the only land access. Gabriola Island is renowned for its petroglyphs dating back over 2,000 years to the original presence of First Nations people. An excellent example can be found at the head of the bay on a slab of sandstone, just 1 m (3 ft) above LW. The most accessible site is on the grounds of the United Church on South Road, about a kilometre from the public wharf. Here you will find over 50 captivating images carved into the bedrock. (For in-depth information, read *Petroglyph Island* by Mary and Ted Bentley.)

Sailboat leaving the shelter of Degnen Bay.

DRUMBEG PROVINCIAL PARK & KENDRICK ISLAND, GABRIOLA PASSAGE   13.5

CHARTS

3475. 3313, page 19. SCN Map C3.

APPROACH

Drumbeg Provincial Park at LW slack, when Rogers Reef and the rocky shoreline are exposed. Approach Kendrick Island from the N, giving ample clearance to a reef that extends NW from its tip.

ANCHOR

Drumbeg: temporary anchorage, exposed to the SE.

Kendrick Island: good all-around shelter.

DEPTHS

Drumbeg: 4 - 6 m (13 - 19.5 ft); holding good in sand and shingle.

Kendrick Island: 5 - 10 m (16 - 33 ft); holding good in sand and mud.

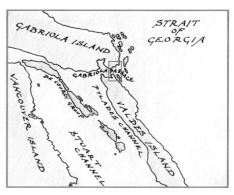

Gabriola Passage: 49°08'N 123°42'W

The delights of Drumbeg Provincial Park can easily be missed as you race through Gabriola Passage en route to other major destinations. It's best to enter the small bay on low, slack water and anchor toward the centre. This temporary anchorage can take 2 to 3 boats quite comfortably, and kayakers or small boats often pull up onto the beach.

It's fun to explore the rocky ledges at low tide, hike the wooded trails or simply picnic on the clean pebble beach.

KENDRICK ISLAND provides an ideal anchorage if you are waiting for the tide to turn in Gabriola Passage or need a sheltered overnight stop. West Vancouver Yacht Club has an outstation on the island with private floats and mooring buoys on its western shoreline.

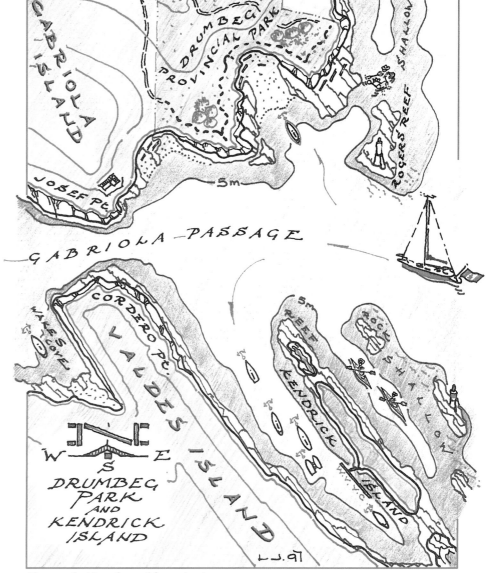

Not to scale. Not to be used for navigation.

Looking north to Drumbeg Provincial Park. A sailboat enters Gabriola Passage.

13.6   SILVA BAY, GABRIOLA ISLAND

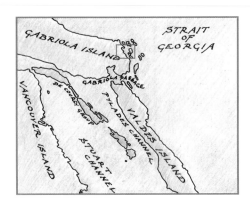

49°09'N   123°42'W

Entrance to Silva Bay between Tugboat and Vance Islands.

This popular rendezvous spot for boaters provides one of the best all-weather anchorages on the Georgia Strait side of the Gulf Islands. It is usually the first port of call for cruising boaters crossing the strait en route to their favourite island destinations. As a provisioning stop the choices are limited, with some fresh produce available.

When entering the bay between Vance and Tugboat Islands be sure to avoid the reef, Shipyard Rock, which extends N from Tugboat Island. Although the reef is well marked, you need to aim for Law Point after rounding the light and before steering toward the marina floats.

The bay has ample anchorage space and 3 marinas to choose from, each with their own distinctive features. PAGE'S RESORT & MARINA offers fuel, moorage, showers and laundry facilities. The industrious owners have a personal interest in books, art and music, and their bookstall features many island authors and topics. Pick up their self-published guide for hikers and bird-watchers if you wish to explore the island. They also host local art exhibitions and the occasional chamber music concert.

SILVA BAY RESORT & MARINA has a generous supply of moorage and fuel. Water, showers, a hot tub, pool and laundry facilities are also available. In the summer months you can lunch on the deck of THE LOOKOUT and enjoy barbecued burgers while watching the fascinating boat traffic (children welcome). Alternatively, pop into the BITTER END PUB or LATITUDE (250-247-8662). A small store also sells basic groceries, books and fishing tackle.

The SILVA BAY BOATEL & STORE provides limited moorage for shallow-draft boats but has a convenient general store that sells basic groceries, some fresh produce and hardware. Laundry facilities are also available, and they will take your garbage, for a fee.

Looking north over Silva Bay.

CHARTS

3475. 3313, page 19. SCN Maps C3 & C5.

APPROACH

The main entrance lies between Tugboat and Vance Islands. Enter Silva Bay by leaving the port-hand day beacon and light on Shipyard Rock and the port-hand buoy, to port.

ANCHOR

Between the marinas and Tugboat and Sear Islands.

DEPTHS

3 - 6 m (10 -19.5 ft). Holding good in mud and sand.

MARINAS

SILVA BAY RESORT & MARINA (250-247-9992). PAGE'S RESORT & MARINA (250-247-8931). SILVA BAY BOATEL & STORE (250- 247-9351). All marinas offer transient moorage; prior booking is advised. Silva Bay Resort & Marina monitors VHF channel 68. Their "shipyard" has repair facilities and a marine railway and travel lift. Reservations required in summer.

FUEL

At Silva Bay Resort & Marina and Page's Resort & Marina.

Note: The N entrance between Lily and Vance Islands and the S entrance between Sear Island and the Gabriola shoreline are considered small boat passes only.

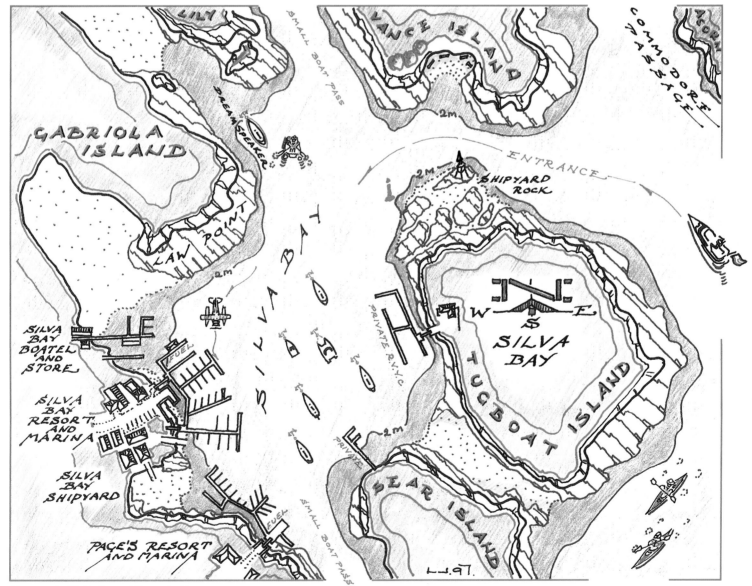

Not to scale. Not to be used for navigation.

Chapter 14
NANAIMO

TIDES
Reference Port: Point Atkinson
Secondary Ports: Harmac & Nanaimo

CURRENTS
Reference Station: Dodd Narrows
Secondary Station: False Narrows

WEATHER
Area: Strait of Georgia
Reporting Stations: Entrance Island, Halibut Bank

Dodd Narrows from Northumberland Channel.

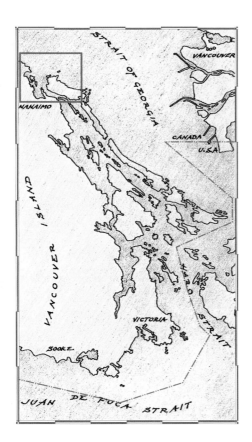

Dodd Narrows is the gateway to the featured destinations of this final chapter, taking you out of the protected Gulf Islands and through the narrowest, fastest and sometimes most hazardous major passage. These narrows should be navigated with extreme caution and at slack water, and a sharp lookout should be kept for slow tugs pulling large barges. Outside of slack water these narrows can become potentially dangerous when large standing waves are formed due to the sheer volume of water that has to push its way through a very restricted channel.

On entering Northumberland Channel you will be greeted by the rolling hills and pasture land of Gabriola Island to the east and the towering smokestack of a large pulp mill to the west. At first this might not look all that inviting, but once you enter the bustling harbour of Nanaimo or pop into the charming anchorages of north Gabriola, your perspective could be altered.

Nanaimo Harbour, with its revitalized downtown waterfront, choice of marinas and variety of shops for provisioning, has once again become the "hub city" of Vancouver Island, providing cruising boaters with a convenient and pleasurable spot to begin or end their voyages.

Enjoy the attractions of downtown Nanaimo or take a hike along the beautiful coast trail that circles Newcastle Island Marine Park, just a stone's throw from the city. Across the water, the spectacular sandstone Malaspina Galleries on the northern tip of Gabriola Island provide a great picnic stop. Taylor and Pilot Bays lie on either side of Gabriola Sands Provincial Park. Here you can spend a lazy day on the small white sandy beaches while enjoying some of the best warm-water swimming in the Gulf Islands. Lock Bay, located on the outside of Gabriola Island, has an inviting crescent-shaped beach with warm-water swimming, hidden petroglyphs and trails through Sandwell Provincial Park.

CAUTIONARY NOTES

Use Charts 3475; 3313, page 20; or SCN Map C5 if transiting Dodd or False Narrows.

Dodd Narrows is best transited at slack water or within 1 hour before or after slack water.

Although False Narrows offers alternative passage, it is a precarious connection. The pass is shallow and runs between reefs, so it is best transited on a rising tide, on or above mid-tide.

FEATURED DESTINATIONS

14.1 Nanaimo Harbour 180

....

14.2 Nanaimo Commercial Inlet,
     Boat Basin & Downtown 182

....

14.3 Newcastle Island Passage & Marinas 183

....

14.4 Newcastle Island Marine Park 184

....

14.5 Taylor & Pilot Bays, Gabriola Island 186

....

14.6 Malaspina Point & Galleries, Gabriola Island 188

....

14.7 Lock Bay, Gabriola Island 189

....

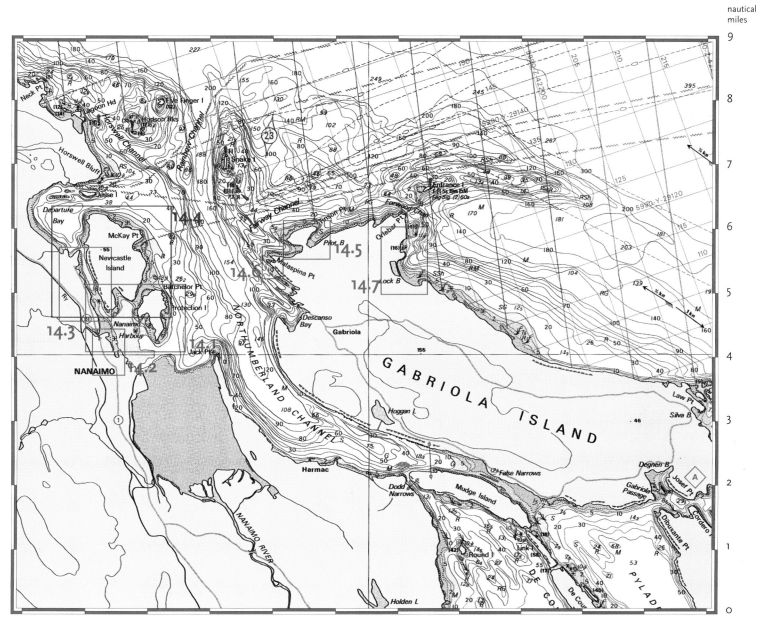

nautical
miles

Reproduced portion of CHS Chart 3463 for passage planning only. Not to be used for navigation.

14.1　NANAIMO HARBOUR

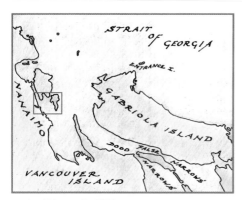

49°10'N 123°56'W

Approach from the south by rounding Gallows Point.

Extensive marine facilities, good anchorage and a rejuvenated downtown waterfront make the bustling and friendly harbour of Nanaimo very attractive to the cruising boater. To top it all, 2 unique and rather charming urban islands, accessible only by water, are just a short hop from the historic city centre. Marinas line the western shores of Newcastle Island Passage (see page 183), and the Commercial Inlet, in the heart of downtown Nanaimo, provides convenient moorage within easy walking distance of the HARBOUR PARK MALL and the charming shops, cafés and bookstores of the city core. THE BOOKSTORE ON BASTION STREET offers 3 floors of books to choose from, as well as comfy sofas to relax on while browsing. Nanaimo's intriguing 4-km (2.5-mi) Harbourside Walkway begins at the Commercial Inlet, follows the shoreline N and ends at the SEALAND OCEANARIUM and the PUBLIC MARKET. A wonderful medley of shops, restaurants and cafés is available en route. Pop into THE DOCK SHOPPE for all your boating needs, or treat yourself to a silver-service high tea at JUST DESSERTS. Stop in at the unusual green-roofed floatplane terminal where patio dining at THE BISTRO offers sumptuous seafood with a view. Alternatively, indulge in "fresh off the boat" fish and chips at TROLLERS on the public wharf. Good crabbing can be found off the public pier at "Swy-a-lana Lagoon" (local name).

If you prefer to anchor, ample protected anchorage is possible in the designated area between Newcastle and Protection Islands, which is well clear of the floatplane operation zone.

Newcastle Island Marine Park also offers plenty of moorage space at its public wharf. A frequent ferry service (SCENIC FERRIES at 250-753-5141) connects the island with Maffeo-Sutton Park (see page 184 for Newcastle Island info). The PROTECTION ISLAND CONNECTION (250-753-8244), which leaves from the Nanaimo Commercial Inlet, services the residential community of Protection Island as well as the DINGHY DOCK PUB, where limited moorage, shower and laundry facilities and great food are available. Access to the island's peaceful lanes can be found beyond the small island store.

Nanaimo is renowned for two quite diverse innovations. First, its traditional "sweet treat," the Nanaimo Bar, which originated in the town's coal mining days, and second, the WORLD CHAMPIONSHIP BATHTUB RACE, which crosses the Strait of Georgia from Nanaimo to Vancouver. The race's accompanying MARINE FESTIVAL lasts for 4 days and takes place in late July.

Nanaimo is world famous for its bathtub races.

CHARTS

3457. 3313, page 21. SCN Map C5.

APPROACH

By rounding Gallows Point, the southern tip of Protection Island, leaving the starboard-hand buoy to starboard.

ANCHOR

Protected anchorage for numerous boats can be found NE of a line drawn between 2 yellow anchor buoys.

DEPTHS

5 - 8 m (16 - 26 ft). Holding good in mud.

PUBLIC WHARF

Public wharves at Good Point and Gallows Point are essentially for residents of Protection Island. For Commercial Inlet, see page 182. For Newcastle Island, see page 184.

MARINAS & BOAT LAUNCH

In Newcastle Island Passage (see page 183).

FUEL

In the Commercial Inlet and Newcastle Island Passage.

CUSTOMS

Port of entry in the Commercial Inlet.

Notes: A floatplane operation zone is located in Nanaimo Harbour.

NANAIMO HARBOUR COMMISSION (250-753-4146) operates a harbour patrol, monitors VHF channel 11 and enforces a speed limit of 5 knots. The Eco Barge sewage reception facility is located on the Commercial Inlet's breakwater float.

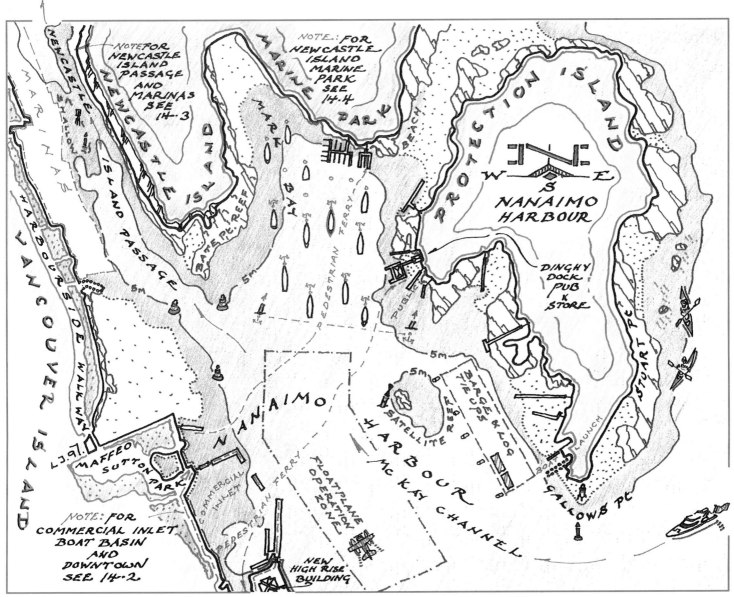

Not to scale. Not to be used for navigation.

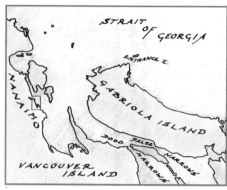

49°10'N 123°56'W

CHARTS

3457. 3313, page 21. SCN Map C5.

APPROACH

From the E to enter between the northern tip of the VISITING VESSEL PIER and the southern end of the breakwater float.

PUBLIC WHARF

The marina facilities, including CAMERON ISLAND MARINA and the VISITING VESSEL PIER, are all administered by the Port of Nanaimo.

FUEL & CUSTOMS

At fuel barge within the Commercial Inlet.

Note: The Commercial Inlet is exceedingly busy, with boats manoeuvring in a very confined space. Prior to entering the boat basin it is advisable to contact the wharfinger on VHF channel 67, or phone (250) 754-5053 to be assigned to a berth. The northern portion of the Commercial Inlet is an active floatplane terminal.

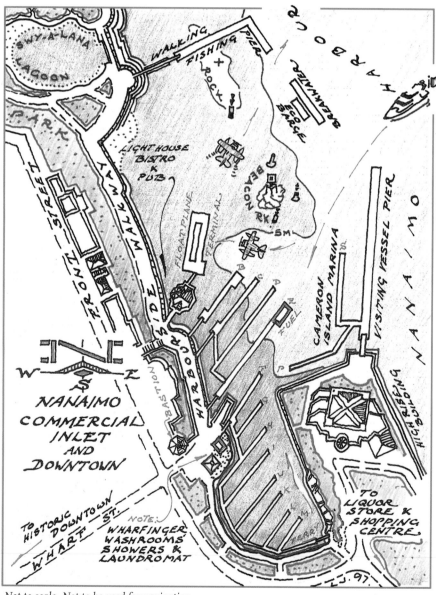

Not to scale. Not to be used for navigation.

This large commercial boat basin lies below THE BASTION, a landmark white tower that was built in 1853. Here, the Port of Nanaimo provides comprehensive marina facilities, which offer showers, laundry and the first 3 hours free if you are just visiting. This is also a good spot to pick up fresh fish and live crab.

Easy provisioning is possible at the downtown HARBOUR PARK MALL, where a variety of shops – including THRIFTY FOODS, LONDON DRUGS and a B.C. LIQUOR STORE – as well as laundry facilities and a post office can be found. For fresh bread and tasty Nanaimo Bars try THE SCOTCH BAKERY on Wharf and Commercial Streets. Take a self-guided heritage tour into the old city quarter. Pick up a map at THE BASTION.

The boat basin looking southwest.

NEWCASTLE ISLAND PASSAGE & MARINAS 14.3

CHARTS

3457. 3313, page 21. SCN Map C5.

APPROACH

From the S, within the inner portion of Nanaimo Harbour, and enter between the starboard and port-hand buoys. Alternatively, approach from the N, between Shaft and Pimbury Points.

MARINAS

Most marinas offer visitors transient moorage (see listings below). Call beforehand.

BOAT LAUNCH

Public at Brechin Point.

FUEL & CUSTOMS

At BRECHIN POINT MARINA.

Note: Two rocks to the W with shallow water between them lie mid-channel, mid-passage. The safe channel lies to the E of both the port-hand buoy that marks Oregon Rock and the port-hand day mark that marks Passage Rock. An arrow above the day mark also indicates this channel.

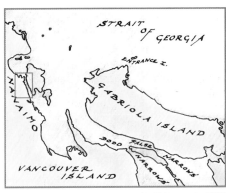

49°11'N 123°56'W

Extensive moorage facilities and boating amenities are available opposite Newcastle Island, on the Nanaimo side of Newcastle Island Passage. A choice of marinas line the shore. From S to N: NANAIMO YACHT CLUB (250-754-7011); TOWNSITE MARINA (250-716-8801); CHANNEL VIEW MARINA; MOBY DICK MARINA (250-753-7111); NANAIMO SHIPYARD (250-753-1151); NANAIMO HARBOUR CITY MARINA (250-754-2732); NEWCASTLE MARINA (250-753-1431); OCEAN MARINE (250-754-3931); ANCHORAGE MARINA (250-754-5585); STONE'S MARINA (250-753-4232); SEALAND MARKET MARINA (250-754-1723); BRECHIN POINT MARINA (250-753-6122).

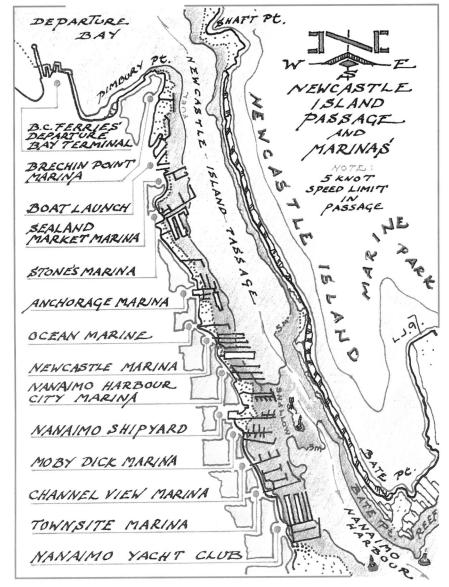

Approach to Nanaimo Harbour via Newcastle Island Passage.

Not to scale. Not to be used for navigation.

14.4   NEWCASTLE ISLAND MARINE PARK

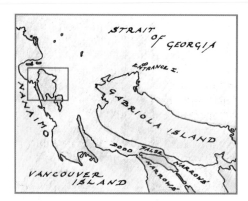

49°11'N   123°55'W

The anchorage in the northern portion of Nanaimo Harbour.

The end of another glorious day.

Accessible by boat only, this entire island is now a provincial marine park with extensive and well-organized facilities. These include a public wharf, campgrounds, playgrounds, picnic areas, a barbecue shelter and the restored park pavilion. Fresh water is available, toilets are numerous and convenient anchorage is close by in Nanaimo Harbour and in Mark Bay. Although the island's popularity increases in the summer months, with boaters, campers and day trippers converging all at once, it becomes surprisingly uncrowded once you venture away from the public service areas.

Just a short walk up from the wharf is a public phone and visitor information shelter where you can pick up a detailed map of the island and its clearly marked, well-groomed trails. These will take you along the island's beautiful shoreline or through its thickly forested interior, where you can stop and enjoy the tranquillity of Mallard Lake. Steep sandstone cliffs tower over the intriguing coast trail. Caves and caverns abound and numerous sand-and-gravel beaches can be found along the way, with fine warm-water swimming in shallow "Kanaka Bay" (local name). Look out for the family of rare champagne-coloured raccoons who often visit the beaches.

SCENIC FERRIES operates a foot-passenger ferry service to and from Nanaimo in the summer months (250-753-5141). The DINGHY DOCK PUB on nearby Protection Island provides excellent pub grub if you're in a sociable mood. Access to the island's small store and quiet lanes is also possible from here.

The Dinghy Dock Pub is just a short row away from the boats at anchor.

CHARTS

3457. 3313, page 21. SCN Map C5.

APPROACH

The anchorage and park float in Mark Bay from the S, within the inner portion of Nanaimo Harbour.

ANCHOR

In the northern portion of Nanaimo Harbour or in Mark Bay. Good all-weather shelter.

DEPTHS

3 - 5 m (10 -16 ft). Holding good in mud.

PUBLIC WHARF

An extensive park float is available to boats under 7 m (23 ft) in length.

Note: If a moderate to strong northwesterly is blowing, gusts will blast into the anchorage between Newcastle and Protection Islands.

A young lookout spots a place to anchor.

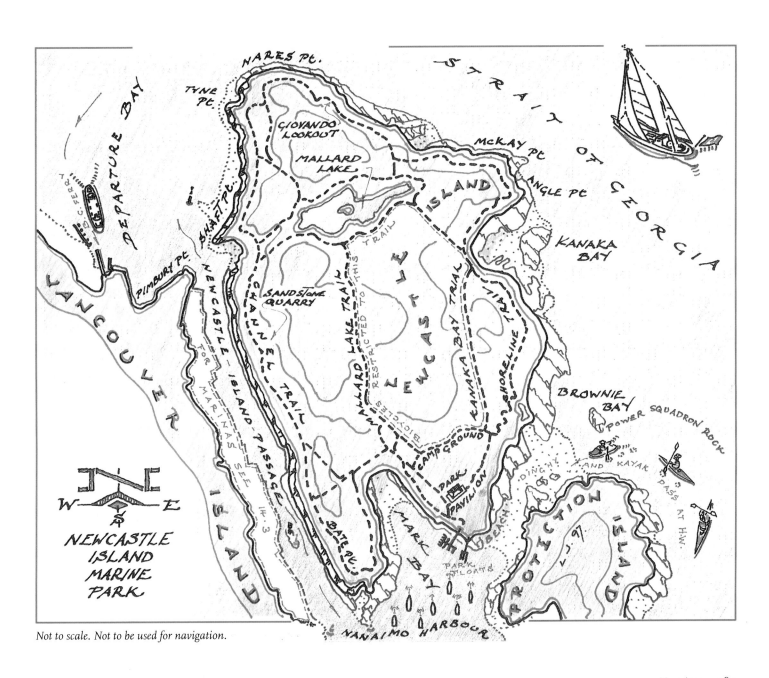

Not to scale. Not to be used for navigation.

14.5 TAYLOR & PILOT BAYS, GABRIOLA ISLAND

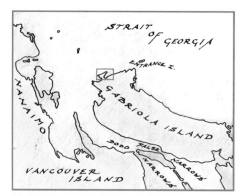

Taylor Bay: 49°12'N 123°52'W
Pilot Bay: 49°12'N 123°51'W

Approach to Taylor Bay.

Rowing to shore in Pilot Bay.

The well-manicured Gabriola Sands Provincial Park straddles a strip of land and a road between Taylor and Pilot Bays, taking in both of the lovely beaches on either side. The wide expanse of grass, shady trees, fine silver-white sand and bleached logs invite you to explore, picnic or just while away a few hours enjoying the view. The park is also popular with local families, who arrive early to claim their favourite spots in the summer months. Pilot Bay affords good shelter from the frequent northwesterlies, and Taylor Bay serves up warm-water swimming and stunning sunsets. You can also visit the Malaspina Galleries by dinghy from here.

The TWIN BEACHES SHOPPING CENTRE is conveniently situated at the junction of Ricardo Road and Berry Point Road, just a few minutes walk away. Here you will find a restaurant and an assortment of shops, including a grocery store and a B.C. LIQUOR STORE. In the summer months you may also find a flea market in progress, in which craft tables are often set up displaying unique and intriguing work. Gabriola Island boasts a wealth of artistic talent, making the GABRIOLA ARTISANS' COOPERATIVE well worth a visit.

Looking west to Pilot Bay.

CHARTS

3458. 3313, page 20. SCN Map C5.

APPROACH

Taylor Bay from the W, N of Malaspina Point. Approach Pilot Bay from the NE after rounding Tinson Point.

ANCHOR

In the centre of both Taylor and Pilot Bays, off the sandy beach.

DEPTHS

2 - 6 m (6.5 - 19.5 ft). Holding good in sand.

Note: If intending to overnight, Taylor Bay is exposed to westerly winds and ferry wash. Pilot Bay offers protection from all but NE winds, although the swell from the Strait of Georgia tends to enter the bay.

The park beach at the head of Taylor Bay.

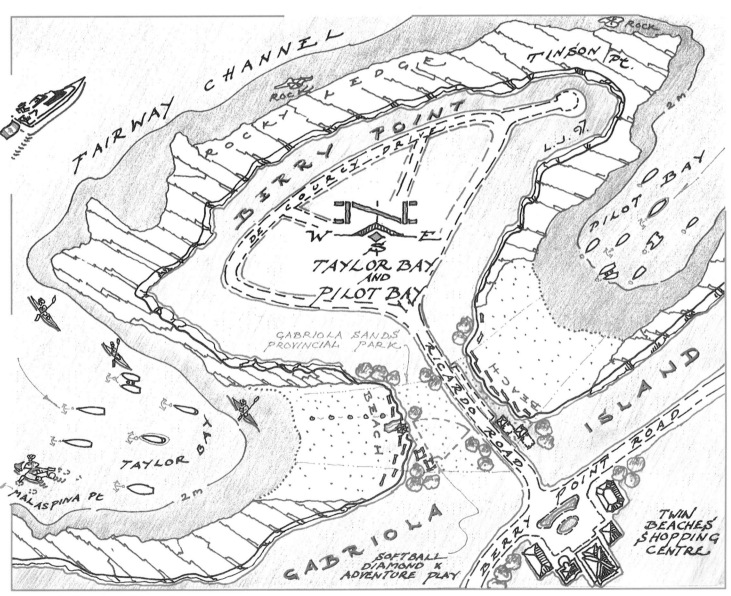

Not to scale. Not to be used for navigation.

14.6 MALASPINA POINT & GALLERIES, GABRIOLA ISLAND

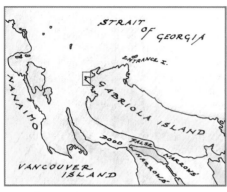

49°12'N 123°52'W

CHARTS

3458. 3313, page 20. SCN Map C5.

APPROACH

Malaspina Point at LW, when the rocky ledges that extend a considerable distance NW of the point are visible.

ANCHOR

Temporary day anchorage may be found S of Malaspina Point, parallel to the Galleries.

DEPTHS

2 - 6 m (6.5 - 19.5 ft). Holding and bottom condition unrecorded.

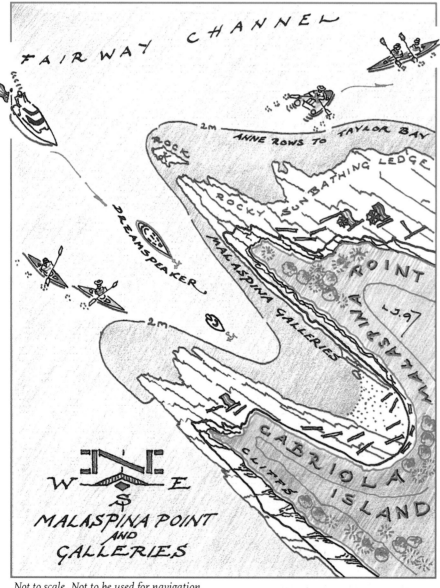

Not to scale. Not to be used for navigation.

The small bay S of Malaspina Point provides an interesting picnic and adventuring day stop. The unique Malaspina Galleries found here were originally a sacred aboriginal burial site and have been a renowned tourist attraction for over 200 years. The galleries are actually a long and eroded sandstone sea cave that sits above the HW mark, resembling a large standing wave. Local islanders keep a low-key but diligent watch over the area and encourage visitors to enjoy the galleries for their natural beauty and spiritual past. Anyone found defacing the site will be prosecuted.

Looking over Malaspina Point and Galleries toward Taylor Bay.

ARTS

58. 3313, page 20. SCN Map C5.

APPROACH

Lock Bay from the E at LW. Temporary picnic anchorage only. Exposed to all weather and sea conditions in the Strait of Georgia.

ANCHOR

Off the sand-and-pebble beach.

DEPTHS

2 - 5 m (6.5 - 16 ft). Holding and bottom condition unrecorded.

Note: Anchoring overnight, even in the most settled conditions, is not recommended.

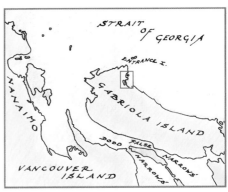

49°11'N 123°49'W

Lock and Leboeuf Bays lie on the outside of Gabriola Island and to the S of Entrance Island. Both are exposed to easterly winds blowing across the Strait of Georgia. However, in fair weather, or when there is an offshore wind, Lock Bay becomes an inviting picnic anchorage. The wide, crescent-shaped beach is strewn with weathered logs, and petroglyphs carved into large boulders lie hidden under piles of driftwood, providing an interesting game of treasure hunt. Sometimes the water is even warm enough for a swim. Peaceful Sandwell Provincial Park backs the beach with a walking trail, picnic area and washrooms. It is worth taking your dinghy into Leboeuf Bay to explore the shoreline and rocky "one tree" islet.

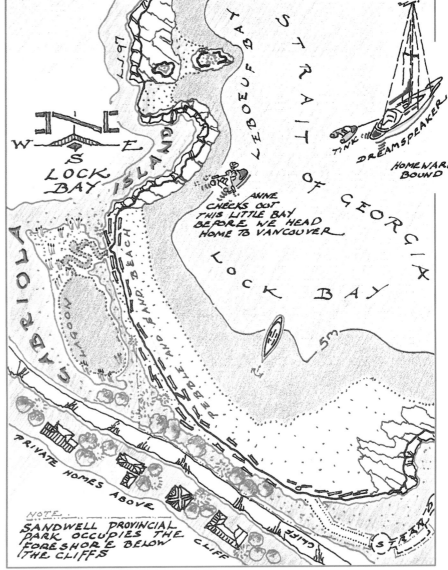

Not to scale. Not to be used for navigation.

Looking southwest from Leboeuf to Lock Bay.

SELECTED READING

Baron, Nancy, and John Acorn. *Birds of Coastal British Columbia*. Edmonton: Lone Pine Publishing, 1997.

B.C. Parks Visitor Pamphlets (*Campground Critters*; *Principal Berries*; *Principal Trees*; *Life at the Edge*; *Things to Do Outdoors*). Call (250) 387-5002.

Chettleburgh, Peter. *An Explorer's Guide to the Marine Parks of British Columbia*. Vancouver: Special Interest Publications, 1985.

Christie, Jack. *Inside Out British Columbia: A Best Places Guide to the Outdoors*. Vancouver: Raincoast Books, 1998.

Grant, Peter. *Victoria from Sidney to Sooke: An Altitude CityGuide*. Canmore, AB: Altitude Publishing Canada, 1994.

Hale, Robert, ed. *Waggoner Cruising Guide*. Bellevue, WA: Weatherly Press, 1997. Updated and published annually.

Hill, Beth. *Guide to Indian Rock Carvings of the Pacific Northwest Coast*. Surrey, BC: Hancock House Publishers, 1984.

Koppel, Tom. *Kanaka: The Untold Story of Hawaiian Pioneers in British Columbia and the Pacific Northwest*. Vancouver: Whitecap Books, 1995.

Lillard, Charles, ed. *The Call of the Coast*. Victoria: Horsdal and Schubart Publishers, 1992.

Loomis, Ruth. *Small Stories of a Gentle Island*. Ladysmith, BC: Reflections, 1986.

McIntosh, Barbara-jo. *Tin Fish Gourmet: Great Seafood from Cupboard to Table*. Vancouver: Raincoast Books, 1998.

Montgomery, Georgina, and Andrea Spalding. *The Pender Palate: Tastes and Flavours from Our Favourite Island*. Pender Island, BC: Loon Books, 1992.

Obee, Bruce. *Coastal Wildlife of British Columbia*. Vancouver: Whitecap Books, 1991.

Pacific Yachting's Marina Guide and Boaters Blue Pages: The Complete Guide to B.C. Marinas and Marine Services. Magazine supplement (January issue), updated and published annually by Pacific Yachting.

Pojar, Jim, and Andy MacKinnon, eds. *Plants of Coastal British Columbia, Including Washington, Oregon and Alaska*. Vancouver: Lone Pine Publishing, 1994.

Snively, Gloria. *Exploring the Seashore in British Columbia, Washington, and Oregon: A Guide to Shorebirds and Intertidal Plants and Animals*. Vancouver: Gordon Soules Book Publishers, 1978.

Snowden, Mary Ann. *Island Paddling: A Paddler's Guide to the Gulf Islands and Barkley Sound*. Victoria: Orca Book Publishers, 1997.

Spalding, David, Andrea Spalding, and Lawrence Pitt. *B.C. Ferries and the Canadian West Coast: An Altitude SuperGuide*. Canmore, AB: Altitude Publishing Canada, 1996.

———, and Georgina Montgomery. *Southern Gulf Islands of British Columbia: An Altitude SuperGuide*. Canmore, AB: Altitude Publishing Canada, 1995.

Turner, Nancy J. *Food Plants of Coastal First Peoples*. Vancouver: UBC Press, 1995.

Vassilopoulos, Peter. *Docks and Destinations: Coastal Marinas and Moorage*. West Coast Cruising Dock-to-Dock Destinations Guides. Vancouver: Seagraphic Publications, 1996.

Wolferstan, Bill. *Gulf Islands and Vancouver Island from Sooke to Courtenay: Cruising Guide to British Columbia, Volume 1*. Vancouver: Whitecap Books, 1987.